TWELFTH NIGHT

Shakespearean Criticism
(Advisory Editor: Joseph G. Price)
Vol. 3

TWELFTH NIGHT
Critical Essays

Stanley Wells

GARLAND PUBLISHING, INC. • NEW YORK & LONDON
1986

Library of Congress Cataloging-in-Publication Data
Main entry under title:

Twelfth night

(Shakespearean criticism ; vol. 3)
Bibliography: p.
1. Shakespeare, William, 1564–1616. Twelfth night—
Addresses, essays, lectures. I. Wells, Stanley W.,
1930- . II. Series.
PR2837.W45 1985   822.3′3   85-13029
ISBN 0-8240-9239-2 (alk. paper)

Printed on acid-free, 250-year-life paper
Manufactured in the United States of America

Contents

General Editor's Preface

The Garland series is designed to bring together the best that has been written about Shakespeare's plays, both as dramatic literature and theatrical performance. With the exception of some early plays which are treated in related combinations, each volume is devoted to a single play to include the most influential historical criticism, the significant modern interpretations, and reviews of the most illuminating productions. The collections are intended as resource companions to the texts. The scholar, the student, the reader, the director, the actor, the audience, will find here the full range of critical opinion, scholarly debate, and popular taste. Much of the material reproduced has been extremely difficult for the casual reader to locate. Original volumes have long since been out of print; definitive articles have been buried in journals and editions now obscure; theatrical reviews are discarded with each day's newspaper.

"The best that has been written" about each play is the criterion for selection, and the volumes represent the collective wisdom of foremost Shakespearean scholars throughout the world. Each editor has had the freedom and responsibility to make accessible the most insightful criticism to date for his or her play. I express my gratitude to the team of international scholars who have accepted this challenge. One would like to say with Keats "that is all/Ye know on earth, and all ye need to know," but the universality of Shakespeare will stimulate new responses, yield fresh meanings, and lead new generations to richer understandings of human nature.

Generally the essays have been reproduced as they appeared originally. Some concessions in punctuation, spelling, and documentation have been made for the sake of conformity. In the case of excerpts, notes have been renumbered to clarify the references. A principle of the series, however, is to reproduce the full text, rather than excerpts, except for digressive material having no bearing on the subject.

Joseph Price

Introduction

Shakespeare was in his mid-thirties and at the height of his powers when, probably in 1601, he wrote *Twelfth Night*. During the previous ten or more years he had written tragedies—*Titus Andronicus, Romeo and Juliet, Julius Caesar,* and *Hamlet*—tragical histories—the three parts of *Henry VI, Richard III, King John, Richard II*—comical histories—the two parts of *Henry IV* and *Henry V*—and comedies—*The Two Gentlemen of Verona, The Comedy of Errors, The Taming of the Shrew, Love's Labour's Lost, A Midsummer Night's Dream, The Merchant of Venice, Much Ado About Nothing, The Merry Wives of Windsor,* and *As You Like It*. He had been a prominent member of the Lord Chamberlain's Men since their foundation in 1594, and had helped them to become the leading English theatrical company. He might have been resting on his laurels, but *Twelfth Night* is the culmination of his work in the form of romantic comedy, a masterpiece which was evidently popular in his own day and is now among the most frequently performed and most highly admired of his plays.

Nevertheless, like most of the comedies, it was not greatly to the taste of the later seventeenth and early eighteenth century. Samuel Pepys, in the 1660s, thought it "a silly play" but managed to sit through it three times. After this period it was largely neglected until its theatrical revival in 1741. For the remainder of the eighteenth century it was frequently included in the repertory at Drury Lane and Covent Garden, and (though Pepys had remarked that it was "not related at all to the name or day") was particularly likely to be performed on or around 6 January. During this time the play was given substantially as written, but in

1820 Frederic Reynolds, along with the composer Henry Bishop, put on at Covent Garden a heavily adapted version introducing "Songs, Glees, and Choruses, the Poetry selected *entirely* from the Plays, Poems, and Sonnets of Shakespeare." This adaptation continued in performance at intervals over several years. Shakespeare's play had been introduced to New York in 1804, and it returned to the London stage in 1846. Since then it has been frequently played not only in the world's theatres but also, more recently, on radio and television.

Except for notices of performances, some represented in this anthology, there is little lasting criticism of the comedy before the present century. Perhaps this is partly because it is easy to enjoy as both drama and literature. Nevertheless, the passage of time has dimmed some of its significance, which may be restored to us through historical criticism. As a product of Shakespeare's mature art, the play may be illuminatingly related to the literary and theatrical conventions and traditions that lie behind it, and to its author's own achievements up to the time of its composition. The history of its performance may be drawn upon for information as to its theatrical potential, and in the attempt to investigate the extent to which our responses to it are liable to be conditioned by its theatrical incarnations and reshapings. And, short though it may be in comparison with some of the other masterpieces of Western literature, the intricacy of its plotting, the resonances of its language, the richness of its ideas, the range and power of its characterization, the complexity of its ironies, the artistry of its dramaturgy, and the reasons for its appeal to later ages are among those aspects of the play that have been valuably explored by generations of critics.

The choice of writings in this volume has been governed, not by historical considerations, but by the aim of presenting to today's reader those discussions of the play which may most profitably enhance his experience of it both in the study and on the stage. The opening essays, concerned with the play's characters, are followed by accounts of its potential and actual theatrical realization and then by a selection from the best of the many scholarly and critical studies of its artistry.

J. B. Priestley's "The Illyrians" comes from his early book *The English Comic Characters* (1925)—a title which itself justifies the concentration on the persons of the play rather than, for instance, its structure, its poetry, or its theatrical effect. Sensitively written, evocative, the work of a born essayist who was to become one of the few English writers to achieve comparable distinction as both novelist and playwright, it is in the belle-lettrist tradition now somewhat out of fashion; yet its very opening paragraphs introduce us to a central critical issue: "we are more likely to regard Malvolio with some measure of sympathy than was Shakespeare" writes Mr Priestley, adumbrating a theme which recurs in many of these essays. From this appreciation of the play's characters in general we pass to a single one: "Feste the Jester" by A. C. Bradley, better known for his writings on Shakespeare's tragedies. This is "character criticism" at its best: not a fantasy taking off from the text but a thoughtful, perceptive view of one of the play's characters based on a scrupulous examination and exploration of the lines.

Though Bradley generally writes about Shakespeare's plays as a reader rather than as a theatregoer, he was—as one of the footnotes to this essay shows—not oblivious to their theatrical impact. In the third essay in this collection John Russell Brown, a scholar-critic who has also been very active in the practical theatre, opens our eyes to the variety of effect of which the play is capable in performance. This essay also looks closely at details of the text, but it draws upon memories and accounts of the play in the theatre. Directors and actors can offer illumination no less than critics; and though their work is transient it may, at least partially, live on in the writings of those who have both described it and been provoked by it to thought about the play itself (in so far as we can talk of a "play" apart from performance).

Whereas John Russell Brown is concerned with the play's general openness to interpretation, Arthur Colby Sprague, in an extract from his book *Shakespeare and the Actors*, aims at a more precise and objective, though not uncritical, chronicling of business employed on the stage from the earliest recorded performances to the end of the nineteenth century. This concise account draws on descriptions and reviews such as those that follow. Charles Lamb's essay "On Some of the Old Actors" is a nostalgic piece of retrospective criticism. It was published in 1823, but Robert Bensley's last performances as Malvolio had been given in 1792, when Lamb was seventeen years old. As we read it we should perhaps be aware that Lamb writes as an essayist, not as a reporter: as one whose aim is to give aesthetic pleasure and who may therefore impose his personality upon the facts. There is reason to believe that Lamb's view that Bensley gave to the role of Malvolio "a kind of tragic interest" is a very individual one, as Sylvan Barnet shows in his "Charles Lamb and the Tragic Malvolio," *Philological Quarterly*, 33 (1954), but it represents a romantic reading of the character that has been adopted by many actors since Lamb's time.

Twelfth Night offers to its performers a wide range of excellent roles. It is essentially a "company" play, but in the star-dominated theatre of the nineteenth century and after, the role of Malvolio has been seen as that which provides the greatest opportunities for virtuosity. Samuel Phelps, who produced most of Shakespeare's plays with great distinction at Sadler's Wells Theatre from 1844 to 1862, was not a selfish actor, yet Henry Morley's account of his *Twelfth Night* concentrates upon Phelps's playing of the role, giving an excellent impression of its individuality. Other great actor-managers played this role, including Sir Henry Irving in his own not very successful production (1894), and Sir Herbert Beerbohm Tree. Tree's half-brother, Max Beerbohm, remarks in his review on the dominance of Malvolio, while inviting us to imagine "what a splendid play [Shakespeare] might have written if he had made Malvolio specifically the central figure!" Like Lamb, Beerbohm was an essayist even in his weekly theatre criticism; he refers in this review to Lamb's essay, which had become influential. In his gently mischievous way, Beerbohm is as provocatively critical of Shakespeare as George Bernard Shaw (who preceded him as theatre critic on the *Saturday Review*) had more aggressively been. But we do not need to endorse Beerbohm's estimate of the play to appreciate the skill and grace with which he evokes Tree's production.

It seems undeniable that one of the finest of all productions of *Twelfth Night* was the one that Harley Granville Barker directed at the Savoy Theatre, London, in 1912. Regrettably, it did not provoke any reviews of great distinction (a historical account is given in Karen Greif's "'If This Were Play'd upon a Stage': Harley Granville Barker's Shakespeare Productions at the Savoy Theatre, 1912–1914," *Harvard Library Bulletin* 28, 2 (April, 1980), 117–145).

Nor is Barker's Preface to his acting edition among his better critical writings. But in 1931 he turned theatre critic and reviewed for the *Observer* (1 January 1922) a Paris production of *Twelfth Night* directed by Jacques Copeau which had been playing in repertory since 1914. Barker's review reflects his opinions on the play after he had had the experience of directing it; he is especially interesting on the interpretation of Viola. (Robert Speaight (*Shakespeare on the Stage*, 1973, p. 189) calls this essay "a classic of dramatic criticism," but it is not listed in the bibliography of Barker's writings in C. B. Purdom's *Harley Granville Barker* (1955), and so far as I have been able to discover has not previously been reprinted.)

Virginia Woolf, the novelist, wrote little about the theatre. In her account of Tyrone Guthrie's production of *Twelfth Night* at the Old Vic in 1931 she writes—like Lamb and Beerbohm—primarily as an essayist; and, also like Beerbohm, she is not entirely adulatory of Shakespeare. But she is wonderfully sensitive to the play's language, and fascinating in the way that she explores her own situation: that of a reader of Shakespeare confronting the difference between reading a play and seeing it performed.

One of the best productions of modern times is Peter Hall's, which opened at the Shakespeare Memorial Theatre (now the Royal Shakespeare Theatre), Stratford-upon-Avon, in 1958. Roy Walker's account demonstrates the more analytical, text-centered approach to the theatre criticism of Shakespeare's plays resulting from the coming together of academic and theatrical study.

From these theatre-based pieces we pass to more purely scholarly and critical writings about the play.

Leslie Hotson's book *The First Night of "Twelfth Night"* propounds a thesis which has not commanded general assent: that the play was written, transcribed, learnt, and rehearsed within the space of twelve days for a conjectural performance before Don Virginio Orsino, Duke of Bracciano, on 6 January 1601. This is improbable, but, like all of Hotson's writings, the book is full of interesting information entertainingly presented, and the chapter reprinted here provides fascinating historical background to the play's language and allusions, particularly in its commentary on the Fool's final song. The chapter from C. L. Barber's *Shakespeare's Festive Comedy* opens with a reference to Hotson's argument and proceeds to a discussion of the play's "festive comic form" emphasizing its ideas and the relationships among its characters. Bertrand Evans's

"The Fruits of the Sport" comes from a book whose concern, according to its Preface, is to present an "account of the dramatist's means and ends in the creation, maintenance, and exploitation of differences in the awarenesses of participants and of differences between participants' awarenesses and ours as audience." *Twelfth Night*, with its many errors and comic misconceptions, responds particularly well to this type of analysis, which increases our understanding of the technical mastery by means of which Shakespeare controls his audience's reactions. Harry Levin concentrates on the contribution to the overall design made by the play's "underplot."

The next two essays focus on Shakespeare's processes of composition. Harold Jenkins examines the play in the light of Shakespeare's earlier comic writings, especially *The Two Gentlemen of Verona*, and of its narrative and dramatic sources. In the course of his essay he offers a particularly illuminating examination of Malvolio, insisting that he is not "the central figure of the play," and supporting his case by close textual reference. L. G. Salingar, in "The Design of *Twelfth Night*," is still more closely concerned with Shakespeare's transmutations of his source materials, helping to reveal the dramatist's purposes through comparison with earlier treatments of related plot material.

A. S. Leggatt and Karen Greif contribute sophisticated forms of character study. The former, in a chapter from his book *Shakespeare's Comedy of Love*, explores the persons of the play in their isolation, "the lovers trying to make contact but with limited success, and the comic figures, either openly hostile or forming relationships based on temporary expediency"; he directs attention also to the play's structure, its language, and its developing action. Karen Greif finds that "Virtually every character . . . is either an agent or a victim of illusion," and examines the way in which "Role-playing, deceptions, disguises, and comic manipulations provide the fabric of the entire action."

This volume ends with two studies of the manner in which Shakespeare draws the action to a close. Jörg Hasler looks closely at the dramaturgy of the last scene, and Anne Barton (in an extract from a longer essay) shows how, in this same scene, "a world of revelry, of comic festivity, fights a kind of desperate rearguard action against the cold light of day."

TWELFTH NIGHT

J. B. Priestley

THE ILLYRIANS

If you take ship from the coast of Bohemia—having made your last bow to Perdita and Florizel—and sail for a day in a westerly direction, you will presently arrive at Illyria. There you will find the love-sick melancholy Duke, seated among his musicians, polishing his images and doting upon the "high-fantastical"; and go but a little way out of the city and you will come upon the stately Countess Olivia among her clipped box-trees, pacing the lawns like some great white peacock, while her steward Malvolio, lean, frowning, and cross-gartered, bends at her elbow. There too, if you are lucky, you may catch a glimpse of the rubious-lipped lovely Viola, stretching her slim legs and swinging her pert page's cloak between the Duke's palace and Olivia's house, delicately breathing blank verse. And if there should come to your ears the sound of drunken catches, and to your nose the smell of burnt sack and pickled herrings, then look for Olivia's uncle, Sir Toby Belch, and his friend, Sir Andrew Aguecheek, and with them, it may be, that dainty rogue, Maria, darting about like some little black and white bird, and Feste the Clown, with his sharp tongue, bright eyes and strange bitter-sweet songs. In and out of doors, there is good company in Illyria, good company whether it is high or low, sober or drunk.

Our present inquiry takes us into the society of the low, the drunken and disreputable company, the comic Illyrians. (It is difficult even to sound the name and remain sober.) Whether Malvolio, who was himself neither drunken nor disreputable but

Reprinted by permission of the Bodley Head Ltd., from *The English Comic Characters* by J. B. Priestley.

essentially a "grave liver," should have place in the company, is a very debatable question. Most of the comic scenes in the play revolve around him, and it is his antics, his sudden rise and his awful collapse, that form the basis of most of the broader comedy of the piece; his self-love and swelling vanity, which make him an easy butt for Maria and her grinning troupe, his gravity and pompous airs, are all served up, without mercy, for our entertainment. Yet Malvolio, strictly speaking, is not a comic character. He stands outside the real comic tradition. Although Shakespeare gives some of his speeches a most delicious flavour of absurdity, he does not treat Malvolio as he treats his purely comic figures, whom he regards not merely with a humorous tolerance but with positive delight and relish, encouraging them, as it were, to indulge their every whim. The difference between, let us say, Malvolio and Sir Andrew Aguecheek is that Shakespeare handles the one and dandles the other. Sir Andrew is really a much more contemptible figure than the serious and capable steward, but then he is so manifestly ridiculous that he evades criticism altogether, escapes into a world of his own, where every fresh piece of absurdity he commits only brings him another round of laughter and applause. Times change, and we are more likely to regard Malvolio with some measure of sympathy than was Shakespeare; indeed, in spite of his vanity, to us he is a figure not untouched by pathos, for the possibility of Olivia falling in love with him (and she admits his value as an employee) appears to us not entirely preposterous, nor do his portentous gravity and puritanical airs seem to us so offensive, now that our Sir Tobies have been steadily rebuked in the manner of Malvolio for at least two generations. Sir Toby's famous reply—"Dost thou think, because thou art virtuous, there shall be no more cakes and ale"—cuts the ground from under the feet of a very large number of our energetic fellow-citizens, whose apparent business it is, Malvolio-like, to attend to our private affairs and superintend our morals; and Sir Toby was fortunate in being able to make such a rejoinder without being suppressed. Malvolio, we may say, has been steadily coming into his own for a long time, so that it is difficult for us to regard him as an unpleasant oddity as Shakespeare did. And perhaps it says something for our charity that, sitting as we are among ever-diminishing supplies of cakes and ale, we can still see something pathetic in this figure.

Shakespeare's sympathies were so wide and his dramatic genius so universal that it is always dangerous to give him a point of view and dower him with various likes and dislikes. Nevertheless it is true to say that certain types of character very clearly aroused his dislike; and it is also true to say that these are the very types of character that appear to have some fascination for our world. In short, his villains are rapidly becoming our heroes. Thus, Shakespeare clearly detested all hard, unsympathetic, intolerant persons, the over-ambitious and overweening, the climbers and careerists, the "get-on-or-get-outs" of this world. When the will and the intellect in all their pride were divorced from tolerance, charity, a love of the good things of this world, they formed the stuff out of which the Shakespearean villains were made. But the Bastard and Iago and Richard the Third are the very characters that some of our modern dramatists would select to adorn three acts of hero-worship. So too, to come down the scale, our friend Malvolio, the pushing puritan, is, under various disguises, the hero of almost one-half of all the American novels that were ever written. Shakespeare, looking steadily at Malvolio with his self-love ("O, you are sick of self-love," cries Olivia to him) and his intolerance, contrives that he shall be covered with ridicule, but never regards him as a comic figure. In spite of his absurdities there are fermenting in him too many of those qualities that Shakespeare detested for him to be a figure of fun. While this conceited and over-ambitious steward struts cross-gartered on the lawn for our entertainment, there flutters across his path, for one fleeting moment, the terrible shadow of that other ambitious underling, Iago. So Malvolio is deceived, abused, locked up and treated as a madman for a short space, and this is his purgation, for Shakespeare saw that his soul was in danger and so appointed for him two angels of deliverance, namely, Maria and Sir Toby Belch.

In the very first speech that Sir Toby makes, when we discover him talking with Maria, he remarks that "care's an enemy to life," and this we may take to be his philosophy. His time is spent in putting a multitude of things, oceans of burnt sack, mountains of pickled herrings, between himself and the enemy, Care; and he may be shortly described as a Falstaff without genius, who would have made the fat knight a very able lieutenant. Undoubtedly, he is a very idle and drunken old rip, who forgets his position, which, as the uncle of the Countess, is considerable, his years and his manners, and passes all his time in low company, in the society of his inferiors, either because, like Maria, his niece's chambermaid, they devise entertainment for him, or because, like Sir Andrew, they serve as butts and cat's-paws. But notwithstanding his devotion to sherris-sack—and it is doubtful if we ever see him sober—unlike Falstaff Sir Toby does not live altogether in an ideal comic world of ease and merriment; by much drinking of healths and singing of catches and fool-baiting, and with the assistance of a kind of rough philosophy, a tap-room epicureanism, he certainly tries to live in such a world; but common-sense and a knowledge of this world's uses keep breaking in from time to time. In spite of his idleness and love of mischief, he is shrewd enough on occasion. Thus, he does not propose to deliver Sir Andrew's ridiculous challenge to the supposed Cesario, because, he declares, "the behaviour of the young gentleman gives him out to be of good capacity and breeding; his employment between his lord and my niece confirms no less: therefore this letter, being so excellently ignorant, will breed no terror in the youth—he will find it comes from a clodpole." He is in no doubt as to the capacity of his admiring dupe, Sir Andrew, who is only encouraged to remain as the suitor of Olivia in order that Toby may amuse himself and mulct the foolish knight of his ducats. His apparently innocent defense of Sir Andrew in the opening dialogue with Maria ("He's as tall a man as any's in Illyria"—and the rest) is, of course, mere impudence, one wag winking at another. Then later, when the confusion between Viola and her brother complicates the action, Sir Toby changes his mind about Cesario, as he has a right to do on the evidence before him, and remarks: "A very dishonest, paltry boy, and more a coward than a hare: his dishonesty appears in leaving his friend here in necessity, and denying him." And he it is who has the wit to see that the joke against Malvolio has gone far enough—"I would we were well rid of this knavery." Although he vastly enjoys stirring up unnecessary strife and egging on two apparent cowards to fight one another, he shows no reluctance to taking part in any quarrel himself and is certainly no coward. When he himself is hurt, it will be remembered, he makes no complaint ("That's all one: 'has hurt me, and there's the end on't.—Sot, didst see Dick surgeon, sot?"), and though this stoicism simply covers a fear of being ridiculed, it does argue a stout nature.

Sir Toby, then, is by no means a simpleton. Nor is he, on the other hand, a comic genius like Falstaff, whose world has been transformed into an ideally comic world, whose whole life, whose every speech and action, are devised to further ease, enjoyment and laughter. Sir Toby, in his own coarse, swashbuckling manner, is witty, but he is not the cause of wit in other men. He does not transform himself into an object of mirth, content so long as men are laughing and the comic spirit is abroad, but like any bullying wag of the tap-room, looks for a butt in the company. He is really nothing more than an elderly schoolboy with a prodigious thirst and far too much spare time on his hands: the type is not uncommon. Having a more than usual amount of energy, both of brain and body, and no serious powers of application and no sensible objects upon which to expend such energy, his one problem is how to pass the time pleasantly. As he happens to have his existence in a romantic and idyllic world of love and dalliance and fine phrases that offers no employment to a robust and prosaic middle-aged gentleman, and as he, unlike our country squires and retired majors, cannot turn to golf and bridge, there is nothing for it but cakes and ale, the roaring of catches, verbal bouts with the chambermaid and the clown, and mischievous antics played at the expense of such creatures as Malvolio and Sir Andrew. Men so situated always seek out low company and are never at ease among their equals. But once among his cronies, Toby enjoys himself with such rollicking abandon that he communicates his enjoyment to us, so that we would not for the world have him different. There is about this drunken, staggering, swaggering, roaring knight such a ripeness and gusto that his humours are infectious, and once we are in his riotous company decency and order seem intrusive and positively ill-natured. He has leave to keep us out of bed all night and we would not stint him of a drop

of sack or a single pickled herring. Falstaff apart, there never was
a better bear-leader of a fool. With what a luxury of enjoyment he
draws out and displays to us the idiocies of the guileless Sir
Andrew:

> *Sir Andrew.* I'll stay a month longer. I am a fellow o' the
> strangest mind i' the world; I delight in masques and
> revels sometimes altogether
> *Sir Toby.* Art thou good at these kickshawses, knight?
> *Sir Andrew.* As any man in Illyria, whatsoever he be, under
> the degree of my betters; and yet I will not compare with
> an old man.
> *Sir Toby.* What is thy excellence in a galliard, knight?
> *Sir Andrew.* Faith, I can cut a caper.
> *Sir Toby.* And I can cut the mutton to 't.
> *Sir Andrew.* And I think I have the back-trick simply as
> strong as any man in Illyria.
> *Sir Toby.* Wherefore are these things hid? wherefore have
> these gifts a curtain before 'em? are they like to take dust,
> like Mistress Mall's picture? why dost thou not go to
> church in a galliard, and come home in a coranto? My very
> walk should be a jig; I would not so much as make water
> but in a sink-a-pace. What dost thou mean? is it a world to
> hide virtues in? I did think, by the excellent constitution
> of thy leg, it was form'd under the star of a galliard.
> *Sir Andrew.* Ay, 'tis strong, and it does indifferent well in a
> flame-coloured stock. Shall we set about some revels?
> *Sir Toby.* What shall we do else? were we not born under
> Taurus?
> *Sir Andrew.* Taurus! that's sides and heart.
> *Sir Toby.* No, sir; it is legs and thighs. Let me see thee ca-
> per. . . .

Once in his cups, how magnificently he overrides mere precision
in speech and common-sense and rises into a poetical kind of
nonsense of his own: "To hear by the nose, it is dulcet in contagion. But shall we make the welkin dance indeed? shall we rouse
the night-owl in a catch that will draw three souls out of one
weaver? shall we do that?" With what gusto does he enter into
the matter of the duel between Sir Andrew and the disguised
Viola, alternately breathing fire into them and then damping it
with a report to each one of the other's fury and prowess. He

bustles from one to the other in a very ecstasy of pleasure. Sir
Andrew, he tells Fabian, "if he were open'd, an you find so much
blood in his liver as will clog the foot of a flea, I'll eat the rest of
the anatomy"—a remark worthy of Falstaff himself—Sir Andrew
is not anxious to fight, but Toby fans his few smouldering embers
of courage into a blaze and compels him to send a challenge:

> Go, write it in a martial hand; be curst and brief; it is no
> matter how witty, so it be eloquent and full of invention:
> taunt him with the license of ink: if thou *thou'st* him some
> thrice, it shall not be amiss; and as many lies as will lie in thy
> sheet of paper, although the sheet were big enough for the
> bed of Ware in England, set 'em down: go, about it. Let there
> be gall enough in thy ink; though thou write with a goose-
> pen, no matter: about it.

Then gives him some further encouragement when the challenge
is written:

> Go, Sir Andrew; scout me for him at the corner of the
> orchard, like a bumbaily: so soon as ever thou see'st him,
> draw; and, as thou drawest, swear horrible; for it comes
> to pass oft, that a terrible oath, with a swaggering accent
> sharply twang'd off, gives manhood more approbation than
> ever proof itself would have earned him. Away!

We can almost bear Toby smacking his lips over the vision of Sir
Andrew letting fly a terrible oath, with a swaggering accent
sharply twang'd off. Then, with an ever-increasing relish for the
situation and with his images swelling at every fresh turn of the
farce, Sir Toby confronts Viola with a tale of her incensed oppo-
nent awaiting her, "bloody as a hunter," "a devil in private brawl:
souls and bodies hath he divorced three; and his incensement at
this moment is so implacable, that satisfaction can be none but by
pangs of death and sepulchre: hobnob is his word; give't or take't
. . ."—a terrifying picture. Back again he goes to Sir Andrew, now
to damp the knight's faint ardour with an equally terrifying
account of his adversary: "Why, man," roars the mischievous old
toper, "he's a very devil; I have not seen such a firago. I had a pass
with him, rapier, scabbard, and all, and he gives me the stuck-in
with such a mortal motion, that it is inevitable; and, on the

answer, he pays you as surely as your feet hit the ground they step on. They say he has been fencer to the Sophy." "Pox on't," cries the startled Sir Andrew, out of his simplicity, "I'll not meddle with him." But there is no escape for him, even though he should part with his horse as the price of that escape. It is only the unexpected entry of Antonio that robs us of the climax and, possibly, Sir Toby of the horse, but the artful and mischievous knight, who has known something of the satisfaction of those lesser gods who prompt our tyrants and prophets and further our wars and revolutions to pass pleasantly their idle aeons, has had his fun. He has contrived a tale that, with humorous embellishment, will keep any company uproarious between one round of sack and the next, between chorus and chorus.

But if we have enjoyed Sir Toby's antics so much that we have no desire for his immediate amendment, we must leave him with some misgiving, for at the conclusion of the piece we plainly see that those very gods of mischief whom he has emulated in this affair of the duel have now selected him as the victim of their sport. They who have allowed him to season his sack with so many herrings in pickle, have now devised for him a rod in pickle. This is nothing less than his marriage with Maria, of which we learn from Fabian's explanation of the joke against Malvolio at the end of the play. We are told: "Maria writ the letter at Sir Toby's great importance (i.e., importunity—though this is not strictly true); in recompense whereof he hath married her." Alas!—poor Toby. We had seen the possibility of such an alliance throughout the play; indeed, scene after scene had shown us Toby edging nearer and nearer to his doom. We had heard him declare, "She's a beagle, true-bred, and one that adores me," in all his fateful masculine complacency. When the Malvolio jest was at its intoxicating height, we had heard him shower compliments on the artful little soubrette, "Excellent wench" and the rest, had caught him declaring to Sir Andrew and Fabian, in the ecstasy of his enjoyment, "I could marry this wench for this device, and ask no other dowry with her but such another jest." We have heard him cry to her, "Wilt thou set thy foot o' my neck?" and "Shall I play my freedom at tray-trip, and become thy bond-slave?" Yet, with the sound of such dangerous speeches, verbal gun-cotton, still ringing in our ears, we had thought that the old fox might yet sniff the air, scent danger and then bolt for freedom. But no, he has walked into the trap. He has been snared, like many another man, not only by a woman but by his own philosophy. "Care's an enemy to life," he has told himself, and with so much idleness on his hands, with so rich an appreciation of japes and jests, with so great a capacity for mischief and the staging of whims, what could be better than an alliance with Maria, who has proved herself the very queen of humorous strategy, a "most excellent devil of wit," and a most generous purveyor of cakes and ale? Alas!—had this been any other man's reasoning, he would have seen the folly of it. As it is, he marries, so that the perfect life of comic ease and merriment that he is always attempting to build up may have another prop, and does not realise that he is simply bringing it all down in one awful crash. Who doubts for a moment that what Olivia, with her stately displeasure, could not do, Maria, the erstwhile accomplice and fellow mischief-maker, but now the wife, will accomplish within a very short space; that Maria the chambermaid, with a comically sympathetic view of sack, catches, and late hours, is one thing, and Maria the wife, with a husband to reform, is another; that the very wit that could devise such unseemly jests will henceforward be occupied, not in devising others, but in schemes, equally efficacious, for preventing husband Toby from reaching the large freedom he hitherto enjoyed? As a last bulwark against care, he has taken Maria to wife, and now, without a doubt, the old freedom has vanished and care is about to return in an undreamed-of measure. Toby's philosophy has undone him, and he falls; but he falls like a great man. We have caught his days at their highest point; nevermore shall we see him, free, spacious, as rich and ripe as a late plum, all Illyria his tavern, a prince of gusto, good living, and most admirable fooling; from now on he will dwindle, take on a cramped and secretive air, and lose his confidence and zest, for now he will always be discovered, his Maria's reproaches still shrilling in his ear, a cup too low.

Of one of Sir Toby's boon companions, Feste the Clown, there is little to be said. Viola, after a bout of wit with him, sums up the matter admirably:

This fellow's wise enough to play the Fool;
And to do that well craves a kind of wit:
He must observe their mood on whom he jests,
The quality of persons, and the time;
Not, like the haggard, check at every feather
That comes before his eyes. This is a practice
As full of labour as a wise man's art:
For folly, that he wisely shows, is fit;
But wise men's folly, shown, quite taints their wit.

This is an accurate description of Feste's own practice, for as he lounges in and out of the scene, it will be noticed that always he plays up to his company. He is a professional entertainer and gives his audiences what he knows will please them. The love-sick Duke feeds upon melancholy, and so to him Feste sings "old and antique" songs and takes delight in his art, but as soon as he has finished the last note of "Come Away, Death," like the brisk professional he is, he himself shows no trace of melancholy or of any emotion, but is his usual self in a moment, detached, observant, critical, taking his leave with a sly dig at the Duke's melancholy and inconstancy. With the other serious characters, he acts the professional fool but always with a certain reserve and dignity and always with one eye upon the main chance, conjuring another coin into his hand with an ingratiating witticism. Malvolio he really dislikes because the proud and puritanical steward has a contempt for both him and his office (a contempt that Shakespeare himself had probably met with in some Malvolio of his acquaintance), and so he does not scruple to play Malvolio the cruellest trick of all by pretending to be Sir Topas the parson. With Sir Toby and Maria, Feste appears at his ease and, as it were, with his wit unbuttoned, bandying broad jests with them; while for the delectation of Sir Andrew, a great admirer of his, he utters the first nonsense that comes into his head. Indeed, in this company of boon companions and midnight caterwaulers, his humour is all for wild nonsense of a Rabelaisian cast. Such ridiculous speeches as "I did impeticos thy gratillity; for Malvolio's nose is no whipstock; my lady has a white hand, and the Myrmidons are no bottle-ale houses" cast a spell over the rural wits of Sir Andrew, who pronounces it to be "the best fooling, when all is done." (There is apparently a lower level of intelligence and humour than

Sir Andrew's; it is to be found in those commentators who have pored for hours over these nonsensical speeches of the Clown's and have then complained that they could make little of them.) And though we may not agree that this "is the best fooling, when all is done," most of us have regretted that we were not present at the previous meeting of Sir Toby, Sir Andrew, and the Clown, when, according to Sir Andrew, the Clown was in very gracious fooling and spoke of Pigrogromitus and of the Vapians passing the equinoctial of Queubus. Perhaps this is one of the delights that Heaven has in store for us, or for those of us who are only fit for a Heaven slightly damaged and humanised. Wind and rain outside; indoors a clear fire and a few tall candles, with sack in plenty; Sir Toby, straddling and with nose aglow, on one side; Sir Andrew gaping on the other; and the Clown before us, nodding and winking through his account of Pigrogromitus and the Vapians passing the equinoctial of Queubus; the whole to be concluded by the catch of "Hold thy peace, thou knave," with the possibility of being interrupted at any moment by a Malvolio in his nightshirt—here is a hint for the commander of the starry revels.

Sir Andrew Aguecheek is one of Shakespeare's family of simpletons: he is first cousin to Slender and Silence. Life pulses so faintly in this lank-haired, timid, rustic squire that he is within a stride of utter imbecility. He is really the very opposite of Sir Toby, who is for ever in mischief simply because he has more energy and brains than he knows what to do with, being without any serious purpose, whereas Sir Andrew follows Toby into mischief simply because he is deficient in both energy and brains, and for ever takes the line of least resistance. Without a shred of either self-respect or self-confidence, without volition, courage or sense, he is any man's prey, a toy-balloon blown hither and thither by the slightest breeze. His social standing and wealth are just sufficient to leave him independent of any occupation or control, a free agent, but being what he is, it means that they are just sufficient to leave him at the mercy of the first rascal he meets. At first sight, it seems astonishing that a comic character of any dimensions could possibly be created out of such material, and, indeed, only a great genius could have taken these few straws and made of them a creature whose every odd remark and quaint caper is a delight. But it is Sir Andrew's amazing simplicity, his almost pathetic naïvety, his absolute lack of guile, that make him so richly absurd. And with these there goes a certain very characteristic quality, the unanalysable factor, that is present in every remark he makes; every speech has a certain Aguecheek flavour or smack that is unmistakable; even as we read we can hear the bleating of his plaintive little voice. His best trait is one that he shares with every simpleton, and that is a childlike capacity for enjoyment, which is really born of a sense of wonder, the ability to marvel at and relish the commonest things, to see the world innocently and freshly, a sense that withers among brighter wits and natures richer in experience but blooms for ever with the extremes of humankind, the utter simpletons and the great geniuses. Sir Andrew has this capacity, and it entitles him to a place at the revels. In spite of his starts and frights, his loss of two thousand ducats and his broken head, it is clear that he has enjoyed himself hugely in the company of his admired Sir Toby, and that he will return to his distant estate bubbling with a confused tale of strange happenings and great personages that will be meat and drink to him for years. It is true that he has been everybody's butt, but then he does not know it; he is happily protected from all such discoveries and will be all his life; so that he might almost be said to have the best of the laugh, for whereas the others are living in this world, he is still dwelling in Eden.

There are a thousand things that could be said of this simple creature, for there is probably no better text than a fool, but one particular aspect of him invites our attention. What really tickles us about Sir Andrew, over and above the unanalysable drollery of his speeches, is not what he thinks and feels but the fact that he should not be able to conceal what he thinks and feels. There is somewhere at the back of all our minds a little Sir Andrew Aguecheek, giggling and gaping, now strutting and now cowering, pluming himself monstrously at one word and being hurled into a fit of depression by the next; but most of us contrive to keep this little fellow and his antics carefully hidden from sight for the sake of decency and our own self-respect. Some of Sir Andrew's ingenuous remarks have the same effect, or should have the same effect, upon us as the sight of a monkey, which presents us with a parody of human life that is highly diverting but that leaves us somewhat shamefaced: after seeing so many things done openly that we ourselves do in secret, we blush, partly for the monkey that it should make a public show of itself, and partly for ourselves who have so much that is better concealed. The mind of Sir Andrew, such as it is, is as plain to sight as the dial of the parish clock. Almost every remark he makes innocently revealing, as it does, the ebb and flow of his poor self-esteem, is not only a piece of self-revelation but also a revelation of all our species: this zany, naked to our sight, is uncovering the nakedness of statesmen and philosophers, popes and emperors. How delicious in its candour is his reply to Sir Toby's bantering charge of being "put down": "Methinks sometimes I have no more wit than a Christian or an ordinary man has: but I am a great eater of beef, and I believe that does harm to my wit." How swiftly following the thought that he may be no better than the ordinary in some particular comes the possible explanation, the eating of beef, to raise the phoenix of his vanity again from its ashes. He remains, at some charge to his purse, with Sir Toby as a suitor to Olivia; and yet it is clear that the whole idea is Sir Toby's, for Olivia plainly does not favour Sir Andrew, and he knows it, nor does he himself feel any passion for the lady: he has simply allowed himself to be persuaded, caught in the web of Sir Toby's imagination and rhetoric. How swiftly too his vanity plumes itself again at Sir Toby's artful prompting in the matter of his accomplishments; he can cut a caper, he tells us with a delicious affectation of detachment, and thinks he has the back-trick simply as strong as any man in Illyria.

In the matter of scholarship, which most gentlemen of his time affected, his simplicity and candour are nothing less than wholesome and refreshing. When Sir Toby declares that "not to be a-bed after midnight is to be up betimes"—and then, plunging into the depths of his learning, brings forth an adage from Lily's grammar—"And *diliculo surgere*, thou know'st—" Sir Andrew provides us with the rare spectacle of a man acting honestly in the face of a classical quotation, by replying: "Nay, by my troth, I know not: but I know, to be up late is to be up late." So too when Sir Toby asks if our life does not consist of the four elements, he replies, indifferently, "Faith, so they say; but I think it rather consists of eating and drinking"—a notable answer. Again, when the Clown asks whether they will have a love-song or a song of good life, and Sir Toby decides for the former, Sir Andrew speaks for all the novel-readers of our circulating libraries but with more sincerity than they can ever muster when he adds: "Ay, ay: I care not for good life." Most excellent too is his critical observation in reply to the Clown's remark that the knight, Sir Toby, is "in admirable fooling": "Ay, he does well enough if he be disposed, and so do I too: he does it with a better grace, but I do it more natural." And what could be more revealing than his cry at the indignation meeting after the visit of Malvolio. Maria has said that the steward is sometimes a kind of Puritan. "O!" cries Sir Andrew, "if I thought that, I'd beat him like a dog." When pressed for his exquisite reason, he confesses to having none: indeed, he has no reason at all, but the excitement of the occasion has heated his poor wits and he wishes to make some full-blooded declaration and stand well with the company, like our Sir Andrews who sit in their clubs and tell one another they would "shoot 'em down." How pathetically he echoes Sir Toby. Even when the latter re-marks that Maria adores him, Sir Andrew, not to be left out, instantly lights a pitiful rushlight of amatory remembrance: "I was adored once." Yes, he, Sir Andrew, was adored once: it is not true, but for the moment he thinks it is and so contrives to take his place among the swaggering fellows, alongside Sir Toby. And perhaps best of all, the very sweet distillation of ingenuousness, is his whisper in the shrubbery when Malvolio, having read the letter, is rehearsing his part as the Countess's husband. As soon as mention is made of "a foolish knight," Sir Andrew is in no doubt as to the person—"That's me, I warrant you." And when his guess is confirmed by the actual sound of his name, he is almost triumphant—"I knew 'twas I, for many do call me fool," a remark that smacks more of complacency than resignation, as if to be known as a fool did at least single him out for some notice. And how revealing, too, is his conduct during the duel episode. He has been told that Olivia has only shown favour to Cesario in order that her more backward suitor, the knight, should be en-couraged to accost: he must redeem his credit either by valour or by policy; and so he declares for valour, for policy he hates. And so he sends a challenge that, notwithstanding his complacent view of its "vinegar and pepper," deserves a prominent place in any collection of diplomatic documents:

> Youth, whatsoever thou art, thou art but a scurvy fellow. Wonder not, nor admire not in thy mind, why I do call thee so, for I will show thee no reason for 't. Thou comest to the Lady Olivia, and in my sight she uses thee kindly: but thou liest in thy throat; that is not the matter I challenge thee for. I will waylay thee going home; where if it be thy chance to kill me, thou kill'st me like a rogue and a villain. Fare thee well; and God have mercy upon one of our souls! He may have mercy upon mine; but my hope is better, and so look to thyself. Thy friend, as thou usest him, and thy sworn enemy,
>
>   Andrew Aguecheek

Never, in the whole history of the duello, was such good citizenship exhibited in a challenge. And when Sir Andrew learns that his adversary has been fencer to the Sophy and is a fire-eater, he is swift to declare that he will not meddle with him, and that had he known that the fellow had been so valiant and so cunning in fence, he would have seen him damned before he would have challenged him. And, of course, Sir Andrew is only talking sense: it would have served the fellow right not to have been challenged. Later, when he has struck Sebastian and has received a pummelling in exchange, he tells Sir Toby to let Sebastian alone: "I'll go another way to work with him; I'll have an action of battery against him, if there be any law in Illyria: though I struck him first, yet it's no matter for that." No matter at all: he feels, as we all do, that the law is on his side. Our last glimpse of him is somewhat moving, for he has a broken head, received in the company of Sir Toby, who has himself been given "a bloody coxcomb," but nevertheless his admiration and faith are undiminished; had Sir Toby not been in drink, he tells the company, things would have fallen out very differently; and at the last, he cries: "I'll help you, Sir Toby, because we'll be dressed together." But his idol turns and rends him, calling him an ass-head and a coxcomb and a knave, a thin-faced knave, a gull. These are hard sayings but not too hard for Sir Andrew to swallow, and perhaps they made

their peace together afterwards. If not, we can only hope that our
simpleton went on his travels and somehow in the end contrived
to find his way into Gloucester and into the orchard of Justice
Shallow, for there he would find company after his own heart,
the great Shallow himself and Silence and Slender, and take his
place among such boon companions, seat himself at the pippins
and cheese and try to disengage from his tangled mind such
confused memories as remained there of Illyria and the royster-
ing Illyrians, his foolish face aglow beneath the unfading apple-
blossom.

A. C. Bradley

Feste the Jester

Lear's Fool stands in a place apart—a sacred place; but, of Shakespeare's other Fools,[1] Feste, the so-called Clown in *Twelfth Night*, has always lain nearest to my heart. He is not, perhaps, more amusing than Touchstone, to whom I bow profoundly in passing; but I love him more.

Whether Lear's Fool was not slightly touched in his wits is disputable. Though Touchstone is both sane and wise, we sometimes wonder what would happen if he had to shift for himself. Here and there he is ridiculous as well as humorous; we laugh *at* him, and not only *with* him. We never laugh at Feste. He would not dream of marrying Audrey. Nobody would hint that he was a "natural" or propose to "steal" him (*As You Like It*, I i 46, 48; I iii 125). He is as sane as his mistress; his position considered, he cannot be called even eccentric, scarcely even flighty; and he possesses not only the ready wit required by his profession, and an intellectual agility greater than it requires, but also an insight into character and into practical situations so swift and sure that he seems to supply, in fuller measure than any of Shakespeare's other Fools, the poet's own comment on the story. He enters, and at once we know that Maria's secret is no secret to him. She warns him that he will be hanged for playing the truant. "Many a good hanging," he replies, "prevents a bad marriage"; and if Maria wants an instance of a bad marriage, she soon gets it: "Well, go thy way; if Sir Toby would leave drinking, thou wert as witty a piece of Eve's flesh as any in Illyria." (Gervinus, on the contrary,

Reprinted from *A Book of Homage to Shakespeare*, ed. Israel Gollancz (Macmillan, 1916).

regarded this marriage as a judgement on Sir Toby; but then
Gervinus, though a most respectable critic, was no Fool.) Maria
departs and Olivia enters. Her brother is dead, and she wears the
deepest mourning, and has announced her intention of going
veiled and weeping her loss every day for seven years. But, in
Feste's view, her state of mind would be rational only if she
believed her brother's soul to be in hell; and he does not conceal
his opinion. The Duke comes next, and, as his manner ruffles
Feste, the mirror of truth is held firmly before him too: "Now, the
melancholy god protect thee; and the tailor make thy doublet of
changeable taffeta, for thy mind is a very opal." In these encounters we admire the Fool's wisdom the more because it makes no
impression on his antagonists, who regard it as mere foolery. And
his occasional pregnant sayings and phrases meet the same fate.
His assertion that he is the better for his foes and the worse for
his friends the Duke takes for a mere absurdity or an inadvert-
ence of expression, though he is tickled by Feste's proof of his
affirmation through double negation.[2] The philosopher may
speak to Sebastian of "this great lubber the world"; he may tell
Viola how "foolery, sir, does walk about the orb like the sun—it
shines everywhere"; he may remark to the whole company how
"the whirligig of time brings in his revenges"; but nobody heeds
him. Why should any one heed a man who gets his living by
talking nonsense, and who may be whipped if he displeases his
employer?

All the agility of wit and fancy, all the penetration and wisdom, which Feste shows in his calling, would not by themselves
explain our feeling for him. But his mind to him a kingdom is, and
one full of such present joys that he finds contentment there.
Outwardly he may be little better than a slave; but Epictetus was
a slave outright and yet absolutely free: and so is Feste. That
world of quibbles which are pointless to his audience, of incon-
gruities which nobody else can see, of flitting fancies which he
only cares to pursue, is his sunny realm. He is alone when he
invents that aphorism of Quinapalus and builds his hopes on it;
and it was not merely to get sixpence from Sir Andrew that he
told of Pigrogromitus and the Vapians passing the equinoctial of
Queubus. He had often passed it in that company himself. Maria
and Sir Toby (who do enjoy his more obvious jests) are present

when, clothed in the curate's gown and beard, he befools the imprisoned Malvolio so gloriously; but the prisoner is his only witness when, for his own sole delight, himself as Sir Topas converses with himself the Fool. But for this inward gaiety he could never have joined with all his heart in the roaring revelry of Sir Toby; but he does not need this revelry, and, unlike Sir Toby and Sir Toby's surgeon, he remains master of his senses. Having thus a world of his own, and being lord of himself, he cares little for Fortune. His mistress may turn him away; but, "to be turned away, let summer bear it out." This "sunshine of the breast" is always with him and spreads its radiance over the whole scene in which he moves. And so we love him.

We have another reason. The Fool's voice is as melodious as the "sweet content" of his soul. To think of him is to remember "Come away, come away, death," and "O mistress mine," and "When that I was," and fragments of folk-song and ballad, and a catch that "makes the welkin dance indeed." To think of *Twelfth Night* is to think of music. It opens with instrumental music, and ends with a song. All Shakespeare's best praise of music, except the famous passage in *The Merchant of Venice*, occurs in it. And almost all the music and the praise of music comes from Feste or has to do with Feste. In this he stands alone among Shakespeare's Fools; and that this, with the influence it has on our feeling for him, was intended by the poet should be plain. It is no accident that, when the Duke pays him for his "pains" in singing, he answers, "No pains, sir; I take pleasure in singing, sir"; that the revelry for which he risks punishment is a revelry of song; that, when he is left alone, he still sings. And, all this being so, I venture to construe in the light of it what has seemed strange to me in the passage that follows the singing of "Come away." Usually, when Feste receives his "gratillity," he promptly tries to get it doubled; but here he not only abstains from any such effort but is short, if not disagreeably sharp, with the Duke. The fact is, he is offended, even disgusted; and offended, not as Fool, but as music-lover and artist. We others know what the Duke said beforehand of the song, but Feste does not know it. Now he sings, and his soul is in the song. Yet, as the last note dies away, the comment he hears from this noble aesthete is, "There's for thy pains"!

I have a last grace to notice in our wise, happy, melodious Fool. He was little injured by his calling. He speaks as he likes; but from first to last, whether he is revelling or chopping logic or playing with words, and to whomsoever he speaks or sings, he keeps his tongue free from obscenity. The fact is in accord with the spirit of this ever-blessed play, which could not have endured the "foul-mouthed" Fool of *All's Well*, and from which Aldis Wright in his school edition found, I think, but three lines (not the Fool's) to omit. But the trait is none the less characteristic of Feste, and we like him the better for it.

It remains to look at another side of the whole matter. One is scarcely sorry for Touchstone, but one is very sorry for Feste; and pity, though not a painful pity, heightens our admiration and deepens our sympathy. The position of the professional jester we must needs feel to be more or less hard, if not of necessity degrading. In Feste's case it is peculiarly hard. He is perfectly sane, and there is nothing to show that he is unfit for independence. In important respects he is, more than Shakespeare's other fools, superior in mind to his superiors in rank. And he has no Celia, no Countess, no Lear, to protect or love him. He had been Fool to Olivia's father, who "took much delight in him"; but Olivia, though not unkind, cannot be said to love him. We find him, on his first appearance, in disgrace and (if Maria is right) in danger of being punished or even turned away. His mistress, entering, tells him that he is a dry fool, that she'll no more of him, and (later) that his fooling grows old and people dislike it. Her displeasure, doubtless, has a cause, and it is transient, but her words are none the less significant. Feste is a relic of the past. The steward, a person highly valued by his lady, is Feste's enemy. Though Maria likes him and, within limits, would stand his friend, there is no tone of affection in her words to him, and certainly none in those of any other person. We cannot but feel very sorry for him.

This peculiar position explains certain traits in Feste himself which might otherwise diminish our sympathy. One is that he himself, though he shows no serious malevolence even to his enemy, shows no affection for any one. His liking for Maria does not amount to fondness. He enjoys drinking and singing with Sir Toby, but despises his drunkenness and does not care for him. His attitude to strangers is decidedly cool, and he does not appear to be attracted even by Viola. The fact is, he recognizes very clearly that, as this world goes, a man whom nobody loves must look out for himself. Hence (this is the second trait) he is a shameless beggar, much the most so of Shakespeare's Fools. He is fully justified, and he begs so amusingly that we welcome his begging; but shameless it is. But he is laying up treasures on earth against the day when some freak of his own, or some whim in his mistress, will bring his dismissal, and the short summer of his freedom will be followed by the wind and the rain. And so, finally, he is as careful as his love of fun will allow to keep clear of any really dangerous enterprise. He must join in the revel of the knights and the defiance of the steward; but from the moment when Malvolio retires with a threat to Maria, and Maria begins to expound her plot against him, Feste keeps silence; and, though she expressly assigns him a part in the conspiracy, he takes none. The plot succeeds magnificently, and Malvolio is shut up, chained as a lunatic, in a dark room; and that comic genius Maria has a new scheme, which requires the active help of the Fool. But her words, "Nay, I prithee, put on this gown and this beard," show that he objects; and if his hesitation is momentary, it is not merely because the temptation is strong. For, after all, he runs but little risk, since Malvolio cannot see him, and he is a master in the management of his voice. And so, agreeing with Sir Toby's view that their sport cannot with safety be pursued to the upshot, after a while, when he is left alone with the steward, he takes steps to end it and consents, in his own voice, to provide the lunatic with light, pen, ink, and paper for his letter to Olivia.

We are not offended by Feste's eagerness for sixpences and his avoidance of risks. By helping us to realize the hardness of his lot, they add to our sympathy and make us admire the more the serenity and gaiety of his spirit. And at the close of the play these feelings reach their height. He is left alone; for Lady Belch, no doubt, is by her husband's bedside, and the thinfaced gull Sir Andrew has vanished, and the rich and noble lovers with all their attendants have streamed away to dream of the golden time to come, without a thought of the poor jester. There is no one to hear him sing; but what does that matter? He takes pleasure in singing. And a song comes into his head; an old rude song about the stages of man's life, in each of which the rain rains every day;

a song at once cheerful and rueful, stoical and humorous; and this
suits his mood and he sings it. But, since he is even more of a
philosopher than the author of the song, and since, after all, he is
not merely a Fool but the actor who is playing that part in a
theatre, he adds at the end a stanza of his own:

> A great while ago the world begun,
>   With hey, ho, the wind and the rain,
> But that's all one, our play is done,
>   And we'll strive to please you every day.[3]

Shakespeare himself, I feel sure, added that stanza to the old
song; and when he came to write *King Lear* he, I think, wrote yet
another, which Feste might well have sung. To the immortal
words,

> Poor fool and knave, I have one part in my heart
> That's sorry yet for thee,

the Fool replies,

> He that has and a little tiny wit
>   With heigh-ho, the wind and the rain—
> Must make content with his fortunes fit,
>   Though the rain it raineth every day.

So Shakespeare brings the two Fools together; and, whether or
no he did this wittingly, I am equally grateful to him. But I cannot
be grateful to those critics who see in Feste's song only an illustration of the bad custom by which sometimes, when a play was
finished, the clown remained, or appeared, on the stage to talk
nonsense or to sing some old "trash"; nor yet to those who tell us
that it was "the players" who tacked this particular "trash" to the
end of *Twelfth Night*. They may conceivably be right in perceiving
no difference between the first four stanzas and the last, but they
cannot possibly be right in failing to perceive how appropriate the
song is to the singer, and how in the line

> But that's all one, our play is done,

he repeats an expression used a minute before in his last speech.[4]
We owe these things, not to the players, but to that player in
Shakespeare's company who was also a poet, to Shakespeare

himself—the same Shakespeare who perhaps had hummed the old song, half-ruefully and half-cheerfully, to its accordant air, as he walked home alone to his lodging from the theatre or even from some noble's mansion; he who, looking down from an immeasurable height on the mind of the public and the noble, had yet to be their servant and jester, and to depend upon their favour; not wholly uncorrupted by this dependence, but yet superior to it and, also, determined, like Feste, to lay by the sixpences it brought him, until at last he could say the words, "Our revels now are ended,"⁵ and could break—was it a magician's staff or a Fool's bauble?

NOTES

1. I mean the Fools proper, i.e. professional jesters attached to a court or house. In effect they are but four, Touchstone, Feste, Lavache in *All's Well*, and Lear's Fool; for it is not clear that Trinculo is the court-jester, and the Clown in *Othello*, like the Fool (a brothel-fool) in *Timon*, has but a trivial part. Neither humorists like Launce and Launcelot Gobbo, nor "low" characters, unintentionally humorous, like the old peasant at the end of *Antony and Cleopatra* or the young shepherd called "clown" in *The Winter's Tale*, are Fools proper. The distinction is quite clear, but it tends to be obscured for readers because the wider designation "clown" is applied to persons of either class in the few lists of Dramatis Personæ printed in the Folio, in the complete lists of our modern editions, and also, alike in these editions and in the Folio, in stage-directions and in the headings of speeches. Such directions and headings were meant for the actors, and the principal comic man of the company doubtless played both Launce and Feste. Feste, I may observe, is called "Clown" in the stage-directions and speech-headings, but in the text always "Fool." Lear's Fool is "Fool" even in the former.
2. Feste's statement of his proof (v i 20) can hardly be called lucid, and his illustration ("conclusions to be as kisses, if your four negatives make your two affirmatives") seems to have cost the commentators much fruitless labour. If anything definite was in the Fool's mind it may have been this. The gentleman asks for a kiss. The lady, denying it, exclaims "No no no no." But, as the first negative (and adjective) negates the second (a substantive), and the third in like manner the fourth, these four negatives yield two enthusiastic affirmatives, and the gentleman, thanks to the power of logic, gets twice what he asked

for. This is not Feste's only gird at the wisdom of the schools. It has
been gravely surmised that he was educated for the priesthood and,
but for some escapade, would have played Sir Topas in earnest.

3. Those who witnessed, some years ago, Mr Granville-Barker's production of *Twelfth Night*, and Mr Hayden Coffin's presentment of the
Fool's part, must always remember them with great pleasure, and not
least the singing of this song.

4. "I was one, sir, in this interlude; one Sir Topas, sir; *but that's all one.*"

5. *The Tempest*, iv i 148.

John Russell Brown

Directions for *Twelfth Night*

After the first dozen *Twelfth Night's* there are still surprises, new guises for the old masterpiece. Directors colour it golden, russet, silver or white; blue for dreams, and sometimes pink; or they allow red and even purple to dominate. They can make it sound noisy as a carnival, or eager, or melodious, or quarrelsome like children; it can also be strained and nervous. In 1958, Peter Hall at Stratford-upon-Avon hung the stage with gauzes and contrived what *The Times* called a "Watteauesque light." And critics report that a year previously, at Stratford, Ontario, Tyrone Guthrie contrasted Feste and Malvolio in "psychological terms," allowing the final song of the "wind and rain" to be "as plaintive and wonderful as Jewish lament." Two years before that, at the English Stratford, Sir John Gielgud brought "a faint chill to the air" of his production; the comics were on their best behaviour in deference to a pervasive "charm"; *The Observer* said that the polite word for this would be "formal," and the exact word "mechanical"; it seemed as if, during rehearsals of the last scene, Sir John had stopped the actors and commanded, "Be beautiful; be beautiful."

This play might have been designed for an age when each director must make his name and register his mark. Yet there is one difficulty: in most productions some part of the play resists the director's control. In Sir John's elegant *Twelfth Night*, Malvolio yielded Sir Laurence Olivier a role in which to exploit his impudent and plebeian comedy, and in his last line—"I'll be reveng'd on

Reprinted by permission of the author and Edward Arnold Publishers, Ltd., from *Shakespeare's Plays in Performance*, by John Russell Brown.

the whole pack of you"—an opportunity for the cry of a man
unmade. The grey and urban setting of the Old Vic's production
in 1950 was enlivened by an untrained ballet of sailors and riff-
raff, but Peggy Ashcroft's clear, white voice was an unechoed
reminder of other directions the comedy can be given. More
commonly, without such trained stars to cross the director's
intentions, robust comics usurp more attention than their part in
the last Act is allowed to satisfy, or an intelligent Sebastian will
deny his own words, a too gentle Orsino devalue Viola's ardour.
There is need for vigilance: Margaret Webster, who sees *Twelfth
Night* as "filled with impermanence, fragile, imponderable," has
found that:

> The director will have to balance and combine his in-
> gredients in carefully graded proportions, compensating
> for weaknesses, keeping a moderating hand on excessive
> strength. This play, above all, he must treat with a light
> touch and a flexible mind, keeping the final goal clearly in
> sight.[1]

What happened, one wonders, before there were directors to give
directions?

For if we refer back, from the theatre to the text of the play,
we shall observe a similar lack of simplicity and uniformity. Malvolio can be a "turkey cock," a common "geck and gull" who is told
to "shake his ears"; or a fantastic who asks what "an alphabetical
position portends" and speaks repeatedly "out of his welkin." Yet
Olivier's petty, ambitious vulgarian is also true to the text when
he addresses his mistress with "Sweet lady, ho, ho!" and with tags
from popular ballads. Even Michael Hordern's tortured Malvolio
at the Old Vic in 1954, "dried up, emaciated, elongated . . . [as] an
El Greco"—his hands, reaching out of the pit in the scene where
Feste visits him as Sir Topas, the curate, suggested to one critic
"the damned in the *Inferno*"—is authorised by Feste's disguise, by
his own first words of "the pangs of death" and "infirmity," his
account of how "imagination" jades him, and his physical and
psychological isolation at the end. And yet again, Olivia's high
regard for Malvolio—she "would not lose him for half her
dowry"—justifies Eric Porter's performance at Stratford-upon-
Avon in 1960, as a solid, efficient steward walking with practical
good sense to worlds unrealised.

Actors seeking to express their originality will find that "new" interpretations rise unbidden from a straightforward study of the text. Sir Toby is usually a domesticated Falstaff, but at the Old Vic in 1958 with tumultuous "gulps and shouts," he was seen as a plain "boor"; and for this there is plenty of support in his name, Belch, and in his talk of "boarding and assailing," making water and cutting "mutton." And the same year, at Stratford-upon-Avon, Patrick Wymark made him young and spry with a sense of style; for this, "she's a beagle, true-bred" was most appropriate language, and his easy confidence in "consanguinity" with Olivia and expertise in swordplay were natural accomplishments. One might imagine too, a melancholy Sir Toby, tried in true service and knowing from experience that "care's an enemy to life": his tricks upon Sir Andrew would then be a compensation for his own retirement, his wooing—off-stage and presumably brief—of Maria, a just and difficult tribute to her service for him; lethargy comes with drunkenness and he "hates a drunken rogue"; he needs company, even that of a fool, an ass, and a servant.

Olivia is another role which can be seen to be of different ages—either mature years or extreme youth; and she can be melancholy or gay. Maxine Audley at Stratford-upon-Avon in 1955 presented a gracious lady, truly grieving for the death of her brother and strong enough to recognise an absolute passion for a boy; this Olivia had the "smooth, discreet and stable bearing," the majesty, to which Sebastian and Orsino testify. And three years later, at the same theatre, Geraldine McEwan presented her as kittenish and cute, saved from triviality by fine timing of movement and verse-speaking, the dignity of "style." And yet another Olivia may be suggested by the text: a very young girl, at first afraid of meeting the world and therefore living in a fantasy capable of decreeing seven years of mourning; then a girl solemnly repeating old saws with a new understanding of their truth:

> Even so quickly may one catch the plague? . . . I do I know not what, and fear to find Mine eye too great a flatterer for my mind. . . . What is decreed must be . . . how apt the poor are to be proud . . . youth is bought more oft than begg'd or borrowed,

and forgetting her "discreet" bearing in breathless eagerness:

> *How* does he love me? . . . *Why*, what would you? . . . not
> too *fast*: soft, soft! . . . Well, *let* it be, . . . That's a degree to
> love. . . . Yet *come* again . . . *I* have sent after him: *he says* he'll
> come. . . . *What* do you say? . . . *Most wonderful!*

Feste, the fool, can be melancholy, or bitter, or professional, or
amorous (and sometimes impressively silent), or self-contained
and philosophical, or bawdy and impotent. Sir Andrew Aguecheek can be patient, sunny, feckless, gormless, animated or neu-
rotic. (In 1958 Richard Johnson gave an assured performance of
this knight as a "paranoid manic-depressive, strongly reminiscent
at times of Lucky in *Waiting for Godot*.") Orsino can be mature or
very young; poetic; or weak; or strong but deceived; or real and
distant. The text can suggest a Viola who is pert, sentimental,
lyrical, practical, courageous or helpless. Shakespeare's words can
support all these interpretations, and others; there are few plays
which give comparable scope for enterprise and originality. The
characters, the situations and the speeches are protean.

This is evident in a director's ability to alter the trend of his
production, even in the very last moments, to achieve what Miss
Webster has called his "balance," to arrive at his chosen "final
goal." If sentiment needs reinforcing, Viola (as Cesario) can be
given a down-stage position and a preparatory pause as the arrangements for her duel with Sir Andrew grow to a comic climax,
and thus her "I do assure you, 'tis against my will" can be, not the
usual laugh-line, but a reminder of her other full-hearted struggles of will and passion; this momentary seriousness, the more
impressive for its incongruous setting, was managed with great
grace by Dorothy Tutin at Stratford, in peter Hall's productions
of 1958 and 1960. Still later in theplay, there is another opportunity for the strong re-emphasis of Viola's depth of feeling: Peggy
Ashcroft mastered this in 1950, and J. C. Trewin has well described its effect in performance:

> At the end, as Sebastian faces his sister, he cries: "What
> countryman? What name? What parentage?" There is a long
> pause now before Viola, in almost a whisper (but one of
> infinite rapture and astonishment) answers: 'Of Messaline'.
> Practically for the first time in my experience a Viola has
> forced me to believe in her past. . . .[2]

More simply and without affecting any established characterisation, the balance of a production can be altered by the Priest's lines in the last scene, with their special idiom and assured syntax and timing:

> A contract of eternal bond of love,
> Confirm'd by mutual joinder of your hands,
> Attested by the holy close of lips,
> Strength'ned by interchangement of your rings
> And all the ceremony of this compact
> Seal'd in my function, by my testimony;
> Since when, my watch hath told me, toward my grave,
> I have travell'd but two hours.

If these lines are spoken in a weighty and measured way, they can restore a sense of awe, an awareness of general and timeless implications, to a dénouement which has become too head-long and hilarious for the director's taste. Or, at the last moment, Orsino can give "guts" to an over-pretty production: the sight of Antonio permits an evocation of the "smoke of war" and "scathful grapple," and can legitimately bring a harsh quality to his voice which has hitherto been tuned to softer themes. When he invites Olivia to live "the marble-breasted tyrant still" and turns to Cesario with:

> But this your minion, whom I know you love,
> And whom, by heaven I swear, I tender dearly,
> Him will I tear out of that cruel eye
> Where he sits crowned in his master's spite.
> Come, boy, with me; my thoughts are ripe in mischief:
> I'll sacrifice the lamb that I do love
> To spite a raven's heart within a dove

the director can call for physical as well as verbal violence towards Viola. The lines imply that Orsino cares more for his seeming boy than for the lady of his dreams and fancy, and thus they may be acted fully and strongly; the release of passion in a desire to kill Cesario shows the true object of that passion, and its power. (This reading of the subtext is authorised by Shakespeare, as by Freud and Stanislavski, for Orsino has just acknowledged that a "savage" jealousy "kills what it loves," not what it *thinks* it loves.) If the production is, at this stage of the play, too solemn rather than too sentimental or hilarious, there are opportunities in plenty for lightening the whole last Act: Olivia's "Where goes Cesario?," after Orsino's outburst, can easily be spoken to invite laughter; and so can her "Most wonderful" as Viola and Sebastian confront each other. Nearly all Sebastian's lines can be tipped the same way, as "I do perceive it hath offended you" . . . "Fear'st thou that, Antonio" . . . and (about the mole on the brow of Viola's father) "And so had mine." Antonio's "An apple, cleft in two is not more twin" can be directed so that it implies laughter rather than rapt amazement, and Orsino's final "Cesario, come" can be a jest at the whole contrivance of the last Act, or even at Viola's expense, rather than recognition of his own long, half-hidden affection for his bride-to-be.

The opportunities for swinging a production round into line with a chosen mood—to make it "what they will," to reverse roles as in a "Twelfth Night" revel—have encouraged directors to tackle *Twelfth Night* and to experiment widely in the search for original interpretations. But a second practical consequence of the free-dom of interpretation is of greater importance: this play chal-lenges us to provide a longer and deeper study than is normally given to a text in the theatre. We may be assured that the diverse ways of playing the characters and controlling the mood are not finally irreconcilable. The experience of seeing many independent productions and reading about many more does not create a multitude of separate memories; each new revelation reflects on earlier ones and, in the mind, a single view of the play is continu-ally growing in complexity and range, and in understanding. We may believe that a single production might, one day, represent to the full our single, developing awareness. Our knowledge of *Twelfth Night* and of human behaviour may assure us that an Olivia is both mature and immature, according to which side of her personality is in view; a Sir Toby energetic *and* melancholic, vulgar *and* well-schooled; and a Viola lyrical *and* practical, *and* helpless. The world of the play is gay, quiet, strained, solemn, dignified, elegant, easy, complicated, precarious, hearty, homely; the con-clusion close to laughter, song, awe *and* simplicity. And this is an understanding which begs not to be hid, but to be realised on the stage.

Of course, in the theatre it is tempting to simplify too early, in order to be effective and make a "strong" impression. But with such a play as *Twelfth Night* we are drawn by another possibility, a more demanding course: five years' study, a repeated return to its problems in a succession of productions under different conditions and for different audiences, might make possible a production which would be original, not by one-sidedness, but by answering more fully than before to Shakespeare's text and combining the excitement of many interpretations. The time necessary to make this attempt would be an expensive investment; and it would be a risky one—for the speculator may not be capable of living up to the developing demands of his enterprise. Yet the business is a practical possibility, and must be considered. An exclusive pursuit of immediate effectiveness and originality leads to immature and insecure achievements, in theatres as in other fields of activity; a play like *Twelfth Night* offers, therefore, an opportunity and a challenge which it would be salutary merely to envisage, regenerative to attempt. Shakespeare's stage-cunning, human understanding and poetic imagination, which are all implicit in the text, would be fine assets.

The necessary conditions for such an achievement would be a concern for, and skill in, all the arts of the theatre—this is required for any sort of theatrical success—but, more peculiarly, a constant return to the details of Shakespeare's text. Here the popular misconception that close textual study is a dull and pedestrian activity, restricting originality and encouraging an exclusively verbal kind of drama—may inhibit the right kind of work, and must be denounced: a prolonged and careful study of Shakespeare's text, in association with other theatre skills, can awaken and enrich a production in all elements of a play's life. If we trust Shakespeare's imagination, we know that *Twelfth Night* was conceived as a whole with each apparently discordant element reconciled to its opposite: and our only clue to that original resolution is the printed words. Every opportunity for visual realisation or elaboration, for movement and variation of grouping, for temporal control, for subtlety of elocution or stage-business, for creation of character and mood, emotion and expression, that the text can suggest should be searched out, tested, practically evaluated and, finally, given its due place in the responsible and mature production which each successive, partial and conflicting production of such a play as *Twelfth Night* invites us to consider, and to hope that one day we may help to stage or witness.

The combination, or growing together, of elements from new interpretations of roles is, perhaps, the best charted part of a difficult task; it calls for a developing sympathy and understanding, and a grasp of the progressive and formal presentation of character, but it does not require, at the beginning of rehearsals, a single limiting choice; moreover the actors are always in obvious contact with Shakespeare's words. Perhaps the problems of a textually responsible production will be most perplexing in choosing the stage setting, especially if the play is to be performed on a picture-frame stage with the full range of modern equipment.

Twelfth Night has received many visual interpretations: the elegant, controlled and overtly dramatic, as a Tiepolo fresco, is a common one; or domestic with dark shadows, like the Jacobean interiors in Joseph Nash's *Mansions of England in the Olden Times*; or Italianate, free and colourful in the fashion of the *commedia dell'arte*. Or the stage may be spacious and clean, like one modern notion of what an Elizabethan platform stage was like, or pillared, tiered and substantial, like another. Some designers have introduced the satins and laces of Restoration England, and others the boaters and billows of the theatre of *Charley's Aunt*. The main difficulty is that all these, and others, are in some degree appropriate, usually in different parts of the play; and yet it would be distracting to a modern audience to move from one to another during a single performance, even if this were technically possible. If a mature production of *Twelfth Night* is to be considered, this problem will have to be solved in a single way—the more urgently because the proscenium arches and lighting devices of modern theatres have made the visual embodiment of a play, in setting, costumes and effects, a dominating—often *the* dominating—element of a production.

A recourse to the text in the search for a comprehensive style and single stage setting does not involve the director in an antiquarian production which tries to reproduce original stage conditions; those are, in any case, irrecoverable in their full complexity, which involves specially trained actors and historically accurate audiences, as well as theatres which no longer exist. The study of the text can be of help in utilising the modern technical devices of a picture-frame stage, and in answering the expectations of any particular audience. The verbal imagery can, for example, give valuable help towards deciding which setting is most appropriate; it can tell the director the kind of visual images which were associated with the action and characters in the author's mind and which he may usefully transmit to the audience in visual stage terms.

Illyria, the world of *Twelfth Night*, is obviously a land of love, music, leisure, servants, a Duke and a Countess; it must have dwellings, a garden, a seacoast and a "dark house" or temporary prison. Its institutions include a church and a chantry, a captain and officers of the law, an inn; and there must be doors or gates. Thus far the choice of a setting is not circumscribed; it might be English, Italian, French, Russian (before the revolution), or, with some adaptation, American or Utopian; medieval, renaissance or modern. But incidental details of speech and action at once limit the setting to something resembling, or representing, English countryside and domesticity. In the first scene there are mentioned a bank of violets, a hunt, sweet beds of flowers, and these are followed by wind and weather, a squash and a peascod, a willow, the hills, a beagle, roses, a yew, a cypress and box tree, and more flowers; familiar living creatures are a hart, a sheep-biter, a horse, a trout, a turkey-cock and a wood-cock, a raven, lamb and dove, and hounds; daylight, champaign (or open fields), harvest, ripeness, and oxen and wain-ropes easily come to mind; the songs of nightingales, daws and owls have been heard. The characters of the play do not talk of an elegant or fanciful scene, although the violets and beds of flowers might be interpreted in that way; their wain-ropes, sheep-biter and daws belong to a countryside that knows labour and inconvenience, as well as delights. Speaking of horrors and danger, they are neither sophisticated nor learned; they refer to tempests, the sea, fields, mountains, barbarous caves, and hunger. The domestic note is almost as persistent as that of the countryside: early in Act I, canary-wine, beef, a housewife and a buttery-bar are mentioned; even the Duke, Orsino, speaks of knitters in the sun; there is talk of pilchards and herrings (fresh and pickled) and of vinegar and pepper. If a director is to attempt a responsible production of the play, he should give substance to these references in his setting— not in an illustrative way which provides objects for the actors to point at, but in a manner which echoes, extends and, where appropriate, contrasts with the dialogue and stage business. This is the mental and emotional world of the *dramatis personae* as revealed by their language, and the stage picture can help to establish this, not insistently, but with subtlety.

It is the world of the play's action too, and its visual recreation will, therefore, aid the director towards an appropriate rhythm and acting style: an Italianate setting, which is often chosen, suggests the wrong tempo—the wrong temperature even—and insists on distracting contrasts between dialogue and visual effect. An English summer takes three months to establish itself, through April, May and June, and so does the action of this play— as Orsino states explicitly in the last scene. It would be convenient, therefore, to show this passage of time in modifications to the setting during the course of the play: the first Acts green and youthful, the last coloured with roses in bloom and strong lights; the same setting but at different times of the year. In the first scene Orsino would be seeking the earliest violets; later "beauty's a flower," "women are as roses," "youth's a stuff will not endure" would sound properly precarious in view of the visual reminder of the changing seasons; a "lenten answer" would seem more restrictive and "let summer bear it out" a fuller and more inevitable judgement. Orsino might stand in white, as the young lover in Nicholas Hillyarde's miniature (dated about 1590), over against frail, twining roses: this association represented for the painter his motto—*"Dat poenas laudata fides,"* or "My praisèd faith procures my pain"—and it might serve in much the same way today. "Midsummer madness" and "matter for a May morning," which are spoken of in Act III, would be in key with the setting, and the talk of harvest, the grave and the immutable yew-tree would sound in significant contrast.

The course of single days might also be suggested in the lighting of the stage picture. Talk of hunting in the first scene establishes the time as early morning. In the third, Maria's remonstrance to Sir Toby about returning late "a'nights" belongs to the first meeting of a new day, and then coming "early" by one's "lethargy" implies preprandial drinking. In II iii, the chaffing about "being up late," Malvolio's chiding about "respect of . . . time," and "it's too late to go to bed now" all suggest midnight; so one "day" is completed in due order. (Again Feste's song in this last mentioned scene, about "present mirth" and "what's to come" and "youth's a stuff will not endure," will be more poignant if it seems indeed to have been sung before the "night-owl," nature's reminder of death, is roused.) The following scene, II iv, is clearly a new day with its first lines of "good morrow" and "we heard last night"; and the truth that ". . . women are as roses, whose fair flower Being once display'd doth fall that very hour" is more fully expressed if spoken in the transitory light of dawn. The next scene, II v, beginning with "Come thy ways . . ." and with news that Malvolio has been "i' the sun practising behaviour to his own shadow this half hour," is still early morning. Act III, scene i, which follows with Feste speaking of the sun shining everywhere, may be at noon, and later, when Malvolio supposes Olivia invites him to bed, his outrageous presumption would be more apparent if it were obviously not that "time of day." At the end of IV ii, Feste visits Malvolio in prison and sings:

> I'll be with you again,
>   In a trice,
>   Like to the old Vice,
> Your need to sustain;
>
> Who, with dagger of lath,
> In his rage and his wrath,
>   Cries, Ah ha! to the devil. . . .

—here stage lighting could simulate a sudden, passing storm, such as interrupts an easy summer's afternoon in England; it might culminate in thunder. This would be an elaboration impossible to stage in an Elizabethan theatre, but it would be appropriate in a play which is continually concerned with the summer countryside of England, with "beauty that can endure wind and weather," and which ends with a song of the rain that "raineth every day." Sir Toby and Maria could take shelter from the storm, while the fool is left to bear it out and "pursue the sport." The sun would shine fully again for Sebastian's "This is the air; that is the glorious sun; This pearl she gave me . . . ," and for the high afternoon of the ending of the comedy. Towards the close shadows might lengthen and, as the marriages are postponed till "golden time convents," the sky might become golden with a sunset's promise of another fair day. Then as the other characters leave, to enter perhaps a lighted house, Feste might be left in the grey-green light of early evening to sing alone of time and youth, and of the beginning of the world and the conclusion of a play.

(There is in fact a double time scheme in *Twelfth Night*: three months for the development and fulfilment of the action, and two consecutive days for the sequence of scenes. The representation of both schemes in the setting and in the lighting may help an audience to accept this double sense of time which suits, on the one hand, the rapid fairy-tale transitions and the "changeable" characterisations, and, on the other hand, the play's suggestion of the season's alterations and the endurance and maturing of affections.)

Such lighting effects require an outdoor setting for almost all the play. And this may be convenient for the action: Olivia's house might be shown to one side, with a terrace and garden before it, a main entrance and a way to the back door; and there might be a dovecote, small pavilion or gazebo on the other side of the stage to do duty as Malvolio's prison. There would be some inconvenience in staging the carousing scene between Feste, Sir Toby and Sir Andrew in a garden, but there is plenty of reference to outdoor affairs in its dialogue and the two knights could fall asleep around their table at the close of the scene and be discovered there next morning to be awakened by Fabian. The scenes at Orsino's court could also be in the open air, and could be set by bringing in tall cypress hedges to mask Olivia's house and garden, and to reveal part of the sky-cloth or cyclorama at the end of a long walk or vista in some spacious park. It would be appropriately affected for Orsino to seek the shade of such a walk in the early morning; there could be a stone seat on one side, and on the other a sculpture of Venus, or some such deity. For the brief scene outside Olivia's gate (II ii) and for the Sebastian scenes, "somewhere in Illyria" (II i and III iii), a "wall" could be let down from the flies, with a gate in its centre: this would locate the action outside Olivia's estate and, if her house and the taller trees were visible over the top of the wall and through the gate, the audience would relish the physical proximity of Sebastian to his journey's end.

There remains one, apparently unrelated, scene (I ii) which begins "What country, friends, is this?" This might also be played "outside Olivia's garden," but Viola's mysterious entry into the play from the sea asks for a different visual presentation. It would be possible to play it in front of gauzes let down to hide the transition from Orsino's park of I i, to Olivia's garden of I iii; these might be lightly painted and lit to suggest a seashore, touched, perhaps with fluorescent material low down, as if catching the surf of a strange sea. If Orsino had been contemplating a statue of Venus in the previous scene that figure might be caught by a higher light as the gauzes came down, and then, in a moment of darkness, Viola might take its place to rise from the sea as the stage is relit. If this were effected tactfully, this scene could easily take its place in the chiaroscuro: its sea-effects might be echoed later as Feste is also isolated in the "storm" of his "vice" song; and echoed differently at the end of the play, as he is isolated in the evening. Moreover the myth-like transition and transference would be in keeping with the "romantic" attraction of the lovers and the solution of their stories—the dream, or fantasy element, of the play.

The colours of setting and costumes could be those of an early English summer: clear, light blues, greens, yellows and pinks, and plenty of white. The buildings could be the honey-coloured stone of the English Cotswolds, with marble ornaments for Orsino's park. Olivia would, of course, wear black while in mourning, and Malvolio always—the only character to take no colour from the sun.

Such is one solution of the visual problems of *Twelfth Night*, and one which tries to answer the demands of the text in terms of the realism of the picture-frame stage—which is perhaps the furthest removed from Elizabethan practice. Other stages and other visual styles would call for different solutions. This way of staging the play is worth consideration chiefly as an example: for if any production is to be undertaken with a belief in the unity and imaginative quality of Shakespeare's text, its choice of setting must answer the same demands and others like them, as more are revealed through further study of the text and further experiments in eccentric productions.

The quest for a responsible direction for *Twelfth Night* will not lead to a series of stereotyped productions: changing stage-conditions, actors and audiences will prevent that. Nor will we rest content with our achievements, for the "idea" of the play, which grows in our minds as we meet it frequently in many guises, is most likely to remain several steps beyond our most truthful production. The desire for an authentic direction will not be satisfied easily, but those who try to respond to it will grow more aware of the wealth of Shakespeare's imagination and perhaps more expert in their attempts to give his masterpiece its theatrical life.

NOTES

1. *Shakespeare Today* (1957), p. 205.
2. *John O'London's Weekly*, 8 December 1950.

Arthur Colby Sprague

Twelfth Night

The fact that this most delightful of Shakespeare's comedies was on the boards in the sixteen-sixties, when Pepys saw it more than once—"a silly play," he calls it, "and not related at all to the name or day"—may well be misleading. For though, in 1703, *Twelfth Night* furnished ideas and a certain number of lines to a negligible piece by William Burnaby called *Love Betray'd*, it was not acted again until 1741, this time, we may be certain, without the slightest guidance from tradition.

It has long been customary for Viola, in the second scene, to be accompanied by two sailors carrying a "trunk" or "chest." Why, by the way, it is perfectly seemly for Viola, landing in Illyria, to have luggage, when it would be slightly ridiculous for Hamlet, setting out for England, to have any, is matter for thought.[1] Miss Helen Hayes, I recall, upon entering pretended to shake sand from her shoe.

Sir Andrew Aguecheek's demonstration of dancing and capering is the most notable bit of business in Scene 3. In one of two *Twelfth Night* promptbooks prepared by George Becks (this one identified by a reference to Adelaide Neilson), when Sir Toby says "Let me see thee caper," "Sir A does so—Sir Toby taps his cane on stage—higher &c.—Sir Toby laughing & applauding"—and the friends go out "laughing & capering." A "Walk Cane each" for the frolicsome knights is called for in Mrs. Shaw's promptbook (c. 1850). For a more subtle touch, one reads of Norman Forbes, the Aguecheek in Tree's production, that "his startled look when

Reprinted from *Shakespeare and the Actors* (Harvard University Press, 1944), by Arthur Colby Sprague.

he caught sight of Maria over Sir Toby's shoulder as the knights embraced, was by itself worth the money." Equally happy was an idea of Kate Terry's in the next scene: Viola's "quick turn at the sound of [Orsino's] voice in the question 'Where's Caesario?'"[2]

Tree as Malvolio entered in state, attended by "four smaller Malvolios, who aped the great chamberlain in dress, in manners, in deportment. He had a magnificent flight of stairs on the stage; and when he was descending it majestically, he slipped and fell with a crash sitting." Mr. Bernard Shaw yet finds that this was not "mere clowning. . . . Tree, without betraying the smallest discomfiture, raised his eyeglass and surveyed the landscape as if he had sat down on purpose." Irving had entered with upturned nose, "and eyes half shut, as if with singular and moody contemplation."[3] Sent to admit Cesario, Malvolio has sometimes returned with him, to linger on the stage for whatever values might be obtained from his silent presence. Thus, Daly made Cesario's "some mollification for your giant, sweet lady" (I, 5, 218) apply to him and not to the little "wren," Maria—and was taken to task by Archer for doing so.[4] Two mid-nineteenth-century prompt notes of John Moore's may be quoted in passing. Sir Toby's entrance is "with slightly unsteady gait—Hat over eyes, and cloak awry," and, before "A plague o' these pickle-herring!" "Pause slight Belch." Later, when Olivia says "I thank you for your pains," it is, "Retreating gradually to wing her eyes fixed on Viola—suddenly and eagerly advances to her and offers a purse."

Malvolio has long carried a wand; but it seems to have been Tree who first used the still familiar business of slipping Olivia's ring over the point of this wand and dropping it, churlishly enough, at Cesario's feet.[5] In Viola's soliloquy, which follows this incident in Act II, Scene 2, Mrs. Charles Kean (Ellen Tree) is criticized by George Henry Lewes:

> The *look* with which she said "I am the man" was perfect; but that little saucy tap on her head, with the playful swagger which followed it, though they "brought down the house," appeared to us to betray a forgetfulness of Viola . . .

a passing into "the lower orbit of a soubrette." Julia Marlowe used regularly to check off on her fingers the several items in Viola's complicated account—"My master loves her dearly," etc.[6]

Voices have been raised from time to time in protest against the farcical extravagances of the so-called Kitchen Scene (II, 3). Thus, Joseph Knight in 1878 was "almost certain" that the traditional business dated back "to the time of the Restoration"— though not to a still earlier period, because there were too few of the elder actors who survived the long years during which the theatres were closed. Even so, he found the behavior of the drunken knights "preposterous, unnatural, inartistic, and wholly out of keeping with the general scope of the play." Mr. G. R. Foss, in 1932, not only spoke out against the same ancient abuses, but advanced reasons for supposing that the scene does not take place in a kitchen at all. He even denies that it is a drinking scene! Rather, Sir Toby and Sir Andrew upon their return from carousing have ventured into a part of the great house where their uproar is audible. Twice they call to Maria "to bring drink, but she never does." The last point seems to me indemonstrable.[7]

Our first glimpse of the scene is pleasant enough. Dunlap saw *Twelfth Night* at Drury Lane about 1785.

> The picture presented, when the two knights are discovered with their pipes and potations, as exhibited by Dodd and Palmer, is ineffaceable.. . . [Dodd's] thin legs in scarlet stockings, his knees raised nearly to his chin, by placing his feet on the front cross-piece of the chair (the degraded drunkards being seated with a table, tankards, pipes, and candles, between them), a candle in one hand and pipe in the other, endeavouring in vain to bring the two together; while, in representing the swaggering Sir Toby, Palmer's gigantic limbs outstretched seemed to indicate the enjoyment of that physical superiority which nature had given him.[8]

A generation later, the drunkenness of Liston's Sir Andrew made "his eyes dim and his feet tremble, without making his idiotism more senseless . . . his attempt to light his pipe was amusingly unsuccessful." Mrs. Shaw's promptbook calls for a "Long Pipe" each, for Sir Toby and his companion—and they were still smoking when Mr. Crosse saw them in Daly's production, and in Benson's wielded churchwardens.[9]

Shortly after Malvolio's entrance, comes this scrap of dialogue:

Clown [*sings*] "His eyes do show his days are almost done."
Mal.   Is't even so?
To.   "But I will never die."
Clown.   Sir Toby, there you lie.

Capell, who thinks often in terms of the stage, calls the last speech "a waggish remark in tune upon a great stumble of sir Toby's which brings him almost upon his nose."[10] Bell's edition (1774) has Sir Toby fall down singing. Of course, Sir Andrew goes to his assistance, and of course, in time, he too falls down. Then, according to Becks's promptnotes ("1864"), "Maria & Clown assist them, put them back to back—&c &c—ad lib." "Mal gets L—Sir A X L tries to light his pipe at Mals candle—comic bus—blows it out"; and, as the intruder turns to go, "Clown crows, flaps his arms as though they were wings. . . ." Moore has Sir Toby cross to Malvolio: "fillips his fingers in his face—and Xes behind back to R.H. kissing his hand to Maria as he passes. Clown Xes in the same manner and round again to his place. Sir A. Xes, but is too drunk or stupid to say anything." Malvolio exits, "shaking his head & hand threateningly," and Sir Toby "throws his pipe" after him.

It would be tedious to dwell on such inanities. A general warning must, however, be offered. It is Malvolio who gives offense here; Malvolio who provokes vengeance. I well remember Maude Adams's angry walking up and down as the plan is taking shape in Maria's mind.[11] "Go shake your ears!" she had flung after him, as he went. If, on the contrary, an excess of physical abuse is meted out to the Steward, in this scene, he may, himself, become the injured party with much loss of meaning to what follows.

Near the end of the scene, Becks's "1864" promptbook has:

> Sir Andrew keeps repeating "Cut" as if it was the best joke in the world, laughing at it holding his sides—both Exeunt laughing loudly, or Sir Toby takes candle (also Sir A) from Table Comic bus—Toby mugs & holds candle to Sir A's face—he blows it out—then Toby tries to light it & fails—then make a desperate *thrust*—fails & both go up stairs—Sir Toby on hand & knees—when at top—rolls down.[12]

Of a performance by the Benson Company at the Lyceum, *The Athenaeum* (March 31, 1900) writes stuffily: "When Sir Andrew thrusts his long churchwarden tobacco-pipe through his belt as a sword, and when he and Sir Toby, after wild farcical business with their candles, stretch themselves out at full length . . . the effect is to us as depressing as it is inspiring to the uneducated portion of the public."

In the scene between Orsino and Viola (II, 4), Ada Rehan, upon receiving the chain which she is to give the Countess, "raised it to her lips and reverently kissed it." Julia Marlowe writes interestingly about another passage, the lines beginning "She never told her love." At one time, she had "endeavored to aid Shakespeare" and bring out the speaker's "shyness by coyly fingering Viola's little red cap. The result was that there was a great deal of red cap and not nearly enough of the maiden's perturbation." When, on the contrary, she had last played the part (this was written in 1901), she had "made an effort to keep everything still"—even to the ends of her fingers.

> Experience has taught me that . . . we cannot go far wrong if we let the lines have the center of the stage and allow them to show the poet's meaning. We cannot aid him by a multitude of gestures or by creating of intricate "business."[13]

On Malvolio's approach, in the Letter Scene, Moore's promptbook has: "Sir A. goes to pick up the letter. Toby pulls him to bush, C." Sometimes, Sir Toby and Fabian have hidden themselves behind a tree, with Sir Andrew actually climbing the tree and putting his head out through the branches—a refinement of which Becks notes, "This is better after duel."[14] The Steward reads—and greatness is thrust upon him. "How he went smiling to himself," Lamb writes of Bensley, "with what ineffable carelessness would he twirl his gold chain; what a dream it was!" Or there was Charles Fisher, at Burton's Theatre in 1853: "When it comes home to him at last that he indeed is the favored of *Olivia* . . . he was inimitable. Already [in fancy] he is clothed in yellow-stockings and cross-gartered; and he smiles, as he struts."[15]

In the third act there is little to detain us until we come to the

Duel Scene. Henry Austin Clapp, writing of a performance by Daly's Company at the Hollis Street Theatre, Boston, protests vigorously against

> the impertinent and monstrously absurd introduction of Sir Andrew silently to threaten Viola with his sword in her chief scene with Olivia, as if Olivia's faintly ironical phrase, "Be not afraid, good youth," needed any explanation when followed without pause by "I will not have you."[16]

There could be no better example, indeed, of "business out of keeping with the plain meaning of what Shakespeare wrote." When, in Scene 4, Malvolio enters, no longer "sad and civil" but "in very strange manner," we hear again of Lamb's Mr. Bensley:

> All his peculiarities of deportment . . . aided his exhibition of the steward—the sliding zig-zag advance and retreat of his figure fixed the attention to his stockings and his garters. His constrained smile, his hollow laugh, his lordly assumption, and his ineffable contempt of all that opposed him in the way to greatness were irresistibly diverting.

Fancy such a Malvolio exposed to the familiarity of Belch's "How dost thou, chuck?" accompanied as it sometimes was by a slap on the back![17]

In the eighteenth-century theatre, two armed grenadiers were posted one on each side of the proscenium, where they remained throughout the performance mute and unregarded. On October 28, 1763, one of these sentries, at Drury Lane, behaved most strangely, falling down "in a kind of fit" during the encounter between Viola and Sir Andrew. Explanations were promptly offered: as that his collapse was due to fear; that it resulted from excessive laughter, which seems somewhat more probable; that it had been arranged beforehand since "it was proper for *Sir Andrew* to place himself in that part of the stage the soldier occupied."[18] Sir Andrew in later times has taken refuge in strange places. Mr. Liston, at Covent Garden in 1820, "violated the whole illusion of his duel-scene with *Viola*, by climbing up a part of the proscenium." Mr. Mason, in Edinburgh five years later, climbed up a rope-ladder—"but even that he makes in perfect keeping with the character."[19] In Moore's promptbook, at line 342, the duellists advance towards centre—swords extended—but neither looking at his adversary. in centre the swords meet this frightens them, and they turn away ["causing Sir Toby and Fabian to bump together" inserted] & again are brought back by Sir Toby & Fabian—Advance as before Viola hits Sir Andrew on the leg—he holloas runs away and begin to climb tree L up stage.

By this time, however, if not before, he was more likely to postpone his climbing until Sir Toby crosses swords with Antonio. Then, when the brawl is over, Sir Toby calls him and he answers from among the branches—"Here I am."[20]

As for Viola, enough perhaps that Madame Modjeska realized that her antagonist was not in the least dangerous, had a good opportunity to hit him, and refrained from doing so, out of "womanly generosity"; whereas Julia Arthur beat her Sir Andrew first "with her sword, and then with her hands across his bent back."[21] One last glimpse of the knight comes from *The Examiner* June 5, 1808, and is probably by Leigh Hunt:

> The fixed and trembling posture of Mr. MATHEWS . . . his hard breathing which tried to recover itself now and then by a heavy sigh, and his occasional side bend of the head accompanied with a munch of the lips, like a person who has just swallowed a crust that had stuck in his throat, presented a perfect picture of feeble despair.

At the beginning of the Dark Room Scene (IV, 2),[22] "Malvolio," according to Becks's notes, "gives a deep groan & passes his head by the window straw beruffled." The miserable man has "chains on wrists," too. Irving exhibited him in "a nerveless state of prostrate dejection . . . stretched on the straw of a dungeon worthy of *Fidelio*."[23]

For relief, there is an account of Sir Andrew's final exit. *John Bull*, September 8, 1839, is grateful to Buckstone, at the Haymarket,

> for cheating us into hearty laughter by his whimsicalities in *Sir Andrew* . . . his parting look at *Olivia*, in the last scene, as if to ascertain whether there might not be a chance left for him, was characteristic, and in excellent keeping with his author.

Dyce, in 1853, could "well remember that, when *Twelfth Night* was revived at Edinburgh many years ago, Terry, who then acted Malvolio . . . had 'straw about him,' on his release from durance." Becks's "Neilson" Promptbook calls for "straws in his hair—one over hanging face—which annoys him for a time—finally pulls it out—Eyes red—terribly in earnest." His exit is a great moment. Phelps's restraint was striking. His Malvolio had gone through the play with half-closed eyes, as if there were "nothing in the world without that is worth noticing." Now "he opens his eyes on learning how he has been tricked," but

> they close again in happy self-content, and he is retiring in state without deigning a word to his tormentors, when, as the fool had twitted him by noting how "the whirligig of time brings in his revenges," he remembers that the whirligig is still in motion. Therefore, marching back with as much increase of speed as is consistent with magnificence, he threatens all—including now Olivia in his contempt—"I'll be revenged on the whole pack of you!"[24]

> Tree tore off his steward's chain—the chain Maria had referred to with derision, early in the play, the chain, too, which he had found himself fingering instinctively in the Letter Scene: "I frown the while, and perchance wind up my watch, or play with my—some rich jewel." Sothern preferred to tear the forged letter into bits, which he threw on the stage as he went. And "there was something of great dignity in the manner of that exit."[25]

NOTES

1. See the mid-century French and Lacy editions, the Moore, Mrs. Shaw, and Becks Promptbooks, Daly's acting edition (1893), and the "William Warren Edition," Boston, 1907 (based on Julia Marlowe's promptbook).

    Madame Modjeska, at Booth's, in 1882, appeared in a boat (William Winter, *Shakespeare on the Stage*, Second Series, New York, 1915, p. 62).

2. Gordon Crosse, *Fifty Years of Shakespearean Playgoing*, London, 1941, p. 48; Henry Morley, *Journal of a London Playgoer*, London, 1891, p. 308.

3. Shaw, in Max Beerbohm (ed.), *Herbert Beerbohm Tree*, New York,

[1920], p. 249, see also W. L. Courtney, *ibid.*, 255, and Percy Fitzgerald, *Shakespearean Representation*, London, 1908, pp. 73, 74; Edward R. Russell, "Mr. Irving's Work," *Fortnightly Review*, September 1, 1884.

4. *Theatrical World of 1894*, p. 30. "*Malvolio goes off in contempt, waved away by Olivia*" is the direction in Daly's edition.

5. Cf. Fitzgerald, *Shakespearean Representation*, 73, "William Warren Edition." The wand itself is called for in Mrs. Shaw's promptbook. It is doubtless older.

6. *The Leader*, October 5, 1850, quoted in *Dramatic Essays of John Forster and George Henry Lewes*, eds. William Archer and R. W. Lowe, London, 1896, p. 106; Charles Edward Russell, *Julia Marlowe: Her Life and Art*, New York, 1926, pp. 123, 124.

7. *Theatrical Notes*, London, 1894, pp. 204, 205; *What the Author Meant*, 92, 93.

8. *History of the American Theatre*, London, 1833, II, 57, 58. The performance would seem to have been shortly after Mrs. Jordan's first appearance as Viola, November 11, 1785.

9. *European Magazine*, December 1820; *Fifty Years of Shakespearean Playgoing*, 144; Charlotte Stopes, in *Poet-Lore*, VIII (1896), p. 343, and cf. page 7, below.

10. *Notes and Various Readings*, London [1779], part IV, p. 146. As Kittredge notes, "'There you lie' gives excellent sense without any such buffoonery" (Ed. *Twelfth Night*, p. 116).

11. Performance at Ogunquit, Maine, July 21, 1934.

12. Seemingly, the candle business was the more recent. Up to "or" the notes are in an earlier hand; what follows, in Becks's own. His "Neilson" book has only this. Cf. also "William Warren Edition."

13. William Winter, *Ada Rehan*, New York and London, 1898, p. 191; "The Essentials of Stage Success," *Theatre* (New York), December 1901.

14. "1864" Promptbook. Mrs. Shaw's also has the tree. Great liberties have often been taken with the convention by which the presence of the conspirators remains unperceived by Malvolio.

15. *Dramatic Essays*, ed. Brander Matthews, New York [1891], p. 51 (he is writing of a performance at Drury Lane in 1790); William L. Keese, *William E. Burton*, New York and London, 1885, p. 79 (for the date, cf. Odell, *Annals of the New York Stage*, VI, 209).

16. *Boston Advertiser*, April 18, 1893, in Blinn Shakespeare Scrapbooks (Harvard Theatre Collection).
    That Aguecheek's "As plain as I see you now" (III, 2, 11) was prompted by his catching Sir Toby exchanging winks with Fabian is at least conceivable (see "William Warren Edition").

17. James Boaden, *Memoirs of the Life of John Philip Kemble, Esq.*, 2 vols., London, 1825, 1, 57; Becks Promptbook, cf. "William Warren Edition."

18. Dougald MacMillan, ed., *Drury Lane Calendar 1747–1776*, Oxford, 1938, p. 99; *London Chronicle*, November 1–3, 1763; *Ibid.*, November 8–10. For the stage sentry as an institution, see W. J. Lawrence, *Old Theatre Days and Ways*, London, Bombay, and Sydney [1935], chapter XXIV.

19. *Theatrical Inquisitor*, for November 1820; *Edinburgh Dramatic Review*, May 17, 1825. Leigh Hunt [?] writes of Liston in *The Examiner*, November 12, 1820, that "the faintness with which he sinks back on *Sir Toby's* breast, is absolute 'dissolution and thaw.'"

20. See Becks and Mrs. Shaw Promptbooks, Lacy's Acting Edition, "William Warren Edition," and cf. Spedding, "Miss Kate Terry in Viola," *Fraser's*, August 1865. For similar business in *The Merry Wives of Windsor*, see page 47, below.

21. C[harlotte] P[orter], in *Shakespeariana*, IV (1887), 236; *New York Dramatic Mirror*, February 20, 1904.

22. At the end of III, 4, Daly introduced a new scene in which Olivia is serenaded. Clement Scott and William Winter liked it immensely.

23. William Archer, "'Twelfth Night' at the Lyceum," *Macmillan's Magazine*, August 1884, see also, *Saturday Review*, July 12, 1884.

24. *Furness Variorum*, 309; Morley, *Journal of a London Playgoer*, 139, 140.

25. *The Athenaeum*, February 9, 1901, Mrs. George Cran, *Herbert Beerbohm Tree*, London, 1907, p. 58; Russell, *Julia Marlowe*, 348, 349, "William Warren Edition," cf. Richard Dickins, *Forty Years of Shakespeare on the English Stage: August, 1867 to August, 1907*, p. 151.

Charles Lamb

On Some of the Old Actors

The casual sight of an old Play Bill, which I picked up the other day—I know not by what chance it was preserved so long—tempts me to call to mind a few of the Players, who make the principal figure in it. It presents the cast of parts in the *Twelfth Night*, at the old Drury Lane Theatre two-and-thirty years ago. There is something very touching in these old remembrances. They make us think how we *once* used to read a Play Bill—not, as now peradventure, singling out a favourite performer, and casting a negligent eye over the rest; but spelling out every name, down to the very mutes and servants of the scene;—when it was a matter of no small moment to us whether Whitfield, or Packer, took the part of Fabian; when Benson, and Burton, and Phillimore—names of small account—had an importance, beyond what we can be content to attribute now to the time's best actors.— "Orsino, by Mr. Barrymore."—What a full Shakspearian sound it carries! how fresh to memory arise the image, and the manner, of the gentle actor!

Those who have only seen Mrs. Jordan within the last ten or fifteen years, can have no adequate notion of her performance of such parts as Ophelia; Helena, in *All's Well that Ends Well*; and Viola in this play. Her voice had latterly acquired a coarseness, which suited well enough with her Nells and Hoydens, but in those days it sank, with her steady melting eye, into the heart. Her joyous parts—in which her memory now chiefly lives—in her youth were outdone by her plaintive ones. There is no giving an account how she delivered the disguised story of her love for Orsino. It

From *Essays of Elia* (1823), by Charles Lamb. Repr. E. P. Dutton, 1954.

49

was no set speech, that she had foreseen, so as to weave it into an harmonious period, line necessarily following line, to make up the music—yet I have heard it so spoken, or rather *read*, not without its grace and beauty—but, when she had declared her sister's history to be a "blank," and that she "never told her love," there was a pause, as if the story had ended—and then the image of the "worm in the bud" came up as a new suggestion—and the heightened image of "Patience" still followed after that, as by some growing (and not mechanical) process, thought springing up after thought, I would almost say, as they were watered by her tears. So in those fine lines—

> Write loyal cantos of contemned love—
> Hollow your name to the reverberate hills—

there was no preparation made in the foregoing image for that which was to follow. She used no rhetoric in her passion; or it was nature's own rhetoric, most legitimate then, when it seemed altogether without rule or law.

Mrs. Powel (now Mrs. Renard), then in the pride of her beauty, made an admirable Olivia. She was particularly excellent in her unbending scenes in conversation with the Clown. I have seen some Olivias—and those very sensible actresses too—who in those interlocutions have seemed to set their wits at the jester, and to vie conceits with him in downright emulation. But she used him for her sport, like what he was, to trifle a leisure sentence or two with, and then to be dismissed, and she to be the Great Lady still. She touched the imperious fantastic humour of the character with nicety. Her fine spacious person filled the scene.

The part of Malvolio has in my judgment been so often misunderstood, and the *general merits* of the actor, who then played it, so unduly appreciated, that I shall hope for pardon, if I am a little prolix upon these points.

Of all the actors who flourished in my time—a melancholy phrase if taken aright, reader—Bensley had most of the swell of soul, was greatest in the delivery of heroic conceptions, the emotions consequent upon the presentment of a great idea to the fancy. He had the true poetical enthusiasm—the rarest faculty among players. None that I remember possessed even a portion

of that fine madness which he threw out in Hotspur's famous
rant about glory, or the transports of the Venetian incendiary at
the vision of the fired city. His voice had the dissonance, and at
times the inspiriting effect of the trumpet. His gait was uncouth
and stiff, but in no way embarrassed by affectation; and the
thorough-bred gentleman was uppermost in every movement.
He seized the moment of passion with the greatest truth; like a
faithful clock, never striking before the time: never anticipating
or leading you to anticipate. He was totally destitute of trick and
artifice. He seemed come upon the stage to do the poet's message
simply, and he did it with as genuine fidelity as the nuncios in
Homer deliver the errands of the gods. He let the passion or the
sentiment do its own work without prop or bolstering. He would
have scorned to mountebank it; and betrayed none of that *clever-
ness* which is the bane of serious acting. For this reason, his Iago
was the only endurable one which I remember to have seen. No
spectator from his action could divine more of his artifice than
Othello was supposed to do. His confessions in soliloquy alone
put you in possession of the mystery. There were no by-intima-
tions to make the audience fancy their own discernment so much
greater than that of the Moor—who commonly stands like a
great helpless mark set up for mine Ancient, and a quantity of
barren spectators, to shoot their bolts at. The Iago of Bensley did
not go to work so grossly. There was a triumphant tone about the
character, natural to a general consciousness of power; but none
of that petty vanity which chuckles and cannot contain itself upon
any little successful stroke of its knavery—as is common with
your small villains and green probationers in mischief. It did not
clap or crow before its time. It was not a man setting his wits at a
child, and winking all the while at other children who are mightily
pleased at being let into the secret; but a consummate villain
entrapping a noble nature into toils, against which no discernment was available, where the manner was as fathomless as the
purpose seemed dark, and without motive. The part of Malvolio,
in the *Twelfth Night*, was performed by Bensley, with a richness
and a dignity, of which (to judge from some recent castings of
that character) the very tradition must be worn out from the
stage. No manager in those days would have dreamed of giving it
to Mr. Baddeley, or Mr. Parsons; when Bensley was occasionally

absent from the theatre, John Kemble thought it no derogation to
succeed to the part. Malvolio is not essentially ludicrous. He
becomes comic but by accident. He is cold, austere, repelling; but
dignified, consistent, and, for what appears, rather of an over-
stretched morality. Maria describes him as a sort of Puritan; and
he might have worn his gold chain with honour in one of our old
round-head families, in the service of a Lambert, or a Lady Fair-
fax. But his morality and his manners are misplaced in Illyria. He
is opposed to the proper *levities* of the piece, and falls in the
unequal contest. Still his pride, or his gravity (call it which you
will) is inherent, and native to the man, not mock or affected,
which latter only are the fit objects to excite laughter. His quality
is at the best unlovely, but neither buffoon nor contemptible. His
bearing is lofty, a little above his station, but probably not much
above his deserts. We see no reason why he should not have been
brave, honourable, accomplished. His careless committal of the
ring to the ground (which he was commissioned to restore to
Cesario), bespeaks a generosity of birth and feeling. His dialect on
all occasions is that of a gentleman, and a man of education. We
must not confound him with the eternal old, low steward of
comedy. He is master of the household to a great Princess; a
dignity probably conferred upon him for other respects than age
or length of service. Olivia, at the first indication of his supposed
madness, declares that she "would not have him miscarry for half
of her dowry." Does this look as if the character was meant to
appear little or insignificant? Once, indeed, she accuses him to his
face—of what?—of being "sick of self-love,"—but with a gentleness and considerateness which could not have been, if she had
not thought that this particular infirmity shaded some virtues.
His rebuke to the knight, and his sottish revellers, is sensible and
spirited; and when we take into consideration the unprotected
condition of his mistress, and the strict regard with which her
state of real or dissembled mourning would draw the eyes of the
world upon her house-affairs, Malvolio might feel the honour of
the family in some sort in his keeping; as it appears not that Olivia
had any more brothers, or kinsmen, to look to it—for Sir Toby
had dropped all such nice respects at the buttery hatch. That
Malvolio was meant to be represented as possessing estimable
qualities, the expression of the Duke in his anxiety to have him

reconciled, almost infers. "Pursue him, and entreat him to a peace." Even in his abused state of chains and darkness, a sort of greatness seems never to desert him. He argues highly and well with the supposed Sir Topas, and philosophises gallantly upon his straw.[1] There must have been some shadow of worth about the man; he must have been something more than a mere vapour—a thing of straw, or Jack in office—before Fabian and Maria could have ventured sending him upon a courting-errand to Olivia. There was some consonancy (as he would say) in the undertaking, or the jest would have been too bold even for that house of misrule.

Bensley, accordingly, threw over the part an air of Spanish loftiness. He looked, spake, and moved like an old Castilian. He was starch, spruce, opinionated, but his superstructure of pride seemed bottomed upon a sense of worth. There was something in it beyond the coxcomb. It was big and swelling, but you could not be sure that it was hollow. You might wish to see it taken down, but you felt that it was upon an elevation. He was magnificent from the outset; but when the decent sobrieties of the character began to give way, and the poison of self-love, in his conceit of the Countess's affection, gradually to work, you would have thought that the hero of La Mancha in person stood before you. How he went smiling to himself! with what ineffable carelessness would he twirl his gold chain! what a dream it was! you were infected with the illusion, and did not wish that it should be removed! you had no room for laughter! if an unseasonable reflection of morality obtruded itself, it was a deep sense of the pitiable infirmity of man's nature, that can lay him open to such frenzies—but in truth you rather admired than pitied the lunacy while it lasted—you felt that an hour of such mistake was worth an age with the eyes open. Who would not wish to live but for a day in the conceit of such a lady's love as Olivia? Why, the Duke would have given his principality but for a quarter of a minute, sleeping or waking, to have been so deluded. The man seemed to tread upon air, to taste manna, to walk with his head in the clouds, to mate Hyperion. O! shake not the castles of his pride—endure yet for a season bright moments of confidence—"stand still ye watches of the element," that Malvolio may be still in fancy fair Olivia's lord—but fate and retribution say no—I hear the mischievous titter of

Maria—the witty taunts of Sir Toby—the still more insupportable triumph of the foolish knight—the counterfeit Sir Topas is unmasked—and "thus the whirligig of time," as the true clown hath it, "brings in his revenges." I confess that I never saw the catastrophe of this character, while Bensley played it, without a kind of tragic interest. There was good foolery too. Few now remember Dodd. What an Aguecheek the stage lost in him! Lovegrove, who came nearest to the old actors, revived the character some few seasons ago, and made it sufficiently grotesque; but Dodd was *it*, as it came out of nature's hands. It might be said to remain *in puris naturalibus*. In expressing slowness of apprehension this actor surpassed all others. You could see the first dawn of an idea stealing slowly over his countenance, climbing up by little and little, with a painful process, till it cleared up at last to the fulness of a twilight conception—its highest meridian. He seemed to keep back his intellect, as some have had the power to retard their pulsation. The balloon takes less time in filling, than it took to cover the expansion of his broad moony face over all its quarters with expression. A glimmer of understanding would appear in a corner of his eye, and for lack of fuel go out again. A part of his forehead would catch a little intelligence, and be a long time in communicating it to the remainder.

I am ill at dates, but I think it is now better than five and twenty years ago that walking in the gardens of Gray's Inn—they were then far finer than they are now—the accursed Verulam Buildings had not encroached upon all the east side of them, cutting out delicate green crankles, and shouldering away one or two of the stately alcoves of the terrace—the survivor stands gaping and relationless as if it remembered its brother—they are still the best gardens of any of the Inns of Court, my beloved Temple not forgotten—have the gravest character, their aspect being altogether reverend and law breathing—Bacon has left the impress of his foot upon their gravel walks—taking my afternoon solace on a summer day upon the aforesaid terrace, a comely, sad personage came towards me, whom, from his grave air and deportment, I judged to be one of the old Benchers of the Inn. He had a serious thoughtful forehead, and seemed to be in meditations of mortality. As I have an instinctive awe of old Benchers, I was passing him with that sort of subindicative token of respect which one is apt to demonstrate towards a venerable stranger, and which rather denotes an inclination to greet him, than any positive motion of the body to that effect—a species of humility and will-worship which I observe, nine times out of ten, rather puzzles than pleases the person it is offered to—when the face turning full upon me strangely identified itself with that of Dodd. Upon close inspection I was not mistaken. But could this sad thoughtful countenance be the same vacant face of folly which I had hailed so often under circumstances of gaiety; which I had never seen without a smile, or recognised but as the usher of mirth; that looked out so formally flat in Foppington, so frothily pert in Tattle, so impotently busy in Backbite; so blankly divested of all meaning, or resolutely expressive of none, in Acres, in Fribble, and a thousand agreeable impertinences? Was this the face—full of thought and carefulness—that had so often divested itself at will of every trace of either to give me diversion, to clear my cloudy face for two or three hours at least of its furrows? Was this the face—manly, sober, intelligent—which I had so often despised, made mocks at, made merry with? The remembrance of the freedoms which I had taken with it came upon me with a reproach of insult. I could have asked it pardon. I thought it looked upon me with a sense of injury. There is something strange as well as sad in seeing actors—your pleasant fellows particularly—subjected to and suffering the common lot—their fortunes, their casualties, their deaths, seem to belong to the scene, their actions to be amenable to poetic justice only. We can hardly connect them with more awful responsibilities. The death of this fine actor took place shortly after this meeting. He had quitted the stage some months; and, as I learned afterwards, had been in the habit of resorting daily to these gardens almost to the day of his decease. In these serious walks probably he was divesting himself of many scenic and some real vanities—weaning himself from the frivolities of the lesser and the greater theatre— doing gentle penance for a life of no very reprehensible fooleries,—taking off by degrees the buffoon mask which he might feel he had worn too long—and rehearsing for a more solemn cast of part. Dying he "put on the weeds of Dominic."[2]

If few can remember Dodd, many yet living will easily forget the pleasant creature, who in those days enacted the part of the

Clown to Dodd's Sir Andrew—Richard, or rather Dicky Suett—for so in his life-time he delighted to be called, and time hath ratified the appellation—lieth buried on the north side of the cemetery of Holy Paul, to whose service his nonage and tender years were dedicated. There are those who do yet remember him at that period—his pipe clear and harmonious. He would often speak of his chorister days, when he was "cherub Dicky."

What clipped his wings, or made it expedient that he should exchange the holy for the profane state; whether he had lost his good voice (his best recommendation to that office), like Sir John, "with hallooing and singing of anthems"; or whether he was adjudged to lack something, even in those early years, of the gravity indispensable to an occupation which professeth to "commerce with the skies"—I could never rightly learn; but we find him, after the probation of a twelvemonth or so, reverting to a secular condition, and become one of us.

I think he was not altogether of that timber, out of which cathedral seats and sounding boards are hewed. But if a glad heart—kind and therefore glad—be any part of sanctity, then might the robe of Motley, with which he invested himself with so much humility after his deprivation, and which he wore so long with so much blameless satisfaction to himself and to the public, be accepted for a surplice—his white stole, and *albe*.

The first fruits of his secularisation was an engagement upon the boards of Old Drury, at which theatre he commenced, as I have been told, with adopting the manner of Parsons in old men's characters. At the period in which most of us knew him, he was no more an imitator than he was in any true sense himself imitable.

He was the Robin Good-Fellow of the stage. He came in to trouble all things with a welcome perplexity, himself no whit troubled for the matter. He was known, like Puck, by his note—*Ha! Ha! Ha!*—sometimes deepening to *Ho! Ho! Ho!* with an irresistible accession, derived perhaps remotely from his ecclesiastical education, foreign to his prototype of,—*O La!* Thousands of hearts yet respond to the chuckling *O La!* of Dicky Suett, brought back to their remembrance by the faithful transcript of his friend Mathews's mimicry. The "force of nature could no further go."

He drolled upon the stock of these two syllables richer than the cuckoo.

Care, that troubles all the world, was forgotten in his composition. Had he had but two grains (nay, half a grain) of it, he could never have supported himself upon those two spider's strings, which served him (in the latter part of his unmixed existence) as legs. A doubt or a scruple must have made him totter, a sigh have puffed him down; the weight of a frown had staggered him, a wrinkle made him lose his balance. But on he went, scrambling upon those airy stilts of his, with Robin Good-Fellow, "thorough brake, thorough briar," reckless of a scratched face or a torn doublet.

Shakspeare foresaw him, when he framed his fools and jesters. They have all the true Suett stamp, a loose and shambling gait, a slippery tongue, this last the ready midwife to a without-pain-delivered jest; in words, light as air, venting truths deep as the centre; with idlest rhymes tagging conceit when busiest, singing with Lear in the tempest, or Sir Toby at the buttery-hatch.

Jack Bannister and he had the fortune to be more of personal favourites with the town than any actors before or after. The difference, I take it, was this:—Jack was more *beloved* for his sweet, good-natured, moral pretensions. Dicky was more *liked* for his sweet, good-natured, no pretensions at all. Your whole conscience stirred with Bannister's performance of Walter in *The Children in the Wood*—but Dicky seemed like a thing, as Shakspeare says of Love, too young to know what conscience is. He puts us into Vesta's days. Evil fled before him—not as from Jack, as from an antagonist—but because it could not touch him, any more than a cannon-ball a fly. He was delivered from the burthen of that death; and, when Death came himself, not in metaphor, to fetch Dicky, it is recorded of him by Robert Palmer, who kindly watched his exit, that he received the last stroke, neither varying his accustomed tranquillity, nor tune, with the simple exclamation, worthy to have been recorded in his epitaph—*O La! O La! Bobby!*

The elder Palmer (of stage-treading celebrity) commonly played Sir Toby in those days; but there is a solidity of wit in the

jests of that half-Falstaff which he did not quite fill out. He was as
much too showy as Moody (who sometimes took the part) was
dry and sottish. In sock or buskin there was an air of swaggering
gentility about Jack Palmer. He was a *gentleman* with a slight
infusion of *the footman*. His brother Bob (of recenter memory) who
was his shadow in every thing while he lived, and dwindled into
less than a shadow afterwards—was a *gentleman* with a little
stronger infusion of the *latter ingredient*; that was all. It is amazing
how a little of the more or less makes a difference in these things.
When you saw Bobby in the Duke's Servant,³ you said, what a
pity such a pretty fellow was only a servant. When you saw Jack
figuring in Captain Absolute, you thought you could trace his
promotion to some lady of quality who fancied the handsome
fellow in his topknot, and had bought him a commission. Therefore Jack in Dick Amulet was insuperable.

Jack had two voices—both plausible, hypocritical, and insinu-
ating; but his secondary or supplemental voice still more deci-
sively histrionic than his common one. It was reserved for the
spectator; and the dramatis personæ were supposed to know
nothing at all about it. The *lies* of young Wilding, and the *sentiments*
in Joseph Surface, were thus marked out in a sort of italics to the
audience. This secret correspondence with the company before
the curtain (which is the bane and death of tragedy) has an
extremely happy effect in some kinds of comedy, in the more
highly artificial comedy of Congreve or of Sheridan especially,
where the absolute sense of reality (so indispensable to scenes of
interest) is not required, or would rather interfere to diminish
your pleasure. The fact is, you do not believe in such characters as
Surface—the villain of artificial comedy—even while you read or
see them. If you did, they would shock and not divert you. When
Ben, in *Love for Love*, returns from sea, the following exquisite
dialogue occurs at his first meeting with his father—

> *Sir Sampson.* Thou hast been many a weary league, Ben, since
> I saw thee.
> *Ben.* Ey, ey, been! Been far enough, an that be all.—Well,
> father and how do all at home? how does brother Dick,
> and brother Val?
> *Sir Sampson.* Dick! body o' me, Dick has been dead these two
> years. I writ you word when you were at Leghorn.

> *Ben.* Mess, that's true; Marry, I had forgot. Dick's dead, as
> you say—Well, and how?—I have a many questions to ask
> you—

Here is an instance of insensibility which in real life would be
revolting, or rather in real life could not have co-existed with the
warm-hearted temperament of the character. But when you read
it in the spirit with which such playful selections and specious
combinations rather than strict *metaphrases* of nature should be
taken, or when you saw Bannister play it, it neither did, nor does
wound the moral sense at all. For what is Ben—the pleasant sailor
which Bannister gives us—but a piece of satire—a creation of
Congreve's fancy—a dreamy combination of all the accidents of
a sailor's character—his contempt of money—his credulity to
women—with that necessary estrangement from home which it
is just within the verge of credibility to suppose *might* produce
such an hallucination as is here described. We never think the
worse of Ben for it, or feel it as a stain upon his character. But
when an actor comes, and instead of the delightful phantom—the
creature dear to half-belief—which Bannister exhibited—displays
before our eyes a downright concretion of a Wapping sailor—a
jolly warmhearted Jack Tar—and nothing else—when instead of
investing it with a delicious confusedness of the head, and a
veering undirected goodness of purpose—he gives to it a downright daylight understanding, and a full consciousness of its actions; thrusting forward the sensibilities of the character with a
pretence as if it stood upon nothing else, and was to be judged by
them alone—we feel the discord of the thing; the scene is disturbed; a real man has got in among the dramatis personæ, and
puts them out. We want the sailor turned out. We feel that his
true place is not behind the curtain but in the first or second
gallery.

NOTES

1. *Clown.* What is the opinion of Pythagoras concerning wild fowl?
   Mal. That the soul of our grandam might haply inhabit a bird.
   Clown. What thinkest thou of his opinion?
   Mal. I think nobly of the soul, and no way approve his opinion.

2. Dodd was a man of reading, and left at his death a choice collection of old English literature. I should judge him to have been a man of wit. I know one instance of an impromptu which no length of study could have bettered. My merry friend, Jem White, had seen him one evening in Aguecheek, and recognising Dodd the next day in Fleet Street, was irresistibly impelled to take off his hat and salute him as the identical Knight of the preceding evening with a "Save you, *Sir Andrew*." Dodd, not at all disconcerted at this unusual address from a stranger, with a courteous half-rebuking wave of the hand, put him off with an "Away, *Fool*."

3. *High Life Below Stairs*.

Henry Morley

Samuel Phelps as Malvolio (1857)

The aspect and behaviour of the pit and gallery at SADLER'S WELLS during the performance of one of Shakespeare's plays cannot fail to impress most strongly every visitor who is unaccustomed to the place. There sit our working-classes in a happy crowd, as orderly and reverent as if they were at church, and yet as unrestrained in their enjoyment as if listening to stories told them by their own firesides. Shakespeare spoke home to the heart of the natural man, even in the same words that supply matter for nice judgment by the intellect; he was as a cook, who, by the same meat that feeds abundantly the hungry, tickles with an exquisite delight the palate of the epicure. It is hard to say how much men who have had few advantages of education must in their minds and characters be strengthened and refined when they are made accustomed to this kind of entertainment.

Upon a stage thus managed Mr. Phelps has of late years been the personator of about thirty of the characters of Shakespeare. Great men or small, heroes or cowards, sages or simpletons, sensual or spiritual men, he has taken all as characters that Shakespeare painted, studied them minutely, and embodied each in what he thinks to be a true Shakespearean form. Bottom the Weaver, Brutus, Falstaff, Macbeth, Christopher Sly, are characters assumed by the same man, not to display some special power in the actor, but the range of power in the poet to whose illustration he devotes himself. Good tragedian as he is, we suppose that it is in a sort of comedy, vaguely to be defined as dry and

Reprinted from *The Journal of a London Playgoer 1851–1866* by Henry Morley (Repr. Humanities Press, 1974).

intellectual, but in his hands always most diverting, that Mr. Phelps finds the bent of his genius as an actor to be most favoured. Thus in Malvolio he would appear to have a part pretty exactly suited to his humour, none the less so because there is perhaps no character in which he is himself lost sight of so completely; substance vanishes, and shadow lives.

Malvolio lives at SADLER'S WELLS in bearing and attire modelled upon the fashion of the Spaniard, as impassive in his manner as a Spanish king should be. In one of the first sentences addressed to him we are told his character: "O, you are sick of self-love, Malvolio, and taste things with a distempered appetite." Such a man is the Malvolio we see. When in his tasting of Maria's letter he betrays his distempered appetite for greatness, we are not allowed to suppose for a moment that he loves his mistress. Seeing that, as Maria says, "it is his ground of faith that all that look on him love him," he accepts easily the hope of greatness thrust upon him, and his rejoicing is in the love of Olivia, not in the way of sympathy, but as a way to "sitting in his state, calling his officers about him in his branched velvet gown." Such a man, as Mr. Phelps represents him, walks not with a smirk and a light comic strut, but in the heaviness of grandeur, with a face grave through very emptiness of all expression. This Malvolio stalks blind about the world; his eyes are very nearly covered with their heavy lids, for there is nothing in the world without that is worth noticing, it is enough for him to contemplate the excellence within; walled up in his own temple of the flesh, he is his own adorer. If his ears are assailed with irreverences by the fool, he counts the fool as naught, and is moved therefore but to the expression of a passing shade of pity for his ignorance. Upon the debasement of Sir Toby and Sir Andrew he looks down with very calm disdain. When in the latter half of the play he has been bidden, as he thinks, by her who will thrust greatness upon him, to be opposite with a kinsman, surly with servants, and, if he entertain her love, to let it appear in his smiling; though he had been practising behaviour to his shadow, all the smile he can produce is one of intense satisfaction with himself, and all the surliness but a more open expression of disdain for those who do not pay him homage. When locked up as a madman he is sustained by his self-content, and by the honest certainty that he has been notoriously abused; and when at last he, for once, opens his eyes on learning how he has been tricked, they close again in happy self-content, and he is retiring in state without deigning a word to his tormentors, when, as the fool has twitted him by noting how "the whirligig of time brings in his revenges," he remembers that the whirligig is still in motion. Therefore, marching back with as much increase of speed as is consistent with magnificence, he threatens all—including now Olivia in his contempt—"I'll be revenged on the whole pack of you!"

Other Malvolios seen by the playgoers of this generation have been more fantastical and caused more laughter—although this one causes much—but the impression made by them has been less deep. Few who have seen or may see at SADLER'S WELLS the Spanish-looking steward of Countess Olivia, and laughed at the rise and fall of his *château en Espagne*, will forget him speedily. Like a quaint portrait in which there are master-strokes, his figure may dwell in the mind for years.

Max Beerbohm

Beerbohm Tree's *Twelfth Night*

What would one think if Mr. Haddon Chambers had called his new comedy (of which I shall write next week) *February 6th*, or *Anything Else That May Occur To You?* Yet that were a precise modern equivalent to Shakespeare's title *Twelfth Night*, or *What You Will*. So perfunctory and formless an affair was *Twelfth Night*, and so contemptuous of it its maker, that he called it merely by the date of its production, giving leave to anyone else to re-christen it if he thought it worth the trouble. A few years later, it actually was produced as *Malvolio, tout court*. The Elizabethans, evidently, perceived that the character of Malvolio was, for all its slightness, by far the most interesting feature of it. And their opinion has been upheld by posterity. Malvolio is alive and attractive because he sprang from Shakespeare's own brain. Sir Toby, too, and Sir Andrew, and Maria, are, in their lesser degrees, genuine creations. But the rest of the characters (except, indeed, the Duke, who is remarkable, extraneously, as a study in aesthetic sensuousness) are merely steppers in one of those familiar quadrilles of which Shakespeare was not less sick than we are. The main plot of the play was, as usual, "lifted" from elsewhere—from Venice, to be exact. And Shakespeare, on this occasion, took even less pride than usual in his booty. Various discrepancies of time and place in the scheme of the play testify to the hurry in which this *Twelfth Night* was knocked off. Of course, there are many lovely and immortal passages of poetry in it. Shakespeare radiated such passages whatever his theme; he could not help himself. But

Reprinted by permission of Rupert Hart-Davis, from *More Theatre* (1969), by Max Beerbohm.

not all the exquisite things that Viola has to say could prevent the
main plot from appalling even the gentlest reader with its tedious
and frigid artificiality. If only Shakespeare had taken himself
more seriously, our dramatic literature would have been as much
the richer as it would have been the poorer had he never existed
at all. If, in his comedies, he had given the go-by to the farcical
inventions of fifth-rate playwrights, and had relied on his own
transcendent genius, how much happier we should all be! Imagine
what a splendid play he might have written if he had made
Malvolio specifically the central figure! That he was as much
interested in Malvolio as in Shylock, as indifferent to Viola as to
Portia, nobody with the slightest artistic instinct can have any
doubt. It is amazing that he should have cast Malvolio, as he cast
Shylock, into a deliquium of extraneous nonsense. Artistic conscience and artistic genius usually go hand in hand. Shakespeare,
who had more genius than any other writer that ever lived, seems
to have been without the faintest rudiment of a conscience. He is
immortal despite himself. That he, with his methods of working,
should yet cut the most impressive figure in the world's literature, is the most striking testimony to the miraculousness of his
gifts. What pedestal would be exalted enough for him, what eyes
unshaded could gaze up at him, what syndicate of intellects and
temperaments could measure him, if he had possessed as much of
the artistic conscience as is possessed by any of the Toms or Dicks
or Harrys whose names are printed in the theatrical advertise-
ment to-day?

Twelfth Night, I suggest, is in some degree redeemed by its
accessory characters. The play is worth seeing across footlights,
for sake of them. If the figures in the quadrille—Orsino and
Viola, Sebastian and Olivia—be acted by mimes who look nice,
and move gracefully, and make the most of the words allotted to
them, rendering the music musically, then even they become
tolerable. You are able to forget the frigid convention of the
quadrille, steeping yourself in the verbal poetry. Of such plays as
The Tempest, which Shakespeare wrote for his own pleasure, and in
which the drama is throughout exquisitely consonant with the
poetry, indifferent or even positively bad interpretations are
worth seeing. Them nothing can mar utterly. But plays like
Twelfth Night, which consist mainly of hack-work, should be inter-

preted with real charm and ability, or not interpreted at all. It were well also that they should be shown to us against beautiful backgrounds. With those critics who rail against beautiful backgrounds I concur so far as to admit that the really good Shakespearean plays are tolerable even when they are skimpily produced. But such pills as *King John* and *Henry V*, as *The Merchant of Venice* and *The Taming of the Shrew*, ought to be gilded as richly as possible. This metaphor is unfortunate, perhaps. It implies that I crave gorgeous display; whereas, of course, I crave merely beauty, which is quite another thing. I maintain that Shakespeare's masterpieces are not at all degraded by a setting of beauty, that they deserve such setting, and by it are made more beautiful, and that anyone who by it is distracted from their own intrinsic beauty betrays in himself a lack of visual sense. Visual beauty is complementary to beauty of sound and thought. Some people have no taste for it, just as others have no ear for music. To them, no doubt, an effect of visual beauty, being unintelligible, is an obstacle, a distraction. But they should not make a virtue of their defect, even though they cannot hope to remedy the defect "by taking thought." At any rate, they should not try to deduce and impose from it a general law in the aesthetics of drama. However, I admit readily that Shakespeare's masterpieces, skimpily produced, are well worth seeing. What I protest is that his inferior plays ought to be done elaborately or not at all. One ground on which the pedants base their objection to scenic elaboration is that the expense involves long runs, and that accordingly the public does not get constant chances of paying fresh homage to the bard. To this argument the answer is simple: the public does not go to Shakespearean plays unless they are elaborately produced. At least, it does not go to such plays as *King John*, &c. If we consider the edification of the public, we find this elaboration of scenery to be indispensable. And if we take a broadly aesthetic view of the matter, we come to the same conclusion. And so, in either case, we cannot but plump for the modern mode.

At Her Majesty's Theatre is an excellent production and performance of *Twelfth Night*. The garden of Olivia, in which most of the figures of the quadrille are gone through, is a very lovely Elizabethan-Illyrian garden, lying at the foot of an infinite staircase of green grass, and from it, in the distance, a little arched bridge leads to a lovely park whose trees loom blue through the haze of summer. And the dancers in the quadrille perform their evolutions with grace and skill. True, Miss Maud Jeffries, who is Olivia, does not appreciate the beauty of blank verse so well as the audience appreciates the beauty of her appearance; she speaks her lines, indeed, as though they were bad prose. But a new-comer, Miss Brayton, who is Viola, acts delightfully, and masquerades as the page in a spruce and mettlesome way that is most refreshing after the mincing coyness of other actresses in similar case. She has a quaint humour, too, and a pretty voice which she uses in strict accord to metre. As Sebastian, Mr. Quartermaine has the advantage of looking really like her twin-brother. He, too, speaks his lines musically. And Mr. Taber, as the Duke, strikes just the right note of delicate sensuousness. Thus the quadrille becomes tolerable.

The Clown is a kind of link between the merely conventional and the properly Shakespearean characters in the play. With his jibes and his warnings, he pervades the whole scheme. It was an excellent idea that he, at the fall of the curtain, should be on the stage, blowing a trill on his secular flute, when the other characters have trooped off to the sound of marriage-bells. "After all," he seems to pipe, "what does it all amount to?" just as Shakespeare threw in that *What you will*. Both as actor and as singer, Mr. Courtice Pounds is an admirable Clown, infusing always a touch of sinistry into his mirth. Mr. Lionel Brough and Mr. Norman Forbes are well matched against each other as Sir Toby and Sir Andrew—a contrast of the fruity with the scrannel grotesque. The drinking-bout is done by them in thoroughly Shakespearean fashion. At the end of it comes an effect which Shakespeare did not, perhaps, adumbrate in his stage-directions, but which rounds it off very prettily. As the two topers reel off to bed, the uncanny dawn peers at them through the windows. The Clown wanders on, humming a snatch of the tune he has sung to them. He looks at the empty bowl of sack and the overturned tankards, smiles, shrugs his shoulders, yawns, lies down before the embers of the fire, goes to sleep. Down the stairs, warily, with a night-cap on his head and a sword in his hand, comes Malvolio, awakened and fearful of danger. He peers around, lunging with his sword at the harmless furniture. One thinks of Don Quixote and "the notable adventure of the wine-skins." Satisfied, he retraces his footsteps up the staircase. A cock crows, and, as the curtain falls, one is aware of a whole slumbering household, and of the mystery of an actual dawn. Pedants might cavil at such imaginative glosses in a production of Shakespeare. To me the question is simply whether the imagination be of a good or bad kind. In this instance the imagination seems to me distinctly good.

The analogy between Malvolio and Don Quixote occurs inevitably. For both men were of lofty bearing, cursed with an exaggerated sense of their missions, and in both of them this sense was used by irreverent creatures to entice them into ludicrous plights. But the analogy does not go further than that. I cannot subscribe to Charles Lamb's ingenious paradox that Malvolio was in himself a fine fellow, whose dignified bearing had solid basis in a dignified nature. Malvolio does not, indeed, at the beginning of the play, say anything which would contradict this theory. But that is due to Shakespeare's slap-dash technique. Shakespeare's real opinion of Malvolio is shown in the words which he puts into the mouth of Olivia: "O, you are sick of self-love," &c. Malvolio is meant to be an egomaniac—a state quite inconsistent with true dignity. He is intrinsically absurd. This, evidently, is the view of Mr. Tree, whose dignity throughout is of an absurdly foppish and fantastical kind. So much for Mr. Tree's conception of the part. As for his execution of it, I think I can safely say . . . but I must not break a certain self-imposed rule with which my readers are already familiar.

9 February 1901

Harley Granville Barker

Twelfth Night at the Vieux Colombier (1921)

It is very cheering to an Englishman to see a crowded French audience carried away in spontaneous enjoyment of a Shakespeare play. It was as cheering, and even more remarkable, for the Englishman to find his own enjoyment of the performance just, apparently, as spontaneous. The good cause of Anglo-French friendship is (quite seriously) in debt to Jacques Copeau for his production of *Twelfth Night*. It seems to be a sterling success. It was first staged in May, 1914, and now has a firm place in the repertory; there was hardly a vacant seat at this particular performance. I do not suggest that the production makes the Briand-Lloyd George conversations of the moment any easier; I certainly do not wish to imply that an officially-organized theatrical propaganda of friendship would do anything but defeat its own too obvious end. But Shakespeare is a good ambassador. And he has colleagues, dead and living, who could do their country greater service abroad than most politicians contrive to. Truly it is a simpler, in that it can be a more disinterested, service. No use in thrusting such an embassy across the Channel, but all our thanks to the Frenchmen who make a lodging for it and extend a welcome.

The translation of any play is a plaguily difficult matter; of a poetical play one must admit that in any logical completeness the thing can't be done. When I opened *La Nuit des Rois* to discover that—

> If Music be the food of Love—play on;
> Give me excess of it, that, surfeiting,
> The appetite may sicken and so die,

From *The Observer*, 1 January, 1922.

71

had become—

> Si la musique est la nourriture de l'amour, qu'elle reprenne!
> Donnes-m'en à l'excès, et que ma gourmandise défaille de
> nausée,

I feared the worst. It was so perfectly right that it could not fail, I
thought, to be utterly wrong. But before Monsieur Jean le Goff
had spoken ten lines (even though he looked a little too like a
blend of le Grand Monarque and Charles II) I had forgotten what
I was missing. And the French audience had never any need to
know. And for all I can tell, of course, "le son savourex qui souffle
sur un parterre de violettes, dérobant et rendant un perfum," may
mean as much to them as

> . . . the sweet South
> That breathes upon a bank of violets
> Stealing and giving odour.

This is no criticism of the translation; I am indeed not qualified to
make one. And, as I say, Monsieur le Goff resolved my doubts
without more ado by the distinction, the passion, the sense of
beauty with which he informed his opening scene. One made, in
fact, the appalling discovery that French actors can speak Shakespeare better than English actors—let us say—usually do. This is
not a paradox. It is demonstrable, I think, that the Elizabethan
theatre demanded a fire and rapidity of diction which Elizabethan
actors presumably possessed, which Georgian actors have quite
undoubtedly lost the habit of, in which, alas, Georgian audiences
do not appear to delight. (How should they, one may ask? No
audience can demand the supply of such a commodity.) But
French audiences do unaffectedly appreciate beautiful speech and
French actors are expected to give it them. Swiftness, intensity,
precision, variety, clarity, and above all, passion, the passion informing a beauty of thought and feeling that only just does not
defy expression—it was with these, the fine sound and poise of
these, that the actors of the Vieux Colombier, even at a translated
distance from the fount of their inspiration, thrilled their audience again and again. It is no use; English actors must go to
school again in their matter of Shakespearean verse; and—this,
indeed, is a paradox!—here in France, apparently, is the school.

An explicable paradox, perhaps. Shakespeare was a child of the Renascence, of its quiet unquestioning approbation of things, of its ruthlessness, of the readiness to pay Nature the price of her favours. In France the Renascence is not spent. In England our 17th-century Puritans doused its artistic side with cold water, and, though we are at last just about dry, the rheumatic effects remain. We move stiffly still in these matters.

Twelfth Night is not a perfect production; one should not expect such a thing. Jacques Copeau uses the platform stage, with an apron lower by a few steps, but he does not seem to have thought out its full application to the play. He does not see the importance, where mere indications of time and place are given, of their being precise and constant indications; nor how the structural integrity of the play, and therefore the mental comfort of the audience, depend upon obedience to this. He does not clearly define his opening masses—the Court of Orsino, the household of Olivia— nor differentiate sufficiently between the conduct of the main and the conjunctive scenes. This is not pedantry; the right order-ing of such things quite naturally makes for the better enjoyment of the play. And in one important matter he has been, I regret to say, shamefully betrayed by his English designer, Mr. Duncan Grant.

Whatever may be M. Copeau's disabilities for the full under-standing of Shakespeare's intentions, Mr. Duncan Grant has none. If he does not know that Olivia and all her household are in deep mourning, a cursory reading of the play will inform him. It may be very good fun to dress her up in a harlequinade of colour (a most attractive dress, the lady herself a temptation to any dress-designer!); it may be equally amusing to turn Sir Andrew Aguecheek into the likeness of a rag doll, and Malvolio into a mechanically outrageous figure of fun that even the wildest horse-play cannot animate. But Mr. Duncan Grant, I take it, was not called in to amuse himself, but to interpret Shakespeare. It is worthwhile to speak plainly on this point. We all want to bring artists of distinction to the service of the theatre, but if they cannot recognise that it is a service as strictly conditioned for them as for any other of the play's interpreters, if their one idea is to show off at the expense of the dramatist and actors (it is really very much as if the actor playing Orsino insisted upon rewriting

the part and singing a song and dancing a breakdown occasionally), then they had better amuse themselves elsewhere. And it is
perhaps worthwhile to speak plainly in this instance, as Mr. Duncan Grant, even in his most inappropriate efforts, shows just such
a talent as the theatre needs. His line might be finer and more
precise (formless effects are no use upon a platform stage), but
his colour is enchanting, gay and reposeful, too, the combinations
always a little unexpected, but never disturbing.

One more grumble, and I only hope I may have space left for
half the praise I could spend. Will M. Copeau for his next Shakespeare production not only follow the play's text, as he commend-
ably does in this instance (I could not detect a line cut, and the
audience, with *les jeunes filles* much in evidence, laughed heartily
and naturally even at the few jokes now considered too indelicate
for English ears.) The Renascence, as I say, is still alive in France,
but will he study it as well, to the exclusion of the pseudo-
traditions of the English stage? Had he done so in this instance he
would have saved himself from the capital errors of a Maria more
like a kitchen-maid than a companion to Olivia, of the village-
idiot Sir Andrew, and of a Malvolio incomprehensibly clowning.
French audiences, quite naturally, do not take their Shakespeare
for granted as we do. So much the better; they are likely to get
the more out of him. But the divine William has enough lapses of
his own to answer for without being burdened by the accumula-
tion of his interpreters' misdeeds. The one occasion in *Twelfth
Night* upon which this audience displayed inappropriate hilarity
was when Olivia and Sebastian made their lightning match.
Shakespeare, as was his wont in such cases, attempted (though he
hardly succeeded) to carry this off with a fine flourish of verse.
But, deprived of this, the French actors were helpless; and though
the audience did its best to consider their feelings and to be polite
to the venerable ecclesiastic who came in off the mat (so to speak)
to tie the knot, it was evident that Olivia lost caste a little by the
incident.

But for all this—and, indeed, just because of this—I would beg
M. Copeau to trust to Shakespeare and to no one else in more
important matters. It will not have escaped him that, while the
audience delighted in his comedians for the play's first hour,
thereafter they had to work ever harder, to strain at effects, to

coarsen the comedy in what was still, on the whole, a failing attempt to command attention. It need not have been so. One has only to face the simple fact that Shakespeare's Malvolio, Feste, Maria, Sir Toby, and Andrew will last out the play, whereas the arbitrary funniments of actors will probably not. Shakespeare, for all his faults, M. Copeau, did know his business as a playwright, and as long as he enjoyed writing a character we may be pretty sure that the actor has more to gain by interpreting it than by using it as a peg upon which to hang his own, or anyone else's, ideas.

Albert Savry's Malvolio was, indeed, for half the time quite excellent. He had taken, I should say, Maclise's picture for the figure of the man. The self-sufficiency that can only be sustained upon contempt for one's fellow-creatures, the quick transition from the sarcastic immobility of his attitude of service to the hiss of waspish tyranny when he is released from it, the diseased over-quick apprehension in the letter scene, running like fire among stubble, till it bursts into a blaze of egomania—all legitimately studied and excellently done. Why, then, Monsieur Savry, let one pair of cross-fastened yellow stockings (Shakespeare asked no more, for all that Mr. Duncan Grant so over-obliged him!) lure you into those skipping atrocities? An excellent, if rather sentimental, Antonio (made up, I think, after Charles Kemble as Brutus), a good Sebastian, a first-rate Fabian, Fabian being by no means a third-rate part; Romain Bouquet a richly coloured, totally unexaggerated, really amusing Sir Toby; and for a Viola, the most distinguished actress I have seen, it seems to me, since Duse ceased playing.

As, from personal taste, I can write no higher praise, I look back upon the words with slight hesitation. But my recollection of Madame Susanne Bing's performance confirms the opinion and, in particular, the choice of that epithet. One could dispute several aspects of her reading of Viola. She emphasises the background of tragedy in the girl's life at the expense of the youthful high spirits—the cheerfulness that would come creeping in, and that Shakespeare needed, here and there, for the sustaining of his comedy. As a consequence some important passages—such, notably, as the soliloquy with the ring—slip rather disastrously into a minor key, not only lose their significance, but endanger the

contrasting effects around them. This (to my mind) too sustained note of half-pathetic irony is arguably legitimate from a
Viola's point of view, but it needs more accommodation to the
general purpose of the play. There are times when this failing
turns virtue, as when Madame Bing definitely does not accommodate herself to the accustomed clowning of the duel scene, and so
preserves the romantic interest of the story at a time when—with
the Olivia-Sebastian incident looming—it is about to be severely
shaken.

But, granted her reading of the part—which possesses besides
the extrinsic virtue that it is both a direct reading of the text and a
sympathetic divination of Shakespeare's great tenderness towards women in general at this time of his writing—one can have
nothing but praise for the art with which Madame Bing presents
it. You may know her in just one minute for a supreme actress,
not only by her perfect physical repose, but by the lack of all
anxiety to impress the part—far less herself—upon you. An actor's anxiety to impress you is in direct ratio to his generally
justified fear that he can't; his hurry to show you that he knows
all about the part he is playing is invariably a sign that he knows
very little. But there are not many actors or actresses so sure of
themselves that by doing nothing at all for two minutes—by
doing, that is to say, what they do so simply that it seems nothing,
seems, as they wish it to, a simple "being"—can so raise your
interest that you wait anxiously for their reappearance, watch for
every rare gesture or movement of feature, try to note the
significance of the tone of every sentence they speak, are impa-
tient yourself for the character's development.

It is in the power to arouse and sustain and fulfil such interest
that the art of great acting lies. And while almost anyone who is
sufficiently attractive can display themselves attractively and earn
innocent applause, the infinitely different power to draw you out
of your royal self, sitting there in the consciousness of an honestly paid-for seat to be kow-towed to, away from the theatre and
into the world of the play, comes not (for the actor) but by the
stern suppression of that easily and obviously exhibitive self in
favour of that part of him, of his mind, of his emotions, that can
effect a communion with the intangible stuff of the play. It will
then be surprising—and how one is always surprised and deligh-

ted afresh by fine art!—of what comparatively small account the more material things become. Madame Bing, for instance, spoke very beautifully; she moved with grace. But the movements did not exist apart from their meaning, and every sentence (another sure sign of the supreme actor) came out conceived as a whole, as a thought and a feeling, not as a variously valued collection of words. And so complete the assimilation of the personality of the actress to the idea of the part, and so far, by such an example, did she lead her audience into the world of the play and into the inner world of the imagined Viola, that after a while, by watching as we did for the magnetic moment when thought and feeling were, it seemed, ever freshly conceived, the moment before speech gave them form, one could so nearly oneself conceive what they would be, as to partake with her of her sorrow or joy, one's watching and listening becoming as subsidiary a mechanical matter as the mechanism of the acting itself.

Yet a further gain from the sacrifice of the exhibitive self. The imagined Viola, released, so to speak, from the constant demand upon her to do credit to an actress' performance, can passively reflect, by a critical attitude or two, other aspects of her fellow-characters than those they can actively present. In this lies, doubt-less, one of the last refinements of the actor's art. But in Viola, "knowing all, herself unknown," there are peculiar chances of exemplifying it. And certainly one learnt as much more about Orsino by following the lights and shades of this Viola's love for him as Orsino himself declared. And as much more about Olivia; though here Shakespeare has been verbally downright, and Viola's attitude to Olivia is one of the obvious tests of the part's playing. Madame Bing's was almost impeccable in this. Her main conception of a Viola whose real sorrows, carried so lightly, infinitely outweigh the fantastic griefs of which she is the mes-senger, much helped her—though just once there was a tolerant smile where, I thought, no smile should be. But, needless to say, she did not make Olivia either a butt or the excuse of working off a few purple passages; on the contrary, her shy humility at the beauty's unveiling set the relations between the two in a key in which she could and did do much more than if she had tried to assume the mastery of the scenes from the beginning. And to that other test passage, the recognition of Sebastian—but, truly,

the Viola who cannot make your eyes swim here does not know
the beginning of her business—Mme. Bing responded, not with a
more emotional effect, but more admirably by rounding the character to its completion. Here again was the Viola who could not
glibly tell her love, whom outward life had used so hardly that she
must keep her treasures secretly in her heart. Shakespeare indeed
rounded off his play pretty cavalierly, but he had completed his
Viola nearly enough.

For a final word of most respectful praise to Mme. Bing—her
Viola is fine, I think, chiefly because it is fine all through. There
are no purple passages, no doubtful ones. She has visualized a
Viola, and with certain art, by complete self-abnegation, she
makes her vision ours.

As a final word of compliment to Jacques Copeau—but it
would take many words of discerning praise to express my appreciation of his work at the Vieux Colombier. And he does not need
them. If he wants to sense his achievement (still, let it be granted,
in the achieving) he has but to mingle with his audience as it
leaves the theatre. It is a very mixed audience—workmen, stu-
dents, some foreigners, a taste of literary and learned Paris, a
sprinkling of fashionable Paris. But they have coalesced in enjoyment of the play and—this is the test, this is why managers
should always mingle with a departing audience—they separate
again exhilarated, not exhausted, not as having seen a show, but
as having helped, they too, even actively, in the consummation of
a worthy work of art.

Virginia Woolf

Twelfth Night at the Old Vic (1933)

Shakespeareans are divided, it is well known, into three classes; those who prefer to read Shakespeare in the book; those who prefer to see him acted on the stage; and those who run perpetually from book to stage gathering plunder. Certainly there is a good deal to be said for reading *Twelfth Night* in the book if the book can be read in a garden, with no sound but the thud of an apple falling to the earth, or of the wind ruffling the branches of the trees. For one thing there is time—time not only to hear "the sweet sound that breathes upon a bank of violets" but to unfold the implications of that very subtle speech as the Duke winds into the nature of love. There is time, too, to make a note in the margin time to wonder at queer jingles like "that live in her; when liver, brain, and heart" . . . "and of a foolish knight that you brought in one night" and to ask oneself whether it was from them that was born the lovely, "And what should I do in Illyria? My brother he is in Elysium." For Shakespeare is writing, it seems, not with the whole of his mind mobilized and under control but with feelers left flying that sport and play with words so that the trail of a chance word is caught and followed recklessly. From the echo of one word is born another word, for which reason, perhaps, the play seems as we read it to tremble perpetually on the brink of music. They are always calling for songs in *Twelfth Night*, "O fellow come, the song we had last night." Yet Shakespeare was not so deeply in love with words but that he could turn and laugh at them. "They that do dally with words do

Reprinted by permission of the Author's Literary Estate and The Hogarth Press, from *The Death of the Moth* by Virginia Woolf.

quickly make them wanton." There is a roar of laughter and out
burst Sir Toby, Sir Andrew, Maria. Words on their lips are things
that have meaning; that rush and leap out with a whole character
packed in a little phrase. When Sir Andrew says "I was adored
once," we feel that we hold him in the hollow of our hands; a
novelist would have taken three volumes to bring us to that pitch
of intimacy. And Viola, Malvolio, Olivia, the Duke—the mind so
brims and spills over with all that we know and guess about them
as they move in and out among the lights and shadows of the
mind's stage that we ask why should we imprison them within
the bodies of real men and women. Why exchange this garden for
the theatre? The answer is that Shakespeare wrote for the stage
and presumably with reason. Since they are acting *Twelfth Night* at
the Old Vic, let us compare the two versions.

Many apples might fall without being heard in the Waterloo
Road, and as for the shadows, the electric light has consumed
them all. The first impression upon entering the Old Vic is
overwhelmingly positive and definite. We seem to have issued out
from the shadows of the garden upon the bridge of the Par-
thenon. The metaphor is mixed, but then so is the scenery. The
columns of the bridge somehow suggest an Atlantic liner and the
austere splendours of a classical temple in combination. But the
body is almost as upsetting as the scenery. The actual persons of
Malvolio, Sir Toby, Olivia, and the rest expand our visionary
characters out of all recognition. At first we are inclined to resent
it. You are not Malvolio; or Sir Toby either, we want to tell them;
but merely impostors. We sit gaping at the ruins of the play, at
the travesty of the play. And then by degrees this same body or
rather all these bodies together, take our play and remodel it
between them. The play gains immensely in robustness, in solidity. The printed word is changed out of all recognition when it is
heard by other people. We watch it strike upon this man or
woman; we see them laugh or shrug their shoulders, or turn aside
to hide their faces. The word is given a body as well as a soul.
Then again as the actors pause, or topple over a barrel, or stretch
their hands out, the flatness of the print is broken up as by
crevasses or precipices; all the proportions are changed. Perhaps
the most impressive effect in the play is achieved by the long
pause which Sebastian and Viola make as they stand looking at

each other in a silent ecstasy of recognition. The reader's eye may have slipped over that moment entirely. Here we are made to pause and think about it; and are reminded that Shakespeare wrote for the body and for the mind simultaneously.

But now that the actors have done their proper work of solidifying and intensifying our impressions, we begin to criticize them more minutely and to compare their version with our own. We make Mr. Quartermaine's Malvolio stand beside our Malvolio. And to tell the truth, wherever the fault may lie, they have very little in common. Mr. Quartermaine's Malvolio is a splendid gentleman, courteous, considerate, well bred; a man of parts and humour who has no quarrel with the world. He has never felt a twinge of vanity or a moment's envy in his life. If Sir Toby and Maria fool him he sees through it, we may be sure, and only suffers it as a fine gentleman puts up with the games of foolish children. Our Malvolio, on the other hand, was a fantastic complex creature, twitching with vanity, tortured by ambition. There was cruelty in his teasing, and a hint of tragedy in his defeat; his final threat had a momentary terror in it. But when Mr. Quartermaine says "I'll be revenged on the whole pack of you," we feel merely that the powers of the law will be soon and effectively invoked. What, then, becomes of Olivia's "He hath been most notoriously abused?" Then there is Olivia. Madame Lopokova has by nature that rare quality which is neither to be had for the asking nor to be subdued by the will—the genius of personality. She has only to float on to the stage and everything round her suffers, not a sea change, but a change into light, into gaiety; the birds sing, the sheep are garlanded, the air rings with melody and human beings dance towards each other on the tips of their toes possessed of an exquisite friendliness, sympathy, and delight. But our Olivia was a stately lady; of sombre complexion, slow-moving, and of few sympathies. She could not love the Duke nor change her feeling. Madame Lopokova loves everybody. She is always changing. Her hands, her face, her feet, the whole of her body, are always quivering in sympathy with the moment. She could make the moment, as she proved when she walked down the stairs with Sebastian, one of intense and moving beauty; but she was not our Olivia. Compared with her the comic group, Sir Toby, Sir Andrew, Maria, the fool were more than ordinarily

English. Coarse, humorous, robust, they trolled out their words, they rolled over their barrels; they acted magnificently. No reader, one may make bold to say, could outpace Miss Seyler's Maria, with its quickness, its inventiveness, its merriment; nor add anything to the humours of Mr. Livesey's Sir Toby. And Miss Jeans as Viola was satisfactory; and Mr. Hare as Antonio was admirable; and Mr. Morland's clown was a good clown. What, then, was lacking in the play as a whole? Perhaps that it was not a whole. The fault may lie partly with Shakespeare. It is easier to act his comedy than his poetry, one may suppose, for when he wrote as a poet he was apt to write too quick for the human tongue. The prodigality of his metaphors can be flashed over by the eye, but the speaking voice falters in the middle. Hence the comedy was out of proportion to the rest. Then, perhaps, the actors were too highly charged with individuality or too incongruously cast. They broke the play up into separate pieces—now we were in the groves of Arcady, now in some inn at Blackfriars. The mind in reading spins a web from scene to scene, compounds a background from apples falling, and the toll of a church bell, and an owl's fantastic flight which keeps the play together. Here that continuity was sacrificed. We left the theatre possessed of many brilliant fragments but without the sense of all things conspiring and combining together which may be the satisfying culmination of a less brilliant performance. Nevertheless, the play has served its purpose. It has made us compare our Malvolio with Mr. Quartermaine's; our Olivia with Madame Lopokova's; our reading of the whole play with Mr. Guthrie's; and since they all differ, back we must go to Shakespeare. We must read *Twelfth Night* again. Mr. Guthrie has made that necessary and whetted our appetite for the *Cherry Orchard, Measure for Measure*, and *Henry the Eighth* that are still to come.

Roy Walker

Peter Hall's Production of *Twelfth Night* (1958)

Twelfth Night . . . hardly seems to have a central character, prominent or retired, unless we follow, as most star actors and modern productions do, the theatrical logic of opportunity that led to the comedy's being called, as early as 1623, "Malvolio." It has, of course, the two elements usual in a Shakespeare comedy, a romantic plot and a comic plot, usually played for contrast and counterpoint rather than brought to any final resolution and harmony. In the programme note to Peter Hall's production at Stratford in 1958, Ivor Brown speaks of the comic plot as "secondary" but that hardly does justice to what may have been the producer's intention in keeping Malvolio in his place. Yet to select any one of the endearingly familiar characters as central and to balance the comic and romantic plots accordingly may seem, at best, an arbitrary attempt at novelty. Something of the sort, however, was what Hall seemed to be attempting. In making Feste the centre of the whirligig of time that brings in its revenges he had, at any rate, the authority of the New Cambridge edition. "We must hold," declared, Q,[1] "and insist on holding Feste, Master of the Revels, to be the master-mind and controller of *Twelfth Night*, its comic spirit and president. . . ." In the absence of a full supporting argument the assertion may seem arbitrary. A parallel to stimulate imagination in this direction might be found in the comparison of the bitter-sweet figure of Feste alone on the stage at the end, when the three couples go off, with that of the Merchant at the end of the earlier comedy when three

Reprinted from *Shakespeare Survey*, vol. 12 (1958), by permission of Cambridge University Press. Copyright © 1958 by Cambridge University Press.

other couples go off leaving alone the man to whom they owe, in some degree, their wedded happiness. There is also the fact that the title of *Twelfth Night* may be more indicative than it seems to us, who have lost any sense of twelfth night as a red-letter day in the calendar, the time of the Saturnalia which was also once the true date of Christmas. As John Stow[2] tells us,

> In the feast of Christmas, there was in the king's house, wheresoever he was lodged, a lord of misrule, or master of merry disports; and the like had ye in the house of every noble man of honour, or good worship, were he spiritual or temporal.

Is there more to that ubiquitous comic-sad spirit of Feste, a fool who lives by the church and masquerades as a veritable Abbot of Unreason, in this saturnalian comic romance of the snobbish steward who aspires to be his mistress' master and the faithful servant who becomes her master's mistress, than was apparent to Pepys[3] when he wrote it off as "not related at all to the name or day" (and as "a silly play") and to such moderns as J. Q. Adams[4] when they agree with him, on the first point at any rate? The merit of Peter Hall's production, tentative rather than definitive, aspiring rather than assured, was that it gave new life to such a question. Perhaps Feste, whose song of the wind and the rain is heard next on the lips of Lear's Fool, has grown in the succession of Shakespeare's jesters, from the Touchstone who matches the motley of court and country to something more like the sadly wise Old Clown of such a modern Christian artist as Rouault?

Peter Hall's focus on Feste met the audience entering the theatre, on the drop-curtain painted by Lila de Nobili, who designed his 1957 Stratford production of *Cymbeline*. The central feature was a silvery aureoled figure in clown's costume descending into a dark world in which the faces of other characters seen in shadow were touched with the radiance. With his ass's ears he might well have been a disguised Mercury whose winged cap enabled him to go into whatever part of the universe he pleased with the greatest celerity. As music sounded a front spot focused on this coolly glowing figure, which dissolved as lights came up behind to make the curtain transparent. There a small group of musicians harmonized the music which is the food of love and, on the forestage, a group of gentlemen stood motionless in silhouette. The tableau of the drop had been transposed from the vertical to the horizontal, but nothing went well for love until Feste (Cyril Luckham) appeared. As soon as his quicksilver wit proved his young and feather-brained Olivia (Geraldine McEwan) a fool, this mature Feste[5] gave us a shrewd hint that this was not altogether fool. "There is no slander in an allowed fool" and "Now Mercury endue thee with leasing, for thou speakest well of fools" responds the wise fool whom Mercury's winged cap fits.

From the romantic mistress to the comic kinsman; at the end of the first "act" Feste found out the bully-boy Sir Toby (Patrick Wymark) and the fool absolute, Sir Andrew (Richard Johnson) for the drinking-scene, set not in a wine-cellar but in a glowing Warwickshire walled garden where these laughing cavaliers were rebuked by Malvolio (Mark Dignam)—"the devil a puritan that he is"—kill-joy of comic and romantic plots. As has been observed,[6] Maria's plan to "let the fool make a third" in the gulling of this peacock is contradicted later, in the letter scene, when Fabian unaccountably deputizes for Feste. This production minimized the inconsistency by letting Feste feign sleep, head on arm, at a table. As the others went out he raised his head and stared thoughtfully after them. The stage darkened rapidly on this picture, wood-pigeons cooing amorously in the distance, for the "act" interval. That at least left the emphasis on Feste, but what could he have been thinking so seriously about, unless it was why Fabian had been allowed to usurp his place later in the play? The present writer wonders if this was not the actors' doing at some time before 1623. Might not an actor of Malvolio object that besides having more than his share of the comedy, and songs besides, Feste was stealing his best scene by business behind the box-tree? All Fabian's lines and entrances are somewhat suspect,[7] and the problem is not solved, as in this production, by introducing him with Olivia, in I, v.

The second "act" began with the Duke's "Give me some music . . ." acceptably echoing the opening of the first. Feste's sad song seemed to woo Orsino to accept the death of a hopeless love that new and true might be born, he is lost unless the melancholy god make his doublet of changeable taffeta. After the letter scene, from which Feste was so unaccountably absent, Viola met the fellow "wise enough to play the fool," whose keen eyes seemed to penetrate her disguise. But then Feste was, as usual, missing from the mock duel. Surely he, and not Fabian, was to be Viola's second, well assured this cock would not fight? Was not that the point of Feste's shock when, taking Sebastian for his sister in the next scene, he finds the young man now had mettle enough? This scene, ending with Olivia suddenly smitten with Sebastian, closed the second "act" and the brief final "act" began with an abbreviated version of Feste's visitation of Malvolio, in rapid succession as Sir Topas and as himself, the dungeon being a cellar in the garden.

The play ended as it began, with music, all the romantic and comic characters, except Malvolio, dancing together in a golden distance behind a gauze curtain in love's now triumphant harmony, with Feste, the goer-between of the worlds of romance and comedy, and perhaps also of the gods and human kind, seated on the fore-stage in gathering dusk, sadly remembering how the world began. Now it was their light that just touched his figure, forlorn at the thought that there was no more for him to do in this world. Even a god who plays the wise fool may be left lonely at the dance of human love.

The producer had made the romantic plot more consistently light comedy by treating Olivia as a feather-brained little goose; he had kept the comics well on the subtle side of farce, and so made it possible for his Mercury to modulate between the two worlds of the play and make them one. His choice of Cavalier costume gave the maximum thematic contrast with Malvolio's Puritan habit served the opposition of amours and austerity, and brought out what is most English in Shakespeare's Never-Never Land of Illyria. It also eased the problem of the identical twins[8] with a hair-style equally suitable to boy and girl. He had, in Dorothy Tutin, a Viola of irresistible freshness and charm. The rest of a Stratford company for once not star-studded was of its own fairly high standard with none outstanding. This was a *Twelfth Night* that did not altogether succeed, but a production that continually threw fresh light on a comedy about which most of us have long ceased to think freshly, which we too easily accept as a cherished but somewhat shapeless romantic-comic routine.

NOTES

1. A. Quiller-Couch (and J. Dover Wilson), ed. *Twelfth Night* (1930, 1949), p. xxvi. See also L. G. Salingar, "The Design of *Twelfth Night*" in *Shakespeare Quarterly*, IX (Spring 1958): ". . . saturnalian spirit invades the whole play" (p. 118). "There are discordant strains, then, in the harmony of *Twelfth Night* . . . As far as any actor can resolve them, this task falls on Feste . . . it is precisely on this finely-poised balance of his that the whole play comes to rest" (pp. 135–6).

2. John Stow, *The Survey of London*, Everyman Library ed. (1912, etc.), p. 89. He is describing customs in pre-Elizabethan London.

3. Pepys' comment on the performance he saw on "Twelfth Day" 1663 is quoted by Harold Child in his stage-history of the play in the New Cambridge edition, pp. 173–4.

4. "Possibly it was in honor of this grand occasion [the Twelfth Night revel of 1600] that Shakespeare rechristened the comedy with the otherwise irrelevant title *Twelfth Night*." (A footnote cites Pepys in support of this description of the title.)—J. Q. Adams, *A Life of William Shakespeare* (n.d.), pp. 292.

5. Ngaio Marsh, "A Note on a Production of *Twelfth Night*," in *Shakespeare Survey*, 8, p. 72, argues for a young Olivia. Allardyce Nicoll told the writer that he recalls seeing a comic Olivia in a production by the Habima Players. Granville-Barker, in his 1912 Savoy Theatre production of *Twelfth Night* "gave the part [of Feste] to an actor no longer young."—Norman Marshall, *The Producer and the Play* (1957), p. 160. The actor, Hayden Coffin, was fifty in 1912.

6. J. Dover Wilson, New Cambridge ed. *Twelfth Night*, pp. 93–4.

7. They can mostly be plausibly distributed, or returned, to Feste, Sir Andrew and Maria. The opening of the final scene, V, i, is particularly suspect. Why introduce the business of the letter only to leave it aside for some 300 lines, during which Fabian neither speaks nor is spoken to and may or may not be on stage? Was not Maria, rather than Fabian, meant to say "myself and Toby set this device against Malvolio here," V, i. 367–8?

8. The writer has seen powdered wigs used with even greater effect, and at closer quarters, in an enchanting production on Twelfth Night 1954 in the spacious late-eighteenth century Old Dining Room of Attingham Park, Shropshire, a property belonging to the National Trust.

Leslie Hotson

Illyria for Whitehall

The cant of the age, . . . an obscure proverb, an obsolete custom, a hint at a person or fact no longer remembered, hath continually defeated the best of our *guessers*.
Richard Farmer, 1767.

Why Illyria? Transparent domestic topicalities are always more amusing under the pretense of some distant scene. Ben Jonson set the Whitehall of his *Cynthia's Revels* in Diana's "fustian country," Gargaphie. What reasons appropriate to Twelfth Night led Shakespeare to choose Illyria—that sea-coast far away, beyond the Adriatic? Were the connotations of *Illyria* for him and his audience the lyric, the idyll, or the illusion which the romantic sound of the name so often suggests in a modern ear?

Far from it. Something more robustious. What the Dalmatian-Croatian *Illyria* brought to mind was thoughts of wild riot and drunkenness, and the lawless profession of piracy. "Their riotous neighbours, the Illyrians."[1] "Of the wine bibbing of the . . . Illyrians: Neither are the Illyrians clear of this beastly abuse."[2] The Italian byword for a drunken toss-pot or sound quaffer was *un morlacco*—an Illyrian. For sea-thievery, we find Shakespeare elsewhere citing "Bargulus, the strong Illyrian pirate" and the Ragusan "Ragozine, a most notorious pirate," and aptly bringing that "notable pirate, salt-water thief," Antonio, into *Twelfth Night*'s Illyria.

All in all, a boisterous coast, Illyria. A fit stage for what Dowden happily called "the reeling heights of Sir Toby's bacchanals." Its character as "drunk and disorderly" made it just the

Misrulia or Wassailia in which to set the revelrout, the "sport, the
Devil and all," and the licensed Twelfth Night tippling of spiced ale
and burnt sack—fetched from the bar of the wide-open Buttery—
to such ditties as

> Lusty, lusty boys and free—
> And very, very lusty boys are we.
> We can drink till all look blue,
> Dance, sing, and roar, never give o'er
> As long as we've e'er an eye to see—

though Sir Toby represents his wassailing as healths to Lady
Olivia. "I'll drink to her as long as there's a passage in my throat
and drink in Illyria. He's a coward and a coystrill that will not
drink to my niece till his brains turn o' th' toe like a parish top."
His rhetorical demand of Sir Andrew, his fellow-toper, "Were we
not born under Taurus?" is thoroughly sound. For Taurus—"Bull
Jove"—governed those avenues of drink, the neck and throat.
Jovial by birth, the precious pair are drunkards destined by zodia-
cal predominance. But to flatter him into showing his excellence
in capering, Sir Toby assures the simpleton that Taurus governs
"legs and thighs"—blandly passing off *Cen*taurus (Sagittarius) as
Taurus.

Slovenly Toby, whom Lady Olivia calls a "rudesby," found a
prompt imitator in Chapman's Sir Cut. Rudesby, who "will come
into the Presence, like your Frenchman, in foul boots."[3] By bra-
zenly defending his boots as "good enough to drink in," Sir Toby
recalls the great leathern blackjacks for drink at Court, or perhaps
the heroic boot-carouse—"whole boots-full to their friends' welfare"—achieved by compatriots of Hans van Belch, the drunken
Dutchman of *Northward Ho*.

But the prime aura of suggestion clinging to Sir Toby's name
and nature is the Biblical one, from the Apocrypha: in itself an
affront to Puritan-sympathizers such as *'Mal'-voglio* and Mr. Controller Knollys. For the Puritans vehemently rejected the Apocry-
phal books. As Jonson's Zeal-of-the-land Busy exclaims, "Peace,
with thy Apocryphall wares, thou prophane Publican: thy *Bells*,
thy *Dragons*, and thy *Tobie's Dogges*." Queen Elizabeth nevertheless
had the objectionable Toby—Tobias, son of Tobit or Tobias—
actively displayed before the courtiers' eyes. At Hampton Court
hung "two pieces of rich arras of the story of Thobie," and at

Westminster, a dozen more "pieces of tapestry of the story of Tobie." In 1602 Henry Chettle wrote for the public stage a play (now lost) entitled *Tobias*. Aside from the Angel, and the Devil— who killed his bride's seven previous grooms—, the salient points in Toby's story were two: (a) his fish, and (b) his postponed wedding-night.

First, the fish. Not forgetting the fumigatory power of the very ancient and fish-like smell, the fishy fume which the devil himself couldn't abide, the fish is firmly held by all devout can-suckers, bang-pitchers, and elbow-lifters to be the happiest of living things—for it can drink at will. It is no accident that the drunken coachman in Fletcher's *Night-walker*, with his "Give me the bottle! I can drink like a fish," is called Toby; or that Lady Olivia's cousin, who "is in the third degree of drink—he's drowned," is that deboshed fish, Sir Toby.

As for the Biblical Toby's postponed wedding-night, it became a rule of the Church A.D. 398—marital abstinence for the first night or nights after marriage. The "Toby-night" custom was so well known to the Elizabethans that Chapman brought it into his play *Alphonsus, Emperor of Germany*. Here the groom is encouraged to console himself on his Toby-night by drinking "a dozen or two of these bowls," for "it is the use That the first night the bride-groom spares the bride."[4]

The trouble with Sir Toby Belch, from Mistress Maria's leap-year point of view, is that this Toby will hardly stop drinking long enough to let her jockey him into the Toby-night situation—turn him from fish into flesh. Feste condoles with her: "If Sir Toby would leave drinking, thou wert as witty a piece of Eve's flesh as any in Illyria." With the Toby-night in mind, the audience cannot fail to relish the other meaning of Maria's plea, "Sweet Sir Toby, be patient for to-night," or to cheer her triumphal progress through Sir Toby's "I could marry this wench for this device!" to her well-earned success: "In recompense whereof he hath married her." But the marriage does not take place until poetic justice, in the shape of bloody coxcombs given them by Sebastian, has sobered both the drunkards, Sir Toby and Sir Andrew. How neatly their punishment fits their crime appears by the contemporary euphemism "cut in the head" for *drunk*: "twice cut in the head, once with a pottle-pot, and now with cold iron."[5]

If Shakespeare fitted his Aguchica and his Toby with such

well-tailored and significant names, he suited the Illyrian gentle-man-reveller who joined them in the mad jest on Malvolio equally well: for we find *Fabian* as a favourite current nickname for "a riotous, lavish roister, a careless fellow"—"a flaunting fabian."[6]

Wise men hold that there is no great wit without a mixture of madness. Further, that "there is a pleasure sure in being mad which none but madmen know." "Wild, madding, jocund, and irregular," the world of Twelfth Night is a very mad world, exceeding mad. Small wonder that the epithet *mad* appears here more often than in any other play of Shakespeare's. Sir Toby in drink speaks nothing but madman; witty Maria is a finder of madmen; self-loving Malvolio, both sad-mad and madly-used; Lady Olivia in love, merry-mad; the startled Sebastian not only asks "Are all the people mad?" but is forced to the conclusion, "I am mad, or else the lady's mad." And Feste, mad by vocation, seconds the notion by calling her *Mad-donna*.[7] The piece is shot through with the mad mood of hilarity—only heightened by a humourless Malvolio, who holds with the Preacher: "I said of laughter, it is mad; and of mirth, what doeth it?"

Twelfth Night's high spirits irresistibly call to mind "that merry man Rablays." Like Shakespeare, Rabelais had a mint of phrases in his brain; and it would be strange if he had afforded Shake-speare no suggestion beyond the name *Holofernes* for the pedant in *Love's Labour's Lost*, from Gargantua's Latin-master, *Thubal Holoferne*. Swinburne was not alone in finding this affinity strongly in the learned fooling of Feste. The aphorism of Rabelais, *Un fol enseigne bien un sage*—"A fool may teach a wise man wit"—is capped by Feste's "For what says *Quinapalus*? 'Better a witty fool than a foolish wit.'" And as for Feste's Pigrogromitus and his voyaging Vapians, Dr. Furness confessed that

> However settled the conviction that these are mere non-sense names invented by the Clown on the spur of a convivial moment, it is vain to deny that a curiosity, almost invincible, possesses us all to know something more of these Vapians, whose passing of the Equinoctial of Queubus was so infinitely droll that the humour thereof permeated even the thin and watery wits of Sir Andrew. Almost instinctively, we all turn to Rabelais; I am sure that I have merely followed many editorial predecessors in reading his volumes

> from the first line to the last on a keen but futile scent for the
> possible originals of these fictions of the Clown.

In brief, they *sound* Rabelaisian; but there is no real reason for
denying them to Shakespeare's invention, stimulated by that gay
companion, the *Curé* of Meudon.

But to call such gracious fooling "incoherent jargon" or "mere
high-sounding emptiness" is fatally easy for the modern reader
nourished on nonsense. It may however be doubted that the
Elizabethans could be content with meaningless nonsense. Certainly Rabelais had meaning even in his strangest locutions. And
so had Shakespeare. Our failure to find the meaning here is no
excuse for continuing to sidle past "As slyly as any commenter
goes by hard words, or sense." The only respectable course left us
is to launch one more assault, for what it is worth, on this *château
gaillard*, this *feste Burg* of Feste.

"For what says *Quinapalus*?" Surely the Fool's guide and philosopher, whom he consults for sage corroboration, can be no other
than his inseparable bauble, his *marotte*, the absurd little figure on
a stick. *That* is Quinapalus. And the form suggests derivation
from an Italianate *Quinapalo*—"There on the stick"—on the model
of *quinavalle* and *quinamonte*. On his stick, *Quinapalo* is of course in
the best position to leap nimbly *di palo in frasca*—from pole to
bush—which is the Italian for "cock-and-bull," skipping, discon-
nected talk, the Fool's stock-in-trade.[8] As for *Pigrogromitus*, he
seems to be compounded of the Italian for *lazy* and *scab or scruf*.
Lazyscurvius is contemptuous enough, recalling both Sir Toby's
"Out, scab!" and Sir Andrew's "thou art but a scurvy fellow," but
we miss a clear reference.

Can we do better with the *Vapians* passing the equinoctial of
Queubus? A *Va-pian* should be an Easy-goer, a Leisurely, a Fair-
and-softly—from *Chi va pian piano va lontano*: "Fair and softly goes
far in a day." And the astonishing distance these *Va-pians* cover is
beyond the Equinoctial or Equator of *Cubus*—which, in Plato's
cosmology, is the Earth: The Easygoers passing the Earth's Equator—below the burning Line. Inevitably there is an ingeniously
indecent meaning as well, which however may readily be
dispensed with. Stripped of scholarly whimsy, Feste's *festina lente*
embodies a sound maxim of statecraft. Queen Elizabeth herself

told the French ambassador that "one should go gently and do nothing in haste."

Though the *Va-pians* are Shakespeare's coinage, perhaps the influence of Rabelais is otherwise present in *Twelfth Night*, or *What You Will*, and in a subtler shape than we have guessed. For the essential spirit of the saturnalian feast of misrule lives in its jovial freedom or licence, well set out by Ben Jonson in his Twelfth Night merriment, *Time Vindicated*:

> O, we shall have his Saturnalia, his days of feast and liberty again: where men might do, and talk all that they list—slaves of their lords, the servants of their masters. . . . Time's come about, and promiseth all liberty—nay, licence. We shall do what we list!

That is, not only "drink as in the days of Pantagruel" but "Flout 'em and scout 'em, And scout 'em and flout 'em. Thought is free." In flouting Sir Andrew, the fair shrew Maria tells him, "*Now*, sir, thought is free."

Here we find ourselves at the very door of Gargantua's House of Will or Pleasure, the Abbey of Theleme, if not already inside it, among the enviable Thelemites, in whose rule was but this clause—*Fay ce que vouldras*: What you will! From this vantage-point we now see more in Shakespeare's title than "Call it *Twelfth Night*, or whatever you please"—which is the meaning Marston assigned to his own "slight-writ" *What You Will*. For Shakespeare's title issues the saturnalian invitation, *Twelfth Night*, or *Fay ce que vouldras*, What you will—Liberty Hall. Do what you list with Mr. Controller or anyone else. No excuse is left for the shallow opinion that the play has no connection with Twelfth Night, or that the added title shows a carelessness of the main one. On the contrary, *What You Will* defines and drives home its rollicking message.

And where did Sir Toby find his ironical and preposterous description of Sir Andrew—"He's as tall a man as any's in Illyria . . . he plays o' th' viol de gamboys, and speaks three or four languages word for word without book"? Where but in the description of Gargantua's Thelemites, the Knights of his Abbey of What You Will? "Never were seen knights so worthy, so valiant . . . more vigorous, more nimble. . . . So nobly were they taught that there was neither he nor she amongst them but could . . . sing, play on musical instruments, speak five or six languages."[9]

Since Twelfth Night is the Feast of the Christmas Lord of Misrule, many have joined Quiller-Couch in accepting the festive Feste, with his long green robe of mingled motley and his bauble-sceptre, as "the master-mind and controller of *Twelfth Night*." Yet if that were so, Feste would plan and conduct the brilliant campaign against "Mr. Controller" Malvolio. But no such matter. On the contrary, it is the quick, deviceful, strong-brained little gentle-woman, Maria, whom Shakespeare sets up as rightful ruler of the sport royal, and she richly deserves her crown at the Buttery-bar as a finder of madmen. His excellent ground for this—and, as we have seen, for the choice fitness of the play's main plot as well—is the date of his production, 1600: leap-year, woman's year. "Dian doth rule, and you must domineer." Inevitably Maria reigns as Lady of Misrule, and inevitably she hooks and lands her fish, Toby.[10]

Sovereign for a night, Maria receives us into her holiday realm—a land teeming with Christmas and Epiphany legend, folk custom, and traditional feasting, dance, jesting, and game. For Twelfth Night is not only the joyful Feast of Light for the return-ing sun, but also *Le Jour des Rois*, the anniversary of the Three Kings:

> Be merry, all that be presënt,
> Reges de Saba venient—
> Now is the Twelfth Day come—
> God send us good New Year!

According to Florio, the name *Maria* signifies *Illumination*: not inappropriate for the queen of the Feast of Light.

Sir Toby brings in a well-known piece of Twelfth Day folklore by hailing the neat little sovereign's approach with "Look where the youngest Wren of mine comes." For the tiny Wren is both universally known as King of the Birds, and connected with this feast in a fashion as familiar as it is baffling. Under "Wren" in the *Encyclopædia Britannica*, Alfred Newton writes,

> The curious association of this bird with the Feast of the
> Three Kings, on which day in South Wales—or in Ireland
> and in the South of France on or about Christmas Day—

men and boys used to "hunt the wren," addressing it in a
song as "the king of the birds," is remarkable.

The wren, the wren, the King of all birds
On Saint Stephen's Day he was caught in the furze.

Has anyone ever explained the mystery? Was the Wren King the
enemy of the Three Kings? And must he be yearly slain to clear
their road, when "the Kings of Arabia and Saba shall bring gifts"?

Who can tell? But there are some striking coincidences here.
"Happy Arabia, nature's spicery," which as the Elizabethan Fynes
Moryson reports "yields frankincense, myrrh—grains of gold as
big as acorns are found here," contained two kingdoms: Saba
(Sabæn) and Ma'in. (Minæan). *Mineo* and *Minea* are Florio's words
for frankincense and myrrh. Here then is *Mine* connected both
with the country and with two gifts of the Three Kings. Is the
country possibly the original *Mine* of gold or gold-mine as well?
Who knows? At all events, it is certain that the ancients called the
people of Araby-the-blest "Troglodytes" or cave-dwellers.[11] Furthermore, the country "abounds in small birds," and the name of
the Wren is *Troglodytes parvulus*, "the tiny cave-dweller." However
far we may still be from fathoming the mysterious relation of
King Wren the cave-dweller to the Three Kings of cave-dwelling
Saba and Mine, we can now begin to see light in Sir Toby's "Wren
of Mine."

Wren Maria discharges her role as mock ruler, Twelfth Night
queen, to admiration. But Shakespeare does not therefore neglect
two other features of the ancient Christmas folk-play—the
sword-dance or sham combat, and the mumming. Of the first he
reminds us with the bloodless passage-at-arms between Viola and
Sir Andrew, and of the second with Feste's dressing up as a
counterfeit Sir Topas the curate "to visit Malvolio the lunatic."
And Maria, though she put Feste up to this bit of tradition,
recognizes it as functionless: "Thou mightst have done this without thy beard and gown. He sees thee not."

Another Twelfth Night custom of high antiquity which her-
alds the wassail is *Hunt the Fox*. Obviously a process of "killing the
old Devil for good luck," in former times it was accomplished by
the hullabaloo of hunting down and killing a fox or a cat released

in the Court. "The night is our own, for the Devil is dead!" As late as 1572 a fox was killed at Whitehall on Twelfth Night. The death of the devil-fox gave the joyful signal for wassail so notoriously that drunkards were termed *fox-catchers*, and to be drunk was called *to whip the cat, to hunt the fox*, or to be *foxed*. In a less sanguinary form this Twelfth Night custom survived in the rough sport of "Fox in the Hole," with hue and cry after a luckless human quarry, hunted with yelps of "Fox, fox, go out of thy hole!" As Herrick has it,

> . . . thy wassail bowl,
> That's toss'd up after Fox-i'-th'-hole.

Hunt the Fox gives point to Feste's defiance of Malvolio: "Sir Toby will be sworn that I am no *fox*; but he will not pass his word for twopence that you are no fool." As much as to say, "I am no Twelfth Night fox to be hunted out; if you are so anxious to chase out a fool, begin with yourself." And Orsino's banishing of that young fox, "Cesario," is in the same vein:

> O thou dissembling cub! What wilt thou be
> When time has sow'd a grizzle on thy case?

Once the wassail and catch-singing have been well launched, the natural course is to stretch to the limit the last gaudy night of the holidays, mocking the midnight bell. But Sir Toby's "Not to be abed after midnight is to be up betimes" and " 'Tis too late to go to bed now" inevitably bring the thought of the morning after, when the world will go back to work. And since the universal, ceaseless, and typical work was drawing the fibres and whirling the spindle, the morrow of Twelfth Night was Saint Distaff's or Rock Day:

> Give Saint Distaff all the right,
> Then bid Christmas sport good night.[12]

This prospect of "spinning tomorrow" underlies Sir Toby's broad jest on Sir Andrew's thin and "flaggy" or flat-lying hair, which betrays his foolishness—*His thin-set hair along did sit, Which represents a woodcock's wit*[13]:

To. It hangs like flax on a distaff; and I hope to see a housewife take thee between her legs and spin it off.
And. Faith, I'll home tomorrow, Sir Toby.

But tomorrow, Saint Distaff, and the hussy are futurities. Sir
Andrew still has his hair, such as it is, and Twelfth Night is here—
dancing time of revels. These make the delight of Sir Andrew,
who is good at gambols, capers, and sprawling "kickshawses,"
quelquechoses of papier-maché in Toby's pun, kick-"shows" for
show, not eating. The knightly Aguchica-Littlewit even claims
Illyrian excellence in the acrobatic *salto indietro* or "back-trick," of
which the Italian masters describe no fewer than nineteen distinct
and astonishing varieties.[14]

General freedom of dicing, under the regulation of her Majesty's Groom Porter, was a further Court liberty during Christmas, in which the Queen herself joined. If we think it credible, we
may believe what Ben Jonson is reported to have said, that she
"had always about Christmas evens *set dice*, that threw six or five,
and *she knew not they were other*, to make her win and esteem herself
fortunate." More credible is the story of Elizabeth's gamester's-
humour in calling Pope Sixtus Quintus, her admiring enemy, by
the winning nickname of "Sice-cinq." A favourite holiday game
with the "square rattling bones" was *trey-trip*, in which a three was
the winning throw. *Twelfth Night* brings this in twice. First with
Toby's "Shall I play my freedom at trey-trip, and become thy
bond-slave?" and punningly again, when Feste tries to beg a third
gold-piece of Orsino (as a Christmas present) with "Primo, se-
cundo, tertio, is a good play . . . the *triplex*, sir, is a good *tripping*
measure"—only to be told, "You can fool no more money out of
me at this *throw*."

Another popular implement for dicing at this feast was the
four-sided top, whirligig, or teetotum: which survives in use
today at the Hanukah Festival of Lights as the *Drehrädchen* or
Dredel. When "Time's come about," and Malvolio's number is up
and his luck is out, Feste employs this Twelfth Night teetotum or
whirling die to symbolize poetic justice: "and thus the whirligig of
time brings in his revenges."

As for card-play with the dicing, perhaps the leading Christmas game was what Ben Jonson calls "the thrifty and right

worshipful game of Post and Pair." The Knave or Jack in this game held an important place under the name of *Pur*:

> Some, having lost the double Post and Pair,
> Make their advantage on the Purs they have.

"Post and Pair" figures as a character in Jonson's *Christmas his Masque*, "his garment all done over with Pairs and Purs." So familiar were the Twelfth Night *Post* and *Purs* that they furnished Viola with a scornful pun in her refusal of Olivia's gift of money: "I am no fee'd *post*, lady; keep your *purse*"—that is, "your *knavish* gold."

Turning from gambling to Twelfth Night guessing games, we learn from Drayton and Jonson that the latter included Purposes and Riddles:

> In pretty riddles to bewray our loves,
> In questions, purposes, or drawing gloves.

"At Draw-gloves, Riddles, Dreams, and other pretty Purposes"— "For sport's sake, let's have some riddles, or purposes." Purposes (a sort of "Guess what I'm thinking of") receives only passing reference in Maria's admission, "My *purpose* is indeed a horse of that colour." But the Riddle takes centre-stage in *Twelfth Night* with Maria's cunningly-prepared "dish o' poison" for Malvolio: "*M. O. A. I. doth sway my life.*"

Clearly, this fustian riddle must have a simple solution, obvious both to the audience and to all the characters except that dullard, Malvolio. His fatuous, self-absorbed, and fruitless brain-beating furnish the fun:

> What should that alphabetical position portend? If I could make that resemble something in me! Softly! *M. O. A. I.* . . . *M.—Malvolio. M.*, why, that begins my name! . . . *M.* But then there is no consonancy in the sequel. . . . *A.* should follow, but *O.* does.

Can we do any better than Malvolio? Query, what is the most obvious group of four? Answer, the Four Elements—which in her "Armada" prayer Queen Elizabeth defined as "serving to continue in orderly government the whole of all the mass"—and the word *element* comes more frequently into *Twelfth Night* than into any

other play of Shakespeare's. "*M. O. A. I. doth sway my life.*"[15] Maria
has cleverly chosen those "fustian" designations of the elements
whose initials appear in his name: *Mare*-Sea, *Orbis*-Earth, *Aer*-Air,
and *Ignis*-Fire. *M. O. A. I.*

> Fire hot and dry, air moist and hot we call;
> Seas cold and moist, earth dry and cold withal.[16]

Her "dish o' poison" dupes the self-loved *MALVOLIO* into imag-
ining himself Controller of Lady Olivia, although every fool
knows that she is swayed only by *Mare, Orbis, Aer,* and *Ignis*.
And the order of Maria's arrangement of the elemental four is
thoroughly appropriate. According to accepted theory, Woman is
cold and moist, Man, hot and dry; in the elements swaying Olivia,
therefore, *Mare* must take first place. Also she commands Malvolio ("*I may command where I adore*"): consequently *Mare* leads and *Ignis*
comes last. Moreover, in mourning her brother, Olivia's controlling emotion is grief: and "Grief like water cold and moist" is again
Mare.

This riddle is an essential part of the practical joke on Malvolio. Elaborate plots to make somebody look a fool constituted a
principal Court pastime in the holidays. The current courtier's
slang for the jest was to *dor* someone—"that villain dors me"—or
to give someone the *dor*. Like Malvolio's *geck*, the term is obviously
borrowed from the Dutch: *een door*, a fool. Jonson's Twelfth Night
comedy *Cynthia's Revels* exhibits a deal of this *dor*-ing. In Act 5
Scene 2, a trick is described very similar to the one played on
Malvolio: "He follows the fallacy; comes out accoutred to his
believed instructions; your mistress smiles, and you give him the
dor." Shakespeare likewise brings in the *dor*-ing, but so lightly and
deftly that we have failed to notice it—in the foolish Sir Andrew's
innocent echo of Sir Toby's boast of Maria's love for him: "She's a
beagle true bred, and one that adores me: what o' that?"

Sir Andrew: "I was a-*dor*'d once too."

To close up the Illyrian revel with music and moral, Shakespeare gives us Feste's celebrated song, *When that I was and a little
tiny boy*. For lack of understanding of its drift, this song has naively
been received as a tale in rime but little reason: nonsense contemptible or nonsense charming; but nonsense. But is Feste the
man to waste his wit in nonsense? He knows precisely what to

provide as a fitting farewell to wassail and saturnalian excess: and it is not something adapted to a Christmas party for Victorian young persons. As Rupert Brooke observed, "The Elizabethans liked obscenity; and the primness and the wickedness that do not like it, have no business with them."

Must we really be reminded that ribaldry was the proper and age-old function of the Fool? Shakespeare's colleague Robert Armin played not only Feste but Lear's Fool as well. Knavish, licentious speech is common to both roles; and Armin's rendering of Feste's song proved so popular that an additional stanza was sung in *Lear*—*He that has and a little tiny wit*. Historically, the Fool and indecency cannot be parted. To make up for his mental shortcomings, Nature was commonly believed to have endowed the Fool with an excess of virility, symbolized by his *bauble*. "Fools please women best." "A fool's bauble is a lady's playfellow." "A foolish bed-mate, why, he hath no peer." Priapus used to be described as *that foolish god*; and Mercutio's cynical notion of Love is a *great natural* with his *bauble*.

Feste's lascivious lapses earn him Lady Olivia's sharp reproof—"you grow dishonest." We realize that he has not forgotten its sting, when, with the Fool's immemorial trick of "box about"—that is, of passing a received blow on to someone else—he buffets the devil of lechery in Malvolio with this same *dishonest:* "Talkest thou nothing but of ladies? . . . Fie, thou dishonest Satan!" His boastful pun, "He that is *well hang'd* [i.e., *handsomely furnished or adorned with virility*] in this world, needs to fear no colours [*no deceptions or foes*]" is taken up by Maria.[17] She bids him, "Make that good [*Prove that statement in a decent sense*]." And Feste's lenten answer blandly reverts to the gallows-meaning, dismal but decent: a man well hang'd *by the neck* "shall see none to fear."

As for Lear's Fool, he advertises the Fool's characteristic advantage by announcing, "Marry, here's grace and a codpiece: that's a wise man and a fool." To this he adds a complacent boast of his physical irresistibility to the other sex: "ladies too, they will not let me have all the fool to myself, they'll be snatching."[18] And he closes the first act of the tragedy with the witty and bawdy tag

> She that's a maid now, and laughs at my *deporter*,
> Shall not be a maid long, unless things be cut shorter.

The text has *departure*, a word unacceptable both for the rime and for the sense. I suggest that Shakespeare must have written *deporter*, which Cotgrave gives as the French for "a sporting bauble." What roused the wanton wench to hilarity was not the Fool's vanishing but the sight of his immoderate "bauble."[19] *Thing* in its "bauble" sense is the key word, not only here, but also in the first stanza of Feste's song. In the Fool's childish state as a little tiny boy, a *foolish thing* was no more than a harmless trifle. Far otherwise, however, when he was grown "fit for breed"—a lecherous knave and thief of love, on the prowl after other men's wives:

'Gainst knaves and thieves men shut their gate.

Having begun by making sure that in listening to Feste's song we are not like that blockish Rosencrantz, with whom a knavish speech sleeps in a foolish ear, we may now look at the "reason of the rime"—the plan of the ditty as a whole. Feste has already given us his exquisite love songs; now we are to be sent away with "a song of good life." What he trolls out is a Drunkard's Progress, an Elizabethan forerunner of such bibulous confessions as *I'm a rambling wreck of poverty* and *I've been a moonshiner for seventeen long years*: a moral and musical reminder that the wassailing of the Twelfth Night saturnalia had better not be followed as a way of life. That is the road to "wet damnation." He has already told Lady Olivia—as they contemplate the condition of Sir Toby—that a drunken man is like a fool, a madman, and a drowned man: "One draught above heat makes him a fool, the second mads him, and a third drowns him." Now he proceeds to illustration, with a dramatic lyric of rueful reminiscence leading us through the same three familiar degrees—goat-drunk, lion-drunk, and swine-drunk: "now goatishly to whore, now lion-like to roar, now hoggishly in the mire"—whose attendant deadly sins, appropriated to the three ages of manhood (youth, prime, and old age), are Lechery, Wrath, and Sloth.

As we have noticed, in the second stanza—'*Gainst knaves and thieves men shut their gate*—the lecherous knaves find that his goatish vice renders him an outcast, shut out in the rain. In the third stanza, unable to mend his ways on the precept "Leave thy drink and thy whore, and keep in-a-door," he makes a shiftless, beggarly, wrangling marriage. Lion-drunk, he dings the pots about, swaggers with his own shadow, and his screeching wife drives him forth—out in the rain.

The final phase exhibits him in the torpor, the "benumbing apoplectic sleep" of the swine-drunk—*But when I came unto my beds.* *Beds* is inevitably plural: the various spots where he happened to fall. The abandoned drunkard has many beds, as well as a long series of drunken heads in toss-pot company. As John Day puts it, "The last . . . carry their beds o' their backs . . . and go to bed in the kennel . . . and these we call Swine-drunk."[20] The grovelling Sly of *The Taming of the Shrew* is either hog or corpse: "This were a bed but cold to sleep so soundly. O monstrous beast! How like a swine he lies! Grim death, how foul and loathsome is thine image!"

Again, out in the rain. "Through the sharp hawthorn blows the cold wind." With a sorrowful hey-ho, the wind and the rain, and the implied early death they bring with them, form the inevitable burden. *A great while ago the world begun;*[21] and for the drunken fool without the wit to come in out of the rain, it is all but ended. What of it? *But that's all one. . . .* Then turning smoothly into Robin Armin the player, Feste is out of his moral and into an Epilogue, to beg a gracious *plaudite* of the hearers—

> our Play is done,
> And we'll strive to please you every day.

NOTES

1. *Nashe* (ed. McKerrow), 3.367.
2. A. Fleming, *A Registre of Hystories* (1576), Sig. I2^V.
3. *Sir Giles Goosecap*, I.2.126.
4. See T. M. Parrott's note, *The Tragedies of George Chapman* (1910), 699.
5. Dekker and Webster, *Westward Ho*, 5.4.
6. The *O.E.D.* suggests a probable reference "to the Fabian priests of Pan, and the licence permitted them at the Lupercalia." And we may compare Guilpin's *Skialetheia* (1598), sig. D1^V, where an arrogant reveller is reprehended with "out upon thee *Fabian.*"
7. Compare "Mad-dame," in Jonson's *The Devil is an Ass*, 4.3.39; *Tale of a Tub*, 3.5.4; and in Sir George Buc, *The Third Universitie*—Stow-Howes, *Annals* (1615), 987.
8. Compare the French *sauter du coq à l'âne.*

9. *Gargantua*, Book 1, Chapter 57.

10. In Ben Jonson's *New Inn*, Prudence, "The Chambermaid, is elected *Soueraigne* of the *Sports* in the Inne, gouernes all, commands, and so orders, as the *Lord Latimer* is exceedingly taken with her, and takes her to his wife, in conclusion." The contract of marriage is here made without a priest, *per verbum de presenti* before witnesses, which no doubt was Toby's and Maria's method too.

11. "People of Arabia called . . . *Troglodytans*" Topsell, *Four-footed Beasts*, 225; "Arabia bordering vpon Ethyopia by the auncients called Trogloditick" T. Washington, tr. *Nicholay's Voy.* IV.xi.122b; "The Troglodites myne them selues caues in the grounde, wherin to dwell" W. Watreman, *Fardle of Facions*, I.vi.93; qu. *O.E.D.*

12. Herrick, *Hesperides* (1648), "St. Distaff's Day."

13. *Bacchus Bountie* (1593), by "Phillip Foulface."

14. Tomaso Garzoni, *La Piazza Universale* (1589), 454.

15. The elements compose the eternal Unity, the controlling, turning Universe:

> A man to join himself with th'Universe
> In his main sway, and make (in all things fit)
> One with that All, and go on round with it.

Chapman, *Revenge of Bussy*, 4. 1. 139–41.
   The controlling elements also figure in love lyric:

> What else mishap, but longing to aspire,
> To strive against earth, water, fire, and air?

The Phoenix Nest (1593), ed. H. E. Rollins, 81.

16. R. C., *The Times' Whistle* (E.E.T.S., 1871), 117. Chapman likewise employs *Sea* for the element Water—"When sea, fire, air, in earth were indisposed" *The Shadow of Night* (1594), line 42; and Feste uses *Orb* for the Earth: "Foolery, sir, does walk about the Orb like the Sun" 3.1. 39–40.

17. For this sense of *hang'd*, see the fool Pompey in Fletcher and Massinger's *Wit at Several Weapons*, 2.2: "When they saw how I was hang'd . . ." Compare Cotgrave's *Couillatris*: "Well hang'd".
   Maria gives Feste the derivation of his byword: "I can tell thee where that saying was born, of 'I fear no colours' . . . In the wars." *Colours* of course means "military colours" as well as "deceptions." The historical source would seem to be *La Guerre Folle* of 1485 in France. And who more expert on the Mad War than that accomplished "finder of madmen," Maria? Sir Walter Ralegh, writing on the valour of the English fighting man, cites "another place of the same Authour [de Serres], where hee tells, how the *Britons* [i.e., Bretons],

being invaded by *Charles* the eight, King of France, thought it good policie, to apparell a thousand and two hundred of their owne men in *English* Cassacks; hoping that the very sight of the *English* red Crosse, would be enough to terrifie the *French*."—*The Historie of the World*. Another writer, Henry Belasyse, employed the same familiar incident, as follows: "These victoryes [in the Hundred Years' War] made the English so famous, that the Duke of Britanny warring against Charles 8th of France, to strike terror into the French, apparelled fifteen hundred of his owne subjects in English armes and under the English colours. But the asse is never the better for having putt on the lyons skinne, nor the Britons [Bretons] for appearing like English."—H.M.C., *Various*, 2. 196. Feste may be bold to use a phrase extolling the terrific reputation of English military valour.

18. Compare the Fool's song in *Volpone*, 1.2.71:

> Your Fool, he is your great man's darling,
> And your ladies' sport and pleasure;
> Tongue and bauble are his treasure.

19. "Shee is enamour'd on the fooles bable" *Jack Drum's Entertainment* (1600), Act 2, line 308.
20. "Peregrinatio Scholastia" *Works* (ed. Bullen, 1880), 51, 52.
21. Feste's "A great while ago the world begun" recalls the Elizabethan euphemism for coition, "To dance The Beginning of the World."

C. L. Barber

Testing Courtesy and Humanity in
Twelfth Night

. . . nature to her bias drew in that.

The title of *Twelfth Night* may well have come from the first
occasion when it was performed, whether or not Dr. Leslie Hotson is right in arguing that its first night was the court celebration of the last of the twelve days of Christmas on January 6,
1600–1601.[1] The title tells us that the play is like holiday misrule—though not just like it, for it adds "or what you will." The
law student John Manningham, who saw it at the Middle Temple's feast on February 2, 1602, wrote in his diary that it was
"much like the Comedy of Errores, or Menechmi in Plautus, but
most like and neere to that in Italian called *Inganni*." Actually,
Shakespeare used, in addition to Plautine devices with which he
was familiar, not *Gl'Inganni* to which Manningham refers, but
Rich's tale *Of Apolonius and Silla*, a romance perhaps derived indirectly from that Italian comedy. And he used no written source
for the part Manningham specially praised: "A good practise in it
to make the Steward beleeve his Lady widdowe was in love with
him. . . ."[2] So *Twelfth Night* puts together a tale from a romance,
Plautine farce, festivity, and the sort of merry sport or "practice"
which Shakespeare customarily added from his own invention.

Shakespeare can be inclusive in his use of traditions because
his powers of selection and composition can arrange each element

Cesar Lombardi Barber, *Shakespeare's Festive Comedy.* Copyright © 1959
by Princeton University Press. Chap. 10, pp. 240–61, reprinted by permission of Princeton University Press.

so that only those facets of it show which will serve his expressive purpose. He leaves out the dungeon in which Rich's jealous Orsino shuts up Viola, as well as Sebastian's departure leaving Olivia with child; but he does not hesitate to keep such events as the shipwreck, or Sebastian's amazing marriage to a stranger, or Orsino's threat to kill Viola. It is not the credibility of the event that is decisive, but what can be expressed through it. Thus the shipwreck is made the occasion for Viola to exhibit an undaunted, aristocratic mastery of adversity—she settles what she shall do next almost as though picking out a costume for a masquerade:

> I'll serve this duke:
> Thou shalt present me as an eunuch to him;
> It may be worth thy pains, for I can sing
> And speak to him in many sorts of music . . .
>
> (I ii 55–8)

What matters is not the event, but what the language says as gesture, the aristocratic, free-and-easy way she settles what she will do and what the captain will do to help her. The pathetical complications which are often dwelt on in the romance are not allowed to develop far in the play; instead Viola's spritely language conveys the fun she is having in playing a man's part, with a hidden womanly perspective about it. One cannot quite say that she is playing in a masquerade, because disguising *just* for the fun of it is a different thing. But the same sort of festive pleasure in transvestism is expressed.

It is amazing how little happens in *Twelfth Night*, how much of the time people are merely talking, especially in the first half, before the farcical complications are sprung. Shakespeare is so skillful by now in rendering attitudes by the gestures of easy conversation that when it suits him he can almost do without events. In the first two acts of *Twelfth Night* he holds our interest with a bare minimum of tension while unfolding a pattern of contrasting attitudes and tones in his several persons. Yet Shakespeare's whole handling of romantic story, farce, and practical joke makes a composition which moves in the manner of his earlier festive comedies, through release to clarification.[3]

"A Most Extracting Frenzy"

Olivia's phrase in the last act, when she remembers Malvolio and his "madness," can summarize the way the play moves:

> A most extracting frenzy of mine own
> From my remembrance clearly banish'd his.
>
> (V i 273–4)

People are caught up by delusions or misapprehensions which take them out of themselves, bringing out what they would keep hidden or did not know was there. *Madness* is a key word. The outright gull Malvolio is already "a rare turkey-cock" from "contemplation" (II v 28) before Maria goes to work on him with her forged letter. "I do not now fool myself, to let imagination jade me" (II v 145), he exclaims when he has read it, having been put "in such a dream that when the image of it leaves him he must run mad" (II v 173). He is too self-absorbed actually to run mad, but when he comes at Olivia, smiling and cross-gartered, she can make nothing else of it: "Why, this is very mid-summer madness" (III iv 53). And so the merrymakers have the chance to put him in a dark room and do everything they can to face him out of his five wits.

What they bring about as a "pastime" (III iv 132), to "gull him into a nayword, and make him a common recreation" (II iii 127), happens unplanned to others by disguise and mistaken identity. Sir Toby, indeed, "speaks nothing but madman" (I v 100) without any particular occasion. "My masters, are you mad?" (II iii 83) Malvolio asks as he comes in to try to stop the midnight singing. Malvolio is sure that he speaks for the countess when he tells Toby that "though she harbours you as her kinsman, she's nothing allied to your disorders" (II iii 93). But in fact this sober judgment shows that he is not "any more than a steward" (II iii 109). For his lady, dignified though her bearing is, suddenly finds herself doing "I know not what" (I v 292) under the spell of Viola in her page's disguise: "how now?/Even so quickly may one catch the plague?" (I v 278–9). "Poor lady," exclaims Viola, "she were better love a dream!" (II ii 24). In their first interview, she had told the countess, in urging the count's suit, that "what is

yours to bestow is not yours to reserve" (I v 177). By the end
of their encounter, Olivia says the same thing in giving way to
her passion: "Fate, show thy force! Ourselves we do not owe"
(I v 294). And soon her avowals of love come pouring out, over-
coming the effort at control which shows she is a lady:

> O, what a deal of scorn looks beautiful
> In the contempt and anger of his lip!
> A murd'rous guilt shows not itself more soon
> Than love that would seem hid: love's night is noon.
> Cesario, by the roses of the spring,
> By maidhood, honour, truth, and everything,
> I love thee so . . .
>
> (III i 142-8)

A little later, when she hears about Malvolio and his smile, she
summarizes the parallel with "I am as mad as he,/If sad and merry
madness equal be" (III iv 14-15).

The farcical challenge and "fight" between Viola and Sir
Andrew are another species of frantic action caused by delusion.
"More matter for a May morning" (III iv 136) Fabian calls it as
they move from pretending to exorcise Malvolio's devil to pretending to act as solicitous seconds for Sir Andrew. When Antonio enters the fray in manly earnest, there is still another sort of
comic error, based not on a psychological distortion but simply on
mistaken identity. This Plautine sort of confusion leads Sebastian
to exclaim, "Are all the people mad?" (IV i 26). Just after we have
seen "Malvolio the lunatic" (IV ii 22) baffled in the dark room
("But tell me true, are you not mad indeed? or do you but
counterfeit?" IV ii 190-10), we see Sebastian struggling to understand his wonderful encounter with Olivia:

> This is the air; that is the glorious sun;
> This pearl she gave me, I do feel't and see't;
> And though 'tis wonder that enwraps me thus,
> Yet 'tis not madness.
>
> (IV iii 1-4)

The open-air clarity of this little scene anticipates the approaching
moment when delusions and misapprehensions are resolved by
the finding of objects appropriate to passions. Shakespeare, with
fine stagecraft, spins the misapprehensions out to the last mo-

ment. He puts Orsino, in his turn, through an extracting frenzy, the Duke's frustration converting at last to violent impulses toward Olivia and Cesario, before he discovers in the page the woman's love he could not win from the countess.

That it should all depend on there being an indistinguishable twin brother always troubles me when I think about it, though never when I watch the play. Can it be that we enjoy the play so much simply because it is a wish-fulfillment presented so skillfully that we do not notice that our hearts are duping our heads? Certainly part of our pleasure comes from pleasing make-believe. But I think that what chance determines about particular destinies is justified, as was the case with *The Merchant of Venice*, by the play's realizing dynamically general distinctions and tendencies in life.

"You Are Betroth'd Both to a Maid and Man"

The most fundamental distinction the play brings home to us is the difference between men and women. To say this may seem to labor the obvious; for what love story does not emphasize this difference? But the disguising of a girl as a boy in *Twelfth Night* is exploited so as to renew in a special way our sense of the difference. Just as a saturnalian reversal of social roles need not threaten the social structure, but can serve instead to consolidate it, so a temporary, playful reversal of sexual roles can renew the meaning of the normal relation. One can add that with sexual as with other relations, it is when the normal is secure that playful aberration is benign. This basic security explains why there is so little that is queazy in all Shakespeare's handling of boy actors playing women, and playing women pretending to be men. This is particularly remarkable in *Twelfth Night*, for Olivia's infatuation with Cesario-Viola is another, more fully developed case of the sort of crush Phebe had on Rosalind. Viola is described as distinctly feminine in her disguise, more so than Rosalind:

> . . . they shall yet belie thy happy years
> That say thou art a man: Diana's lip
> Is not more smooth and rubious; thy small pipe

Is as the maiden's organ, shrill and sound,
And all is semblative a woman's part.

(I iv 30–4)

When on her embassy Viola asks to see Olivia's face and exclaims about it, she shows a woman's way of relishing another woman's beauty—and sensing another's vanity: "'Tis beauty truly blent. . . ." "I see you what you are—you are too proud" (I v 223, 234). Olivia's infatuation with feminine qualities in a youth takes her, doing "I know not what," from one stage of life out into another, from shutting out suitors in mourning for her brother's memory, to ardor for a man, Sebastian, and the clear certainty that calls out to "husband" in the confusion of the last scene.

We might wonder whether this spoiled and dominating young heiress may not have been attracted by what she could hope to dominate in Cesario's youth—but it was not the habit of Shakespeare's age to look for such implications. And besides, Sebastian is not likely to be dominated; we have seen him respond to Andrew when the ninny knight thought he was securely striking Cesario:

> *Andrew.* Now, sir, have I met you again? There's for you!
> *Sebastian.* Why, there's for thee, and there, and there!

(IV i 24–5)

To see this manly reflex is delightful—almost a relief—for we have been watching poor Viola absurdly perplexed behind her disguise as Sir Toby urges her to play the man: "Dismount thy tuck, be yare in thy preparation. . . . Therefore on, or strip your sword naked; for meddle you must, that's certain" (III iv 214, 240). She is driven to the point where she exclaims in an aside: "Pray God defend me! A little thing would make me tell them how much I lack of a man" (III iv 286–7). What she lacks, Sebastian has. His entrance in the final scene is preceded by comical testimony of his prowess, Sir Andrew with a broken head and Sir Toby halting. The particular implausibility that there should be an identical man to take Viola's place with Olivia is submerged in the general, beneficent realization that there is such a thing as a man. Sebastian's comment when the confusion of identities is resolved points to the general force which has shaped particular developments:

> So comes it, lady, you have been mistook.
> But nature to her bias drew in that.
>
> (V i 251–2)

Over against the Olivia-Cesario relation, there are Orsino-Cesario and Antonio-Sebastian. Antonio's impassioned friendship for Sebastian is one of those ardent attachments between young people of the same sex which Shakespeare frequently presents, with his positive emphasis, as exhibiting the loving and lovable qualities later expressed in love for the other sex.[4] Orsino's fascination with Cesario is more complex. In the opening scene, his restless sensibility can find no object: "nought enters there, . . ./ But falls into abatement . . ./Even in a minute" (I i II–14). Olivia might be an adequate object; she at least is the Diana the sight of whom has, he thinks, turned him to an Acteon torn by the hounds of desires. When we next see him, and Cesario has been only three days in his court, his entering question is "Who saw Cesario, ho?" (I iv 10) and already he has unclasped to the youth "the book even of [his] secret soul' (I iv 13). He has found an object. The delight he takes in Cesario's fresh youth and graceful responsiveness in conversation and in service, is one part of the spectrum of love for a woman, or better, it is a range of feeling that is common to love for a youth and love for a woman. For the audience, the woman who is present there, behind Cesario's disguise, is brought to mind repeatedly by the talk of love and of the differences of men and women in love. "My father had a daughter loved a man . . ." (II iv 106)

> She never told her love,
> But let concealment, like a worm i' th' bud,
> Feed on her damask cheek.
>
> (II iv 109–11)

This supremely feminine damsel, who "sat like patience on a monument," is not Viola. She is a sort of polarity within Viola, realized all the more fully because the other, active side of Viola does not pine in thought at all, but instead changes the subject: " . . . and yet I know not./Sir, shall I to this lady?—Ay, that's the theme" (II iv 120–1). The effect of moving back and forth from woman to sprightly page is to convey how much the sexes differ yet how much they have in common, how everyone who is fully alive has qualities of both. Some such general recognition is obliquely suggested in Sebastian's amused summary of what happened to Olivia:

> You would have been contracted to a maid;
> Nor are you therein, by my life, deceiv'd:
> You are betroth'd both to a maid and man.
>
> (V i 253–5)

The countess marries the man in this composite, and the count marries the maid. He too has done he knows not what while nature drew him to her bias, for he has fallen in love with the maid without knowing it.

Liberty Testing Courtesy

We have seen how each of the festive comedies tends to focus on a particular kind of folly that is released along with love—witty masquerade in *Love's Labour's Lost*, delusive fantasy in *A Midsummer Night's Dream*, romance in *As You Like It*, and, in *The Merchant of Venice*, prodigality balanced against usury. *Twelfth Night* deals with the sort of folly which the title points to, the folly of misrule. But the holiday reference limits its subject too narrowly: the play exhibits the liberties which gentlemen take with decorum in the pursuit of pleasure and love, including the liberty of holiday, but not only that. Such liberty is balanced against time-serving. As Bassanio's folly of prodigality leads in the end to gracious fulfillment, so does Viola's folly of disguise. There is just a suggestion of the risks when she exclaims, not very solemnly,

> Disguise, I see thou art a wickedness
> Wherein the pregnant enemy does much.
>
> (II ii 25–6)

As in *The Merchant of Venice* the story of a prodigal is the occasion for an exploration of the use and abuse of wealth, so here we get an exhibition of the use and abuse of social liberty.

What enables Viola to bring off her role in disguise is her perfect courtesy, in the large, humanistic meaning of that term as the Renaissance used it, the *corteziania* of Castiglione. Her mastery of courtesy goes with her being the daughter of "that Sebastian of

Messalina whom I know you have heard of": gentility shows
through her disguise as does the fact that she is a woman. The
impact on Olivia of Cesario's quality as a gentleman is what is
emphasized as the countess, recalling their conversation, discovers that she is falling in love:

> "What is your parentage?"
> "Above my fortunes, yet my state is well:
> I am a gentleman."
> I'll be sworn thou art.
> Thy tongue, thy face, thy limbs, actions, and spirit,
> Do give thee fivefold blazon. Not too fast! Soft, soft!
> Unless the master were the man.
>
> (I v 273–8)

We think of manners as a mere prerequisite of living decently, like
cleanliness. For the Renaissance, they could be almost the end of
life, as the literature of courtesy testifies. *Twelfth Night* carries
further an interest in the fashioning of a courtier which, as Miss
Bradbrook points out,[5] appears in several of the early comedies,
especially *The Two Gentlemen of Verona*, and which in different keys
Shakespeare was pursuing, about the same time as he wrote
Twelfth Night, in *Hamlet* and *Measure for Measure*. People in *Twelfth
Night* talk of courtesy and manners constantly. But the most
important expression of courtesy of course is in object lessons. It
is their lack of breeding and manners which makes the comic
butts ridiculous, along with their lack of the basic, free humanity
which, be it virile or feminine, is at the center of courtesy and
flowers through it.

   Mr. Van Doren, in a fine essay, observes that *Twelfth Night* has
a structure like *The Merchant of Venice*. "Once again Shakespeare
has built a world out of music and melancholy, and once again this
world is threatened by an alien voice. The opposition of Malvolio
to Orsino and his class parallels the opposition of Shylock to
Antonio and his friends. The parallel is not precise, and the
contrast is more subtly contrived; Shakespeare holds the balance
in a more delicate hand. . . ."[6] One way in which this more delicate balance appears is that the contest of revellers with intruder
does not lead to neglecting ironies about those who are on the
side of pleasure. We are all against Malvolio, certainly, in the great

moment when the whole opposition comes into focus with Toby's
"Dost thou think, because thou art virtuous, there shall be no
more cakes and ale?" (II iii 109–10). The festive spirit shows up
the kill-joy vanity of Malvolio's decorum. The steward shows his
limits when he calls misrule "this uncivil rule." But one of the
revellers is Sir Andrew, who reminds us that there is no necessary salvation in being a fellow who delights "in masques and
revels sometimes altogether" (I iii 106). There was no such ninny
pleasureseeker in *The Merchant of Venice*; his role continues Shallow's, the would-be-reveller who is comically inadequate. To put
such a leg as his into "a flame-coloured stock" only shows how
meager it is. This thin creature's motive is self-improvement: he is
a version of the stock type of prodigal who is gulled in trying to
learn how to be gallant. As in Restoration comedy the fop confirms the values of the rake, Aguecheek serves as foil to Sir Toby.
But he also marks one limit as to what revelry can do for a man: "I
would I had bestowed that time in the tongues that I have in
fencing, dancing and bear-baiting" (I iii 87–9).

Sir Toby is gentlemanly liberty incarnate, a specialist in it. He
lives at his ease, enjoying heritage, the something-for-nothing
which this play celebrates, as *The Merchant of Venice* celebrates
wealth—what he has without having to deserve it is his kinsman's
place in Olivia's household:

> *Maria.* What a caterwauling do you keep here! If my lady
> have not call'd up her steward Malvolio and bid him turn
> you out of doors, never trust me.
> *Sir Toby.* My lady's a Catayan, we are politicians, Malvolio's a
> Peg-a-Ramsey, and [*sings*] "Three merry men be we." Am
> not I consanguineous? Am I not of her blood? Tilly-vally,
> lady.
>
> (II iii 72–5)

Sir Toby has by consanguinity what Falstaff has to presume on
and keep by his wits: "Shall I not take mine ease in mine inn but I
shall have my pocket pick'd?" (*IH.IV* III iii 78–9). So Sir Toby is
witty without being as alert as Sir John; he does not need to be:

> *Olivia.* Cousin, cousin, how have you come so early by this
> lethargy?

> *Toby.* Lechery? I defy lechery. There's one at the gate.
> *Olivia.* Ay, marry, what is he?
> *Toby.* Let him be the devil an he will. I care not; give me faith,
>   say I. Well, it's all one.

(I v 115)

Stage drunkenness, here expressed by wit that lurches catch-as-catch-can, conveys the security of "good life" in such households as Olivia's, the old-fashioned sort that had not given up "housekeeping." Because Toby has "faith"—the faith that goes with belonging—he does not need to worry when Maria teases him about confining himself "within the modest limits of order." "Confine? I'll confine myself no finer than I am" (I iii 8–11). In his talk as in his clothes, he has the ease of a gentleman whose place in the world is secure, so that, while he can find words like *consanguineous* at will, he can also say "Sneck up!" to Malvolio's accusation that he shows "no respect of persons, places nor time" (II iii 90). Sir Toby is the sort of kinsman who would take the lead at such Christmas feasts as Sir Edward Dymoke patronized in Lincolnshire—a Talboys Dymoke.[7] His talk is salted with holiday morals: "I am sure care's an enemy of life" (I iii 2–3). "Not to be abed before midnight is to be up betimes" (II iii 1–2). He is like Falstaff in maintaining saturnalian paradox and in playing impromptu the role of lord of misrule. But in his whole relation to the world he is fundamentally different from Prince Hal's great buffoon. Falstaff makes a career of misrule; Sir Toby uses misrule to show up a careerist.

There is little direct invocation by poetry of the values of heritage and housekeeping, such as we get of the beneficence of wealth in *The Merchant of Venice.* But the graciousness of community is conveyed indirectly by the value put on music and song, as Mr. Van Doren observes. The Duke's famous opening lines start the play with music. His hypersensitive estheticism savors strains that have a dying fall and mixes the senses in appreciation: "like the sweet sound/That breathes upon a bank of violets" (I i 5–6). Toby and his friends are more at ease about "O mistress mine," but equally devoted to music in their way. (Toby makes fun of such strained appreciation as the Duke's when he concludes their praises of the clown's voice with "To hear by the nose, it is dulcet in contagion," II iii 55–6). Back at court, in the next scene, the significance of music in relation to community is suggested in the Duke's lines about the "old and antique song":

> Mark it, Cesario; it is old and plain;
> The spinsters and the knitters in the sun,
> And the free maids that weave their thread with bones,
> Do use to chant it. It is silly sooth,
> And dallies with the innocence of love,
> Like the old age.
>
> (II iv 42–7)

The wonderful line about the free maids, which throws such firm stress on "free" by the delayed accent, and then slows up in strong, regular monosyllables, crystallizes the play's central feeling for freedom in heritage and community. It is consciously nostalgic; the old age is seen from the vantage of "these most brisk and giddy-paced times" (II iv 6).

Throughout the play a contrast is maintained between the taut, restless, elegant court, where people speak a nervous verse, and the free-wheeling household of Olivia, where, except for the intense moments in Olivia's amorous interviews with Cesario, people live in an easy-going prose. The contrast is another version of pastoral. The household is more than any one person in it. People keep interrupting each other, changing their minds, letting their talk run out into foolishness—and through it all Shakespeare expresses the day-by-day going on of a shared life:

> *Maria.* Nay, either tell me where thou hast been, or I will not open my lips so wide as a bristle may enter in way of thy excuse.
>
> (I v 1–3)

> *Fabian.* . . . You know he brought me out o' favour with my lady about a bear-baiting here.
> *Toby.* To anger him we'll have the bear again . . .
>
> (II v 6–8)

> *Fabian.* Why, we shall make him mad indeed.
> *Maria.* The house will be the quieter.
>
> (III iv 127–8)

Maria's character is a function of the life of "the house"; she moves within it with perfectly selfless tact. "She's a beagle truebred," says Sir Toby: her part in the housekeeping and its pleasures is a homely but valued kind of "courtiership."

All of the merrymakers show a fine sense of the relations of people, including robust Fabian, and Sir Toby, when he has need. The fool, especially, has this courtly awareness. We see in the first scene that he has to have it to live: he goes far enough in the direction of plain speaking to engage Olivia's unwilling attention, then brings off his thesis that *she* is the fool so neatly that he is forgiven. What Viola praises in the fool's function is just what we should expect in a play about courtesy and liberty:

> This fellow is wise enough to play the fool;
> And to do that well craves a kind of wit.
> He must observe their mood on whom he jests,
> The quality of persons, and the time . . .
>
> (III i 57–60)

It is remarkable how little Feste says that is counterstatement in Touchstone's manner: there is no need for ironic counterstatement, because here the ironies are embodied in the comic butts. Instead what Feste chiefly does is sing and beg—courtly occupations—and radiate in his songs and banter a feeling of liberty based on accepting disillusion. "What's to come is still unsure . . . Youth's a stuff will not endure" (II iii 48, 51). In *The Merchant of Venice*, it was the gentlefolk who commented "How every fool can play upon the word!" but now it is the fool himself who says, with mock solemnity: "To see this age! A sentence is but a chev'ril glove to a good wit!" (III i 10–11). He rarely makes the expected move, but conveys by his style how well he knows what moves are expected:

> So that, conclusions to be as kisses, if your four negatives
> make your two affirmatives, why then, the worse for my
> friends and the better for my foes.
> *Duke.* Why, this is excellent.
> *Feste.* By my troth, sir, no; though it pleases you to be one of
> my friends.
>
> (V i 17–23)

His feeling for people and their relations comes out most fully
when he plays "Sir Topas the curate, who comes to visit Malvolio
the lunatic" (IV ii 21–2). This is the pastime of "dissembling" in
a minister's gown that led to so much trouble for Sir Edward
Dymoke's bailiff, John Craddock the elder.[8]

Viola, who as "nuntio" moves from tense court to relaxed
household, has much in common with Feste in the way she talks,
or better, uses talk; but she also commands effortlessly, when
there is occasion, Shakespeare's mature poetic power:

> It gives a very echo to the seat
> Where Love is throned.
>
> (II iv 20–1)

"Thou dost speak masterly," the Duke exclaims—as we must too.
Part of her mastery is that she lets herself go only rarely, choosing occasions that are worthy. Most of the time she keeps her
language reined in, often mocking it as she uses it, in Feste's
fashion. Perhaps it is because he finds himself beaten at his own
game that he turns on her ungraciously, as on no one else:

> *Viola.* I warrant thou art a merry fellow and car'st for noth-
> ing.
> *Clown.* Not so, sir; I do care for something; but in my con-
> science, sir, I do not care for you. If that be to care for
> nothing, sir, I would it would make you invisible.
>
> (III i 24–8)

Once when she is mocking the elaborate language of compliment, greeting Olivia with "the heavens rain odours on you," Sir
Andrew overhears and is much impressed: "That youth's a rare
courtier. 'Rain odours'—well?" (III i 82–3). He plans to get her
fancy words by heart. Of course, as a rare courtier, she precisely
does *not* commit herself to such high-flown, Osric-style expressions. Her constant shifting of tone in response to the situation
goes with her manipulation of her role in disguise, so that instead
of simply listening to her speak, we watch her conduct her speech,
and through it feel her secure sense of proportion and her easy,
alert consciousness: "To one of your receiving," says Olivia,
"enough is shown" (III i 117–18).

Olivia says that "'Twas never merry world/Since lowly feign-

ing was call'd compliment" (III i 95–6). As Sir Toby is the spokesman and guardian of that merry world, Malvolio is its antagonist.
He shows his relation to festivity at once by the way he responds
to Feste, and Olivia points the moral: he is "sick of self-love" and
tastes "with a distempered appetite." He is not "generous, guiltless, and of free disposition." Of course, nothing is more helpful,
to get revelry to boil up, than somebody trying to keep the lid
on—whatever his personal qualities. But the "stubborn and un-
courteous parts" in Malvolio's character, to which Fabian refers in
justifying the "device," are precisely those qualities which liberty
shows up. Malvolio wants "to confine himself finer than he is," to
paraphrase Toby in reverse: he practices behavior to his own
shadow. His language is full of pompous polysyllables, of elaborate syntax deploying synonyms:

> Do ye make an alehouse of my lady's house, that ye squeak
> out your coziers' catches without any mitigation or remorse
> of voice? Is there no respect of place, persons, nor time in
> you?
>
> (II iii 86–8)

In "loving" his mistress, as Cesario her master, he is a kind of foil,
bringing out her genuine, free impulse by the contrast he fur-
nishes. He does not desire Olivia's person; *that* desire, even in a
steward, would be sympathetically regarded, though not of
course encouraged, by a Twelfth-Night mood. What he wants is
"to be Count Malvolio," with "a demure travel of regard, telling
them I know my place, as I would they should do theirs" (II v 48–
50). His secret wish is to violate decorum himself, then relish to
the full its power over others. No wonder he has not a free
disposition when he has such imaginations to keep under! When
the sport betrays him into a revelation of them, part of the
vengeance taken is to make him try to be festive, in yellow
stockings, and crossgartered, and smiling "his face into more lines
than is in the new map with the augmentation of the Indies"
(III ii 74–5). Maria's letter *tells* him to go brave, be gallant, take
liberties! And when we see him "acting this in an obedient hope"
(as he puts it later), he is anything but free: "This does make some
obstruction on the blood, this crossgartering . . ." (III iv 20–1).

In his "impossible passages of grossness," he is the profane intruder trying to steal part of the initiates' feast by disguising himself as one of them—only to be caught and tormented for his profanation. As with Shylock, there is potential pathos in his bafflement, especially when Shakespeare uses to the limit the conjuring of devils out of a sane man, a device which he had employed hilariously in *The Comedy of Errors*. There is no way to settle just how much of Malvolio's pathos should be allowed to come through when he is down and out in the dark hole. Most people now agree that Charles Lamb's sympathy for the steward's enterprise and commiseration for his sorrows is a romantic and bourgeois distortion. But he is certainly pathetic, if one thinks about it, because he is so utterly cut off from everyone else by his anxious self-love. He lacks the freedom which makes Viola so perceptive, and is correspondingly oblivious:

> *Olivia.* What kind o' man is he?
> *Malvolio.* Why, of mankind.
>
> (IV 141–2)

He is too busy carrying out his mistress' instructions about privacy to notice that she is bored with it, as later he is too busy doing her errand with the ring to notice that it is a love-token. He is imprisoned in his own virtues, so that there is sense as well as nonsense in the fool's "I say there is no darkness but ignorance; in which thou art more puzzled than the Egyptians in their fog" (IV ii 41–3). The dark house is, without any straining, a symbol: when Malvolio protests about Pythagoras, "I think nobly of the soul and no way approve his opinion," the clown's response is "Remain thou still in darkness." The pack of them are wanton and unreasonable in tormenting him; but his reasonableness will never let him out into "the air; . . . the glorious sun" (IV iii I) which they enjoy together. To play the dark-house scene for pathos, instead of making fun out of the pathos, or at any rate out of most of the pathos, is to ignore the dry comic light which shows up Malvolio's virtuousness as a self-limiting automatism.

Malvolio has been called a satirical portrait of the Puritan spirit, and there is some truth in the notion. But he is not hostile to holiday because he is a Puritan; he is like a Puritan because he is hostile to holiday. Shakespeare even mocks, in passing, the thoughtless, fashionable antipathy to Puritans current among gallants. Sir Andrew responds to Maria's "sometimes he is a kind of Puritan," with "if I thought that, I'd beat him like a dog" (II iii 131–2). "The devil a Puritan he is, or anything constantly," Maria observes candidly, "but a time-pleaser" (II iii 137–8). Shakespeare's two great comic butts, Malvolio and Shylock, express basic human attitudes which were at work in the commercial revolution, the new values whose development R. H. Tawney described in *Religion and the Rise of Capitalism*. But both figures are conceived at a level of esthetic abstraction which makes it inappropriate to identify them with specific social groups in the mingled actualities of history: Shylock, embodying ruthless money power, is no more to be equated with actual bankers than Malvolio, who has something of the Puritan ethic, is to be thought of as a portrait of actual Puritans. Yet, seen in the perspective of literary and social history, there is a curious appropriateness in Malvolio's presence, as a kind of foreign body to be expelled by laughter, in Shakespeare's last free-and-easy festive comedy. He is a man of business, and, it is passingly suggested, a hard one; he is or would like to be a rising man, and to rise he *uses* sobriety and morality. One could moralize the spectacle by observing that, in the long run, in the 1640s, Malvolio *was* revenged on the whole pack of them.

But Shakespeare's comedy remains, long after 1640, to move audiences through release to clarification, making distinctions between false care and true freedom and realizing anew, for successive generations, powers in human nature and society which make good the risks of courtesy and liberty. And this without blinking the fact that "the rain it raineth every day."

Outside the Garden Gate

Twelfth Night is usually placed just before *Hamlet* and the problem plays to make neat groupings according to mood, but it may well have been written after some of these works. In thinking about its relation to the other work of the period from 1600 to 1602 or 1603, it is important to recognize the independent artistic logic by which each play has its own unity. There are features of *Twelfth Night* that connect it with all the productions of this period. There

is the side of Orsino's sensibility, for example, which suggests
Troilus' hypersensitivity:

> Enough, no more;
> 'Tis not so sweet now as it was before.
>
> (I i 7–8)

> How will she love when the rich golden shaft
> Hath kill'd the flock of all affections else
> That live in her; when liver, brain, and heart,
> Those sovereign thrones, are all supplied and fill'd,
> Her sweet perfections, with one self king!
> Away before me to sweet beds of flow'rs!
>
> (I i 35–40)

Troilus carries this sort of verse and feeling farther:

> What will it be
> When that the wat'ry palate tastes indeed
> Love's thrice-repured nectar? Death, I fear me;
> Sounding destruction; or some joy too fine,
> Too subtle-potent, tun'd too sharp in sweetness,
> For the capacity of my ruder powers.
>
> (*Troi.* III ii 19–24)

Troilus' lines are a much more physical and more anxious
development of the exquisite, uncentered sort of amorousness
expressed by Orsino. But in *Twelfth Night* there is no occasion to
explore the harsh anti-climax to which such intensity is vulnerable, for instead of meeting a trivial Cressida in the midst of war
and lechery, Orsino meets poised Viola in a world of revelry. The
comparison with *Troilus and Cressida* makes one notice how little
direct sexual reference there is in *Twelfth Night*—much less than in
most of the festive comedies. It may be that free-hearted mirth, at
this stage of Shakespeare's development, required more shame-
fastness than it had earlier, because to dwell on the physical was
to encounter the "monstruousity in love" which troubled Troilus:
"that the desire is boundless, and the act a slave to limit" (*Troi.* III ii
79–80).

It is quite possible that *Measure for Measure* and *All's Well That
Ends Well* did not seem to Shakespeare and his audiences so different from *Twelfth Night* as they seem to us. Both of them use comic
butts not unlike Andrew and Malvolio: Lucio and Parolles are,

each his way, pretenders to community who are shown up ludi-
crously by their own compulsions, and so expelled. Our difficulty
with these plays, what makes them problem plays, is that they do
not feel festive; they are not merry in a deep enough way. Part of
our response may well be the result of changes in standards and
sentiments about sexual behavior, and of alterations in theatrical
convention. But the fact remains that in both plays, release often
leads, not simply to folly, but to the vicious or contemptible; and
the manipulations of happy accidents which make all well in the
end are not made acceptable by the achievement of distinctions
about values or by a convincing expression of general beneficent
forces in life. Shakespeare's imagination tends to dwell on situations and motives where the energies of life lead to degradation or
destruction:

> Our natures do pursue,
> Like rats that ravin down their proper bane,
> A thirsty evil; and when we drink we die.
> > *(Meas.* I ii 122–4)

> There's not a soldier of us all that, in the thanksgiving
> before meat, do relish the petition well that prays for peace.
> > *(Meas.* I ii 14–16)

> Pompey, you are partly a bawd, Pompey, howsoever you
> colour it in being a tapster. Are you not? . . .
> *Pompey.* Truly, sir, I am a poor fellow that would live.
> > *(Meas.* II i 207–11)

This sort of paradox is not brought home to us in *Twelfth Night.* In
the problem comedies, vicious or perverse release leads to developments of absorbing interest, if not always to a satisfying movement of feeling in relation to awareness. But that is beyond our
compass here.

We can notice here that the fool in *Twelfth Night* has been over
the garden wall into some such world as the Vienna of *Measure for
Measure.* He never tells where he has been, gives no details. But he
has an air of knowing more of life than anyone else—too much, in
fact; and he makes general observations like

> Anything that's mended is but patch'd; virtue that trans-
> gresses is but patch'd with sin, and sin that amends is but

patch'd with virtue. If that this simple syllogism will serve,
so; if it will not, what remedy?

(I v 40–4)

His part does not darken the bright colors of the play; but it gives
them a dark outline, suggesting that the whole bright revel
emerges from shadow. In the wonderful final song which he is
left alone on stage to sing, the mind turns to contemplate the
limitations of revelry: "By swaggering could I never thrive. . . ."
The morning after, the weather when the sky changes, come into
the song:

With tosspots still had drunken heads,
For the rain it raineth every day.

(V i 389–90)

It goes outside the garden gate:

But when I come to man's estate,
With hey, ho, the wind and the rain,
'Gainst knaves and thieves men shut their gate,
For the rain it raineth every day.

(V i 379–80)

Yet the poise of mirth, achieved by accepting disillusion, although
it is now precarious, is not lost:

A great while ago the world begun,
With hey, ho, the wind and the rain;
But that's all one, our play is done,
And we'll strive to please you everyday.

(V i 391–4)

There is a certain calculated let-down in coming back to the play
in this fashion; but it is the play which is keeping out the wind and
the rain.

The festive comic form which Shakespeare had worked out was a
way of selecting and organizing experience which had its own
logic, its own autonomy: there is no necessary reason to think
that he did not play on that instrument in *Twelfth Night* after
making even such different music as *Hamlet*. Indeed, across the
difference in forms, the comedy has much in common with the

tragedy: interest in courtesy and free-hearted manners; consciousness of language and play with it as though a sentence were but a
chev'ril glove; the use of nonsequitur and nonsense. Malvolio
absurdly dreams of such a usurpation of heritage, "having come
from a day bed, where I have left Olivia sleeping," as Claudius
actually accomplishes. The tragedy moves into regions where the
distinction between madness and sanity begins to break down, to
be recovered only through violence; the fooling with madness in
the comedy is an enjoyment of the control which knows what is
mad and what is not. The relation between the two plays, though
not so close, is not unlike that which we have noticed between
Romeo and Juliet and *A Midsummer Night's Dream*.

But there is a great deal in *Hamlet* which the festive comic form
cannot handle. The form can only deal with follies where nature
to her bias draws; the unnatural can appear only in outsiders,
intruders who are mocked and expelled. But in *Hamlet*, it is insid-
ers who are unnatural. There is a great deal of wonderful fooling
in the tragedy: Hamlet's playing the all-licensed fool in Claudius'
court and making tormented fun out of his shocking realization
of the horror of life. For sheer power of wit and reach of comic
vision, there are moments in *Hamlet* beyond anything in the
comedies we have considered. But to control the expression of the
motives he is presenting, Shakespeare requires a different movement, within which comic release is only one phase. After *Twelfth
Night*, comedy is always used in this subordinate way: saturnalian
movements, comic counterstatements, continue to be important
resources of his art, but their meaning is determined by their
place in a larger movement. So it is with the heroic revels in
Antony and Cleopatra, or with the renewal of life, after tragedy, at
the festival in *The Winter's Tale*.

NOTES

1. In *The First Night of "Twelfth Night"* (1954), Dr Hotson has recovered,
   once again, documents that are astonishingly *à propos*. The most exciting is a long letter home written by a real nobleman named Orsino,
   who was Elizabeth's honored guest when she witnessed a play "in the
   Hall, which was richly hanged and degrees placed round about it."

Don Virginio Orsino's account to his Duchess of the way he was
honored gives a vivid picture of the Twelfth Day occasion at court,
which Mr Hotson skillfully supplements with other evidence, much
of it also new, so as to give us the most complete and graphic
description we have of the circumstances of a dramatic performance
at a court holiday. The Duke's candid letter reports that "there was
acted a mingled comedy, with pieces of music and dances" (*una commedia mescolata, con musiche e balli*). But then it adds "and this too I am
keeping to tell by word of mouth." What maddening bad luck! Here,
and everywhere else, the clinching proof eludes Dr. Hotson, despite
his skill and persistence. He himself cannot resist regarding it as a fact
that *Twelfth Night* was the play in question on January 6, 1600–1601.
But a sceptic can begin by asking where, in *Twelfth Night*, are those *balli*
which Don Virginio witnessed—the play is notable, among Shakespeare's gay comedies, for its *lack* of dances. One could go on to ask
whether it would not be more likely that the name Orsino would be
used sometime *after* the great man's visit, when the elegant ring of it
would still sound in people's ears but no offense be done. A devil's
advocate could go on and on, so rich, and so conjectural, is Dr
Hotson's book.

But it makes a real contribution, even if one is not convinced that
the play on that night must have been *Twelfth Night*, and even if one
rejects many of its sweeping conclusions about such matters as staging. Dr Hotson is a "literalist of the historical imagination," to use
Marianne Moore's phrase. He has produced something equivalent to
an "imaginary garden with real toads in" it—real circumstances and
actions of Elizabethan life. He makes us aware of what the high day at
court was like. And he describes and exemplifies many features of
Twelfth Night custom in a fresh way, and so defines for us the *sort* of
thing that Shakespeare refers to by his title. He also provides, from
his remarkable knowledge of the period, a wealth of useful incidental
glosses to hard places in the play.

But useful as this book can be, whether literally right or not, it is
very misleading in one respect. For he writes as though the festive
quality of *Twelfth Night* were wholly derived, on a one-to-one sort of
basis, from its being commissioned for a court revel. He neglects the
fact that, whatever its first night, the play was designed to work, also,
on the public stage, so that it had to project the spirit of holiday into
forms that would be effective every day. He also ignores the fact that
by the time Shakespeare came to write *Twelfth Night*, festive comedy
was an established specialty with him.

2. E. K. Chambers, *William Shakespeare*, II 327–8.

He left this blank

3. I hope that a reader who is concerned only with *Twelfth Night* will nevertheless take the time to read the generalized account of festive comedy in Chapter 1 of *Shakespeare's Festive Comedy*, for that introduction is assumed in the discussion here.

4. The latest treatment of this motif, in *The Two Noble Kinsmen* (especially Act I, scene iii), is as generously beautiful as the exquisite handling of it which we have examined in *A Midsummer Night's Dream* (*Shakespeare's Festive Comedy*, pp. 129–30).

5. *Shakespeare and Elizabethan Poetry*, chap. ix.

6. *Shakespeare*, p. 161.

7. The whole encounter between Talboys Dymoke's revellers and the Earl of Lincoln is remarkably like that between Sir Toby's group and Malvolio. See *Shakespeare's Festive Comedy*, chap. 3, pp. 37–51. The parallels are all the more impressive because no influence or "source" relationship is involved; there must have been many such encounters.

8. See *Shakespeare's Festive Comedy*, pp. 46–8.

Bertrand Evans

The Fruits of the Sport

In the world of *Twelfth Night,* as in the worlds of the comedies just preceding, the spirit of the practiser prevails. Seven of the principal persons are active practisers, and they operate six devices. All action turns on these, and the effects of the play arise from exploitation of the gaps they open. During all but the first two of eighteen scenes we have the advantage of some participant; in seven—an unusually high proportion—we hold advantage over all who take part. In the course of the action, every named person takes a turn below our vantage-point, and below the vantage-point of some other person or persons: in this play neither heroine nor clown is wholly spared. Although Viola shares the great secret with us alone, Shakespeare early establishes our vantage-point above hers, and once even makes her the unwitting victim of another's practice. Although Feste is either "in" on most practices or unaffected by them, he, with all Illyria, is ignorant of the main secret of the play, the identity of "Cesario". Here, then, even heroine and clown stand below us, and below them the others range down to the bottom, where sit Aguecheek and Malvolio in chronic oblivion. Though also victims of others' practices, neither needs deceiving to be deceived—Nature having practised on them once for all.

But if all are exposed at some time in ignorance of their situations, yet all but Orsino and Malvolio have compensatory moments when they overpeer others: even Aguecheek, though a fool the while, briefly enjoys advantage over Malvolio. The aware-

nesses in *Twelfth Night* are so structured that an overpeerer gloat-
ing in his advantage is usually himself overpeered by another participant or by us: thus Sir Toby exults in his advantage over
"Cesario," knowing that Sir Andrew is not the "devil in a private
brawl" he would have "Cesario" believe—but at the same time
"Cesario" holds advantage over him in knowing that "Cesario" is a
fiction; and the last laugh is ours, on Sir Toby, for even he would
hardly have made his jest of a duel had he known "Cesario" truly.
From much use of such arrangements, in which a participant's
understanding is inferior with respect to some elements of a
situation and superior with respect to others, emerge the richest
effects of *Twelfth Night* and some of the finest in Shakespeare.

Of the six practices, the central one is of course the heroine's
masquerade. It is the longest, and, in its relations with the play as
a whole, the most important such masquerade in the comedies.
Julia's practice in *The Two Gentlemen of Verona* affects only two
important scenes, and the only person whose ignorance of it is
exploited is Proteus. Rosalind's impersonation of "Ganymede" in
As You Like It lasts longer than Julia's, but it, too, is exploited in
only two major scenes, and the only victims whose ignorance of it
greatly matters are Orlando and Phebe. Portia's disguise in *The
Merchant of Venice* is worn during only one act, and its consequences furnish the substance of another. Helena's masquerade
in *All's Well that Ends Well* makes the central incident of the plot,
but its only victim is Bertram. Imogen's practice in *Cymbeline*,
though it yields spectacular effects in the climactic moments, is
one among a multitude of intrigues in that play. But the force of
Viola's masquerade in *Twelfth Night* prevails in all but the opening
scenes and relates to every incident and person. Though it most
affects two victims, Viola's is truly a practice on the whole world
of Illyria, as Duke Vincentio's is on the world of *Measure for
Measure*, and as, in tragedy, Iago's is on his world and as Hamlet's
antic disposition is on the whole world of Denmark. Viola rightly
belongs in this company of most notable masqueraders in all the
plays.

Viola takes up her masquerade with somewhat less urgency
and altruism than moved Portia, but with somewhat more of both
than moved Rosalind to perpetrate her fraud in the Forest of
Arden. Washed up on the shore of Illyria, she goes to work at

once. Quickly ascertaining the name of the place, the name of its ruler, and the fact that he is still a bachelor, she makes up her mind:

> I'll serve this duke.
> Thou shalt present me as an eunuch to him.
> It may be worth thy pains, for I can sing
> And speak to him in many sorts of music
> That will allow me very worth his service.
> What else may hap, to time I will commit,
> Only shape thou thy silence to my wit.
>
> (I ii 55–61)

This speech creates at one stroke the discrepancy in awarenesses which will endure until the closing moments of the play, giving advantage to us and disadvantage to all Illyria. And as swiftly as he creates the gap, Shakespeare begins its exploitation. When next we see Viola, in man's attire, after three days at Orsino's court and already his favourite, Valentine's remarks give first expression to the general Illyrian error:

> If the Duke continue these favours towards you, Cesario,
> you are like to be much advanc'd. He hath known you but
> three days, and already you are no stranger.
>
> (I iv 1–4)

But a stranger, of course, this "Cesario" is to the Duke, and to all others. The Duke's unawareness is next exploited: "Cesario," he says, "thou know'st no less but all"—and so she does, more than he dreams. When Orsino directs her to bear his lovesuit to Olivia, his remarks come near enough to strike sparks from the truth, and these flashes of irony are the first to result from the great discrepancy:

> . . . they shall yet belie thy happy years,
> That say thou art a man. Diana's lip
> Is not more smooth and rubious; thy small pipe
> Is as the maiden's organ, shrill and sound;
> And all is semblative a woman's part.
>
> (Ibid. 30–4)

As the scene ends, the basic exploitable gap is opened wider; says Viola,

> I'll do my best
> To woo your lady,—(*aside*) yet, a barful strife!
> Whoe'er I woo, myself would be his wife.

> (Ibid. 40-2)

As suddenly as her adoption of disguise created the first discrepancy, this confession creates a second. Henceforth her advantage, and ours, over the Duke is double: the secret of her right identity and the secret of her love.

The first major clash of the discrepant awarenesses of Viola and Illyria occurs, however, not in the Duke's court but in Olivia's house. Before meeting the recluse, Viola has encountered, in succession, Maria, Sir Toby, and Malvolio, who must be accounted first in the household to fall victims of her disguise even though the meetings are only reported; thus Malvolio: "Not yet old enough for a man, nor young enough for a boy; as a squash is before 'tis a peascod, or a codling when 'tis almost an apple." But the principal exploitation occurs in the interview with Olivia, whose attitude changes in the course of 100 lines from haughty scorn to flirtatious interest and finally to love. The effect of exploitation of the difference between our understanding and Olivia's is here not merely comic, although that is certainly part of the total. Though the play is not yet a full act old, the dramatist has already packed our minds with so much that simple laughter is an inadequate response. In this respect the meeting with Olivia contrasts with the comparable incident in *As You Like It*, when Phebe falls in love with "Ganymede," and the contrast becomes even more marked in the later interviews of Viola with Olivia and with Orsino, which we are required to watch with minds packed with sympathy that forestalls laughter.

Until the end of this scene, when Olivia, moved by a passion she thinks futile to resist—not knowing how futile it is to succumb—dispatches Malvolio to run after "that same peevish messenger" and give him a ring—"He left this ring behind him/Would I or not"—Shakespeare had established only two levels of awareness. These are Viola's, shared with us, and Illyria's ignorance of "Cesario's" identity. Two levels sufficed in *As You Like It*, even during the climactic scenes, when Rosalind's view is equivalent to ours and Orlando's represents that of all the Forest. But this relative simplicity is abruptly abandoned at the opening of Act II in *Twelfth Night* with the introduction of Sebastian. The instant effect of Sebastian's appearance, safe and sound on the very coast where Viola had inquired "What country, friend, is this?" and been advised "This is Illyria, lady" is the creation of a third level, a vantage-point above Viola's, to be held by ourselves alone until the end of Act III—and possibly but not probably until the last moments of Act V.

The placement of the scene informing us of Sebastian's survival and immediate destination—"I am bound to the Count Orsino's court"—is a notable example of Shakespeare's way of handling the awarenesses. It is the more significant for being conspicuously early in the action, and the more conspicuous for its rather awkward interruption of the expected sequence of incident. Our notification of his rescue and arrival in Illyria might readily have been postponed until Act IV, when, in front of Olivia's house, the Clown mistakes Sebastian for "Cesario." Or he might have been introduced inconspicuously between almost any two scenes in either Act II or Act III. Instead, he is thrust between Viola's departure from Olivia's house and her meeting with Malvolio on the street. Ordinarily, no scene would intervene in this space, as is demonstrable many times over in the plays. The closest parallel occurs in *The Merchant of Venice*. At the end of the court scene Bassanio sends Gratiano to overtake Portia and give her a ring; the very next scene shows Portia and Nerissa on the street, overtaken by Gratiano after Portia has spoken only four lines to mark the passage of an appropriate period of time. In contrast, the introduction of Sebastian splits the sequence with a scene of some fifty lines that entails also a shift from the vicinity of Olivia's house to the sea-coast. From the first history play onward, Shakespeare's method avoided violence to the normal order of action unless there was something special to be gained. By the time of *Twelfth Night*, certainly the only disruptions of sequence are calculated ones. In the present case the dramatist evidently wished us to learn as early as possible that Sebastian is alive, and, more precisely, to learn it *just before Viola discovers that Olivia has fallen in love with her.*

In short, Sebastian's introduction is our assurance that all is well and will end well, an assurance which contradicts Viola's distress and recognising what seems a hopeless entanglement:

> She loves me, sure. . . . If it be so, as 'tis,
> Poor lady, she were better love a dream.
> Disguise, I see thou art a wickedness
> Wherein the pregnant enemy does much.
>
> (II ii 23–9)

When we saw her leave Olivia's house, her vantage-point was ours. Now, overtaken by Malvolio—who is himself wrapped in fourfold ignorance—she has slipped below, for we have seen Sebastian. She is nevermore quite the match of Rosalind, who overpeered all and was never overpeered. Yet her mind is packed with almost as much understanding as ours: she realises, by the ring, that Olivia, ignorant of "Cesario's" sex, has fallen in love; she recognises that Malvolio, besides being a fool, is ignorant also of her sex and of his mistress's meaning in sending the ring; and certainly she observes irony's bright flashes about his head when, with intolerable condescension, he announces that Olivia has commanded "Cesario" to come no more "unless it be to report your lord's taking of this"—thereupon tossing Olivia's, not Orsino's, ring on the ground. But her mind is chiefly on Orsino and his oblivion, which includes ignorance of her identity, of her love for him, and of the fact that just now his beloved has given her heart to "Cesario":

> My master loves her dearly;
> And I, poor monster, fond as much on him;
> And she, mistaken, seems to dote on me.
> What will become of this?
>
> (Ibid. 34–7)

By making Viola voice dismay for the several matters that burden her awareness, Shakespeare bids our own be alert; he comes as near as a dramatist can to saying: "Bear this in mind, and this, and yet this." He prods our remembrance also with utterances that illuminate the newly opened gap between our understanding and Viola's:

> As I am woman,—now alas the day!—
> What thriftless sighs shall poor Olivia breathe!
>
> (Ibid. 39–40)

And, finally:

O time! thou must untangle this, not I.
It is too hard a knot for me t' untie!

(Ibid. 41–2)

Viola's distress should be ours also—but we have just seen Sebastian, in the shape of another "Cesario," and his words still sound in our ears: "I am bound to the Count Orsino's court." Olivia's sighs therefore need not be thriftless: the knot is looser than Viola thinks, and time is, indeed, capable.

Sebastian's introduction is thus a strategic move, giving us assurance that all is and will be well. But it is also a tactical move, multiplying the possibilities of exploitation. Sebastian's unawareness—exploitable the instant he appears on the sea-coast, weeping for a "drowned" sister who is in fact doing quite well for herself in Illyria—provides one such possibility. All Illyria's unawareness that Sebastian is not "Cesario"—who, of course, is not "Cesario" either—provides another. Add to these the possibilities already in existence, including the main secret of Viola—"Cesario" and the subordinate ones born of Aguecheek's and Malvolio's chronic oblivions, and it is evident that by the start of Act II the exploitable potentiality is enormous.

Although Sebastian's appearance gives us advantage over Viola, her demotion is hardly damaging to her prestige as heroine and prime practiser. Her ignorance that her brother is at hand does not expose her to ridicule or pity, for the truth that she cannot see is better than the appearance. Though the heroines of comedy always look about them with a wider sweep of the eye than others enjoy, Shakespeare occasionally cuts off their view of a segment of the full circle; only Rosalind and Portia escape such limitation of their vision. Other heroines, though momentarily blind to some specific aspect of a situation, usually retain a commanding view of all else and in any event are spared exposure to laughter. Beatrice is an exception; but she is a secondary heroine, and besides, like Benedick's, her nature invites corrective effect. Later heroines, Isabella, Imogen, and Perdita, are blind to significant facts of their situations, but their ignorance does not make them vulnerable to laughter. Viola stands between these and Beatrice; she is caught in a condition of laughable unawareness during two incidents in Act III.

During Act II, however, except that she does not know about Sebastian, Viola escapes unawareness and enjoys an advantage over Orsino that matches Rosalind's over poor Orlando and Portia's over Bassanio. Indeed, her advantage grows during this period. When she left for her first interview with Olivia, Orsino was ignorant only of her identity. When she returns, he is still ignorant of that, of the fact that she loves him, that she is loved by Olivia, and that therefore his suit to Olivia is truly hopeful. His fourfold ignorance is the exploitable substance of the second Viola—Orsino interview. Shakespeare capitalizes the opportunity fully but tenderly, and the result is an artistic triumph. Lacking the complexity of some later scenes, in which stair-stepped levels of awareness provide the structure for dazzling cross-play, the scene nevertheless makes a powerful demand for simultaneous conflicting responses. Luxuriating in melancholy, loving love, affecting the agony of the disdained lover, feasting on music and song that aggravate his craving, Orsino stands naked to laughter—a foolish plight for a hero, like that into which Shakespeare previously thrust Orlando, rehearsing with "Ganymede" his love for Rosalind.

Like Orlando's, then, a brutally ludicrous representation of romantic masculinity, Orsino's exposure should inspire roaring laughter. Yet as the scene moves on laughter becomes inappropriate and is perhaps finally made impossible by the force of a contradictory impulse. The latter force is enhanced by the music, song, and poetry of the scene—but its original stimulation is the presence of Viola, whose quality is as right for this moment as are the qualities of Rosalind and Orlando for their wooing scene. Whereas Orsino sees nothing, Viola sees too much; her mind is burdened with understanding. "Thus far I will boldly publish her," said Sebastian; "she bore a mind that envy could not but call fair." If she could know that Sebastian lives, that the solution to her dilemma is even now on the road to Orsino's court, her distress would be lightened and the pain of the scene would be eased. Everything that she does know, beyond Orsino's knowledge, hurts her; and what she does not know—that the dramatist has taken care to have *us* know—hurts her also. Deliberately, with a psychologically shrewd manœuvre, Shakespeare has balanced our own awareness between laughter and pain.

These contradictory impulses, equal in power, stimulated by complex awareness, do not cancel each other out, leaving indifference; they battle for supremacy, and the intensity of their struggle determines the degree of our involvement. Shakespeare's way in the great scenes is to involve us deeply, by packing our minds with private awarenesses that confer a sense of personal responsibility toward the action.

> *Duke.* My life upon't, young though thou art, thine eye
> Hath stay'd upon some favour that it loves.
> Hath it not, boy?
> *Vio.* A little, by your favour.
> *Duke.* What kind of woman is't?
> *Vio.* Of your complexion.
> *Duke.* She is not worth thee, then. What years, i' faith?
> *Vio.* About your years, my lord.
>
> (II iv 24–9)

Here the Duke's oblivion, illuminated by each line he speaks, is laughable—but opposing it is Viola's too-feminine awareness, reaching to every corner of the situation, shining brightly in her every utterance, demanding our concern. Toward the end of the scene, when the same sort of exchange is repeated, with the same tension of opposed awareness sustained, the dialogue is laden with pathos:

> *Duke.* What dost thou know?
> *Vio.* Too well what love women to men may owe.
> In faith, they are as true of heart as we.
> My father had a daughter lov'd a man,
> As it might be, perhaps, were I a woman,
> I should your lordship.
> *Duke.* And what's her history?
> *Vio.* A blank, my lord. She never told her love,
> But let concealment, like a worm i' th' bud,
> Feed on her damask cheek. She pin'd in thought,
> And with a green and yellow melancholy
> She sat, like Patience on a monument,
> Smiling at grief. Was not this love indeed?
> We men may say more, swear more; but indeed
> Our shows are more than will, for still we prove
> Much in our vows, but little in our love.

> *Duke.* But died thy sister of her love, my boy?
> *Vio.* I am all the daughters of my father's house,
>   And all the brothers too;—and yet I know not.
>   (II iv 107–24)

Although the exchange glitters with irony, to describe the total effect as that of irony is to leave its rarer metals unassayed. The effect is compounded of many simples; elements of the comic and elements of the pathetic are exquisitely blended, with the final unity conferred by the alchemy of poetry. Innately rich, vibrant, the lyric voices gather resonance from the sounding-board of awareness which the dramatist, with calculated art, constructed and fixed in our minds before the start of the duet. Perhaps Shakespeare never achieved a richer tone—though he rises to this once more in *Twelfth Night*—than with these voices reverberating over the chasm between the speakers' awarenesses.

In the interim between this scene and Viola's second interview with Olivia occur the beginnings, along with much else, of Maria's practice on Malvolio. But it is best to postpone discussion of the antics of the clowns, wits, and dolts who make up Olivia's household, both in order that these may all be examined together and in order that we may follow the progress of the heroine and come at once to a scene which is closely knit to that just reviewed.

In the second Viola—Olivia interview, Shakespeare deals gently with Olivia's unawareness. Here, if he chose, he might cause a lady to look as ridiculous as Orlando rehearsing for "Ganymede." It is not so; we are required to pity Olivia, for she has caught the plague. With Phebe, suddenly smitten by passion for "Ganymede," the dramatist dealt otherwise, making her ignorance of Rosalind's sex a means of mockery. But though Phebe stands to "Ganymede" as Olivia to "Cesario," Phebe and Olivia are contrasting spirits. Phebe's contemptuous treatment of the shepherd who follows her with doglike devotion demands that she be exposed to laughter; she deserves Rosalind's sharpest barbs: "Sell when you can; you are not for all markets." Olivia, though she has rejected Orsino, has not treated him contemptuously, and her "cruelty" is only a figment of Orsino's music-fed imagination; nor, certainly, has she rejected him suddenly, at first sight of a seemingly better match, as Phebe did Silvius. Derisive exploitation of Olivia's disadvantage would be discordant here, and there is none. Moreover as Phebe differs from Olivia, Viola differs from Rosalind. To Rosalind the masquerade in the name of Jove's page is mocking, malicious, high-holiday sport. She relishes her advantage, exploits it with a conscienceless zest for the game that makes boobies of her victims. As the action continues, her exhilaration mounts; appropriating a magician's reputation, promising to make all things even at last, she enjoys astonishing all Arden. No practiser has a more glorious time of it. Devastating in her thrusts at Phebe, perhaps she would claw even Olivia, though not deeply, if that unfortunate were at her mercy. It is otherwise with Viola, who would deal tenderly even with Phebe.

Viola did not take up the masquerade for the love of mockery. Hers is not a mocking nature. The thing she starts threatens to get out of hand almost at once. Hopelessly wooing Olivia for Orsino, hopelessly loving Orsino, hopelessly loved by Olivia, ignorant that Sebastian is alive to make all right at last, she is caught in what is to her a frightening dilemma such as Rosalind would never be caught in—for Rosalind is superior to dilemmas. It is in accord with her nature that Viola bears her advantage mercifully in the second interview, and the gap between the pair is exploited tenderly: "A cypress, not a bosom,/Hides my heart," Olivia begins, and Viola replies, "I pity you." These are not Rosalind and Phebe, the one exuberantly mocking, the other brazen-bold; these are Viola and Olivia, the one bearing her advantage as if it had suddenly become a cross, the other so deeply stricken that laughter at her condition would be gross. Exploitation is concentrated in one principal exchange that finds what is hilarious girt round with pathos:

> *Oli.* Stay!
>   I prithee, tell me what thou think'st of me.
> *Vio.* That you do think you are not what you are.
> *Oli.* If I think so, I think the same of you.
> *Vio.* Then think you right. I am not what I am.
> *Oli.* I would you were as I would have you be!
>
> (III i 149–54)

Olivia's confession of love is a compulsive outburst of such frankness as only rudeness could laugh at:

Cesario, by the roses of the spring,
By maidhood, honour, truth, and everything,
I love thee so, that, maugre all thy pride,
Nor wit nor reason can my passion hide.

(Ibid. 161–4)

Yet the frame of the situation is comic, even grotesque: the reversal of roles, the woman wooing the man, an incongruity in society if not in nature, is a perennial subject of jest; and the fact that this "man" is not even a man adds a joke to what is already a joke. But within this laughable frame the presentation of human qualities stifles laughter. Olivia's nature conflicts with her plight; her genuineness disarms laughter. And the "man" is not only a woman, but a woman of rare sensitivity, who carries her masquerade with uncertainty, in a sprightly manner but with rising alarm and forced bravado. Earlier heroines—Julia, Portia, Rosalind—had no such difficulty with this role. Besides the fact that their capabilities were greater, they had female companions to confide in: before donning men's clothes Julia jests with Lucetta, Portia with Nerissa, Rosalind with Celia. They carry their roles with a certain elation. But in her disguise Viola is as much alone in the great world as when she floundered in the sea. Acutely feminine, she finds the role hard, is distressed by it, comes soon to wish she had not undertaken it: "Disguise, I see thou art a wickedness/Wherein the pregnant enemy does much."

The emotional conflict which rises from this unlaughable treatment of a laughable situation, complex already, is further complicated by the force of the crowning fact in our superior awareness: our knowledge that Sebastian lives and must now be close at hand. If Olivia can love "Cesario," she can love Sebastian. The "thriftless sighs" that arouse Viola's pity and prevent us from laughing need not be thriftless; the hand that can free Olivia will also sever the knot that is too hard for Viola to untie. Thus while the laughter implicit in the situation is drowned in the sympathy demanded by the gentleness of both women, the struggle is also flooded with comforting assurance; all is well and will end well.

And there is more: the total effect of this scene is lightened by the character of the action which surrounds it. The scene which immediately precedes it has ended on a high note of promised hilarity as Maria speaks of Malvolio to her accomplices:

> If you will then see the fruits of the sport, mark his first approach before my lady. He will come to her in yellow stockings, and 'tis a colour she abhors, and cross-garter'd, a fashion she detests; and he will smile upon her, which will now be so unsuitable to her disposition, being addicted to a melancholy as she is, that it cannot but turn him into a notable contempt. If you will see it, follow me.
>
> (II v 217-25)

This invitation is followed by the entrance of Viola, who matches wits with Feste, then proceeds to the interview with Olivia. *Maria's promise of the ludicrous spectacle that is to be the highest point of hilarity in all the action thus hangs over the tender scene.* Though both women are ignorant that a practice on Malvolio is under way and its exploitation imminent, Olivia is integral to it, for the practice on Malvolio is necessarily a practice on her also; hence her mere presence in the interview helps keep awareness of the promised hilarity alive, and this awareness lightens the effect of the interview.

Shakespeare's preparation of our minds for the climactic scene of the yellow stockings and cross-gartering has been long and elaborate. It has included introduction to the back stairs of that household in which Olivia—exhibited in a predicament as deliciously ironical as any in Shakespeare—has vainly vowed to walk for seven years in mourning veil "And water once a day her chamber round/With eye-offending brine: all this to season/A brother's dead love." It is not only Orsino's suit that threatens her solemn purpose; the stamp of futility is set on her vow by the lunatic character of her household: vain dream, to pass seven years in weeping under the same roof with Malvolio, Maria, Belch, and Aguecheek! Before it is visited by Viola, practising as "Cesario," and before Maria devises her practice on Malvolio, Olivia's house harbours another practice: Sir Toby is revelling at Sir Andrew's cost, the bait being Olivia. This practice was begun before the action of the play commences, and it continues until the final scene when, after Sebastian has half killed both the guller and the gull, Sir Toby breaks it off abruptly:

> *Sir And.* I'll help you, Sir Toby, because we'll be dress'd to-
> gether.
> *Sir To.* Will you help?—an ass-head and a coxcomb and a
> knave, a thin-fac'd knave, a gull!
>
> (V i 210–13)

Though inconspicuous, this long-standing practice is central to much action, for it precipitates both Maria's practice on Malvolio and Toby's practice on Sir Andrew and Viola—"Cesario" which brings them near to duelling and very nearly ends Viola's masquerade; indeed it underlies the entire secondary action, which itself provides the comic 'environment for the main "Cesario"— Olivia—Sebastian plot.

This initial practice is introduced to us before we are shown Sir Andrew himself; in our first sight of Olivia's household, Sir Toby alludes to it:

> *Mar.* I heard my lady talk of it yesterday, and of a foolish
> knight that you brought in one night here to be her
> wooer.
> *Sir T.* Who? Sir Andrew Aguecheek?
> *Mar.* Ay, he.
> *Sir T.* He's as tall a man as any's in Illyria.
> *Mar.* What's that to the purpose?
> *Sir T.* Why, he has three thousand ducats a year.
>
> (I iii 15–23)

Nightly, Sir Toby and Sir Andrew drink healths to Olivia: "I'll drink to her," says Toby, "as long as there is a passage in my throat and drink in Illyria." Toby's is a lucrative practice; much later, he estimates the gross:

> *Fab.* This is a dear manikin to you, Sir Toby.
> *Sir To.* I have been dear to him, lad, some two thousand
> strong, or so.
>
> (III ii 57–9)

Before we see him, then, we hold advantage over Sir Andrew in knowing that he is being gulled. At first sight, in I iii, we gain another: we perceive at once that his ignorance of Toby's practice is only an acute manifestation of a native condition. Of the race of

Bottom, Sir Andrew would be at a disadvantage if he were not being gulled; being gulled, he is doubly "out."

The practice on Sir Andrew goes forward in back-room caterwauling; and it is this caterwauling that precipitates the practice on Malvolio, whose high-handed manner of relaying Olivia's command that the bacchanal cease provokes the wrath of the revellers and inspires Maria's genius: "If I do not gull him into a nayword, and make him a common recreation, do not think I have wit enough to lie straight in my bed." Her device is adapted precisely to that singular lack of self-perspective which is Malvolio's whole vice and whole virtue:

> . . . it is his grounds of faith that all that look on him love
> him; and on that vice in him will my revenge find notable
> cause to work.
>
> (II iii 163–6)

Besides other attributes, Maria has a gift for forgery: "I can write very like my lady your niece." Says Toby,

> He shall think, by the letters that thou wilt drop, that
> they come from my niece, and that she's in love with him.
> (Ibid. 178–80)

Such is the practice which places Maria and her accomplices, with ourselves, on a level above Malvolio and Olivia. Our advantage over Malvolio. however, like that over Sir Andrew, is double. Possibly Malvolio's pit is the darker, since Sir Andrew has moments when he apprehends the possibility that he lacks wit: "I am a great eater of beef and I believe that does harm to my wit." Though foolish enough to dream of Olivia's hand, he is scarcely hopeful. He adores Olivia, with an adoration that is hardly bolder than Slender's remote and silent worship of sweet Anne Page. If Toby did not egg him on—"Send for money, knight. If thou hast her not i' the end, call me cut"—he would lose all hope and go home; if Toby had not first prompted him he would never have aspired. Sir Andrew, then, is deceived, and foolish, but not self-deceived.

Malvolio, on the other hand, is self-deceived before he is deceived. Sir Hugh Evans and Justice Shallow together cannot arouse real hope in Slender's breast; Sir Toby's assurances do not allay Sir Andrew's grave doubts. But Malvolio's fire is the product of spontaneous combustion, and his sense of worthiness is unalloyed by misgivings. Shakespeare makes this fact clear by exhibiting the man's vainglory just before he finds the forged letter: "To be Count Malvolio!" and, again:

> Having been three months married to her, sitting in my state. . . . Calling my officers about me, in my branch'd velvet gown, having come from a day-bed, where I have left Olivia sleeping. . . .
>
> (II v 49–55)

This exhibition of self-deception continues until Malvolio picks up the letter, when deception is welded to self-deception by a gaudy flash of irony: "What employment have we here?" The 100 lines that follow, during which Malvolio manages to find his own name in the letters M, O, A, I, and arrives at confirmation—"I do not now fool myself, to let imagination jade me; for every reason excites to this that my lady loves me"—make simultaneous exploitation of deception and self-deception:

> M, O, A, I; this simulation is not as the former. And yet, to crush this a little, it would bow to me, for every one of these letters are in my name.
>
> (Ibid. 151–4)

Exhibiting the seduction of a mind eager to be seduced, the scene surpasses everything resembling it in Shakespeare. In comedy the nearest to it is the scene in which Falstaff hears the wives' propositions recounted by Mistress Quickly; yet Falstaff hears with astonishment and believes in spite of himself so that deception prevails over self-deception. And in tragedy, the nearest is the witches' initial winning of Macbeth—which leaves him, however, not yet wholly committed.

"Observe him, for the love of mockery," said Maria to her accomplices. Hidden in the box-tree, they hold a triple advantage over Malvolio, in that they watch him when he does not suspect, recognize his self-kindled folly, and, of course, know that the letter which sets him ablaze is forged. Yet the master practiser here is Shakespeare, whose way it is to set participants where

they overpeer others while they are also overpeered. The practisers do not suspect, as we are privately reminded when Maria
describes Olivia as "addicted to a melancholy," a disposition which
will render Malvolio's smiles intolerable to her. The fact is that
Olivia is not now addicted to a melancholy, but is in love with
"Cesario"—and her world has changed. Hence even Maria, knowing nothing of the change, drops below our level. As for Sir
Andrew, Shakespeare does not let us forget that the man is a fool
all the while he joyously overpeers Malvolio—and that, besides,
he is practice-ridden. Maria has just described her scheme to gull
Malvolio when we are reminded that Andrew's own gulling continues:

> *Sir To.* Let's to bed, knight. Thou hadst need send for more
> money.
> *Sir And.* If I cannot recover your niece, I am a foul way out.
> *Sir To.* Send for money, knight. If thou hast her not i' the
> end, call me cut.
>
> (II iii 198–203)

And while he is most enjoying his advantage over Malvolio, Sir
Andrew is made to expose the depth of his congenital unawareness:

> *Mal.* "Besides, you waste the treasure of your time with a
> foolish knight,"—
> *Sir A.* That's me, I warrant you.
> *Mal.* "One Sir Andrew,"—
> *Sir A.* I knew 'twas I; for many do call me fool.
>
> (II v 85–90)

Maria's invitation to see "the fruits of the sport," which is the
final word of preparation for the climactic scene of the yellow
stockings, thus carries even higher promise than she intends,
since the gullers as well as their gull will, in our perspective,
contribute to the fun.

The climactic scene does not follow immediately: Maria's
promise, suspended, conditions the environment of three scenes
before it is fulfilled. The first of these, the pathetic interview of
"Cesario" with Olivia, totally encircled by past, continuing, and
promised hilarity, has already been examined. Sentimentally conceived, permeated with emotion, Olivia's declaration of love de-

mands sympathy: yet placed where it is, it gathers an echo from Malvolio's affair: Olivia's passion for "Cesario" is as preposterous as Malvolio's for Olivia. The second scene (III ii) is affected also, but differently: Sir Toby, assisted by Fabian, puffs up Sir Andrew's collapsing hopes of winning Olivia, and Sir Andrew, foolish and practice-ridden, fails to see in Malvolio's delusion the very portrait of his own. At the same time that it exploits the old practice on the brainless knight, this scene also prepares a new one; says Toby,

> Challenge me the Count's youth to fight with him; hurt him in eleven places; my niece shall take note of it; and assure thyself, there is no love-broker in the world can more prevail in man's commendation with woman than report of valour.
>
> (III ii 36-41)

The new practice is in fact born of ignorance, not only Andrew's but the practisers', for Toby and Fabian do not guess that the "favours" which Andrew reports he saw Olivia do "the Count's serving-man" in the orchard were expressions of true love—or that they were misspent, this youth being no man at all. "For Andrew," says Toby, "If he were open'd and you find so much blood in his liver as will clog the foot of a flea, I'll eat the rest of the anatomy." Fabian's reply flares up in irony that marks a hit of error upon truth: "And his opposite, the youth, bears in his visage no great presage of cruelty."

The third scene set between Maria's promise and its fulfillment shows Sebastian on a street in Illyria and confirms our long-held comforting assumption that the solution to Viola's "insoluble" problem is at hand. Placed between the announcement of Sir Toby's practice (the challenge) which will surely terrify "Cesario," and the exploitation of multiple practices in the climactic scene, Sebastian's declaration that he will walk abroad to view the town is our reassurance that all is well. It comes just as the climactic scene of the yellow stockings begins and is the dramatist's last bid to make certain that all useful information is in our minds.

And it is truly an enormous bundle of awarenesses that we must carry into this scene, during the action of which all nine of the persons present are blind to some part of the situation.

Though not the first of Shakespeare's scenes in which everyone stands below our vantage-point, it is the most complex of such scenes until the climactic portion of *Cymbeline*. Four principal situations comprise the scene: first, that in which Malvolio's delusion is central; second, that in which Olivia's unawareness of "Cesario's" identity is central; third, that in which Viola and Sir Andrew's unawareness of Toby's practice is central; fourth, that in which Antonio's mistaking of "Cesario" for Sebastian is central. Yet these are only the basic situations. The total context which has been established in our minds and from which the action draws its full meaning is beyond explicit description; yet it is in the totality that the cream of the jest—or of four jests—lies.

First up for exploitation is Malvolio's unawareness—but Shakespeare delays Malvolio yet again, until we have been reminded of the state of Olivia's mind. Her remarks stand like the topic sentence for what follows:

> (*Aside.*) I have sent after him; he says he'll come. How
> shall I feast him? What bestow of him? For youth is bought
> more oft than begg'd or borrow'd.
>
> (III iv 1–3)

Not Malvolio, as he thinks, or her dead brother, as Maria and her accomplices suppose, but "Cesario" fills her mind: *we are not to be allowed to forget, even at the very edge of it, that Malvolio's outrageous performance before his lady is set within the frame of Viola's masquerade.* Remembrance of Olivia's vain love thus is made to hang darkly over the hilarious spectacle very much as, earlier, Maria's promise of this hilarity hung brightly above the tender and embarrassed interview of Viola and Olivia. The second fold of Olivia's ignorance is next exposed:

> Where is Malvolio? He is sad and civil,
> And suits well for a servant with my fortunes.
> Where is Malvolio?
>
> (III iv 5–7)

Malvolio's gulling is also Olivia's; says Maria:

> Your ladyship were best to have some guard about you, if
> he come; for, sure, the man is tainted in 's wits.
>
> (Ibid. 12–14)

Unaware of Maria's forgery, both servant and lady are victims of the practice. But Olivia stands on the higher level: mystification is up the scale from oblivion. Maniacally smiling, cross-gartered, yellow-stockinged, a veritable bodying-forth of ignorance, Malvolio is the central figure amid circles of error. His smile, his garters, his stockings are unawareness rendered visible; his words, unawareness rendered audible. Orlando's unawareness of "Ganymede" and Orsino's of "Cesario" are exploited mainly by words whose flares illuminate the space between their depths and our height. But Malvolio's is ignorance not so much of another person as of himself, hence is aptly exhibited not only by words but by physical signs—like Bottom's superadded head and Falstaff's horns. "His very genius," says Sir Toby, when the incident is past, "hath taken the infection of the device." The smile, the garters, the stockings—the immediate effects of Maria's practice on him— are ultimately the signs of Malvolio's practice on himself.

Here and in Feste's later practice (IV ii) Malvolio's exposure to derision is well deserved. Not only is his aspiration self-kindled, lacking the excuse that it was set going by an external practice, but it is contemptible in its nature. Sir Andrew, with Toby's prompting, aspires to Olivia's hand because, in his booby fashion, he loves her. But Malvolio sees Olivia as means to Great Place. Shakespeare exhibits four such deceived, futile aspirants: Sir Andrew and Malvolio of *Twelfth Night*, Slender of *The Merry Wives of Windsor*, and, in the tragic case, Roderigo of *Othello*. Sir Andrew's aspiration is nearest Slender's in its innocence; Malvolio's, tainted with self-love and social ambition, nearest Roderigo's, which is lust.

Though a climax in itself, Malvolio's scene is framed by the main situation: it opens with Olivia awaiting the arrival of "Cesario" to dine with her; "Cesario," not Malvolio, is foremost in her mind then and thereafter—and Malvolio's performance, in her perspective, is only an odd episode which occurs while she is waiting. Moreover, the comic effect of Malvolio's scene arises partly from his ignorance of "Cesario's" identity and of Olivia's misspent passion; indeed, in this ignorance Malvolio stands on the same level as his tormentors, for even Maria believes Olivia still to be grieving for her brother. And Toby incites Andrew to challenge "Cesario," not because he thinks there are grounds for his

gull's jealousy but merely for the love of the game. Amid prepara-
tions for Toby's newest practice, Shakespeare sets the third interview of "Cesario" and Olivia, which reminds us—should the
several interludes have obscured the fact—that Olivia's passion is
real enough. Though brief, the interview is indispensable: it looks
before and after, and its twenty lines bind together the four
episodes of this very long climactic scene.

The third of these episodes, which primarily exploits Sir
Andrew's ignorance, is at once the result of Sir Toby's old practice
on him and of "Cesario's" practice on all Illyria. The episode
parallels that of the yellow stockings: his aspiration fed by Maria's
practice, Malvolio makes a spectacle of himself before Olivia; his
aspiration fed by Sir Toby's practice, Sir Andrew makes a spectacle of himself by challenging "Cesario." "Marry," says Toby, when
the opponents are brought front to front, "I'll ride your horse as
well as I ride you." Even Malvolio is not so practice-ridden as is Sir
Andrew at this moment. Victim, first of all, of nature's practice,
he has next been deceived by Sir Toby into supposing that Toby's
dry gullet is the way to Olivia's heart; next, he is deceived by
Viola's practice into supposing that "the Count's serving-man" is
a serious rival; next, edged on to challenge "Cesario," he is abused
when his foolish letter is replaced by Toby's description of his
ferocity: "this letter, being so excellently ignorant, will breed no
terror in the youth; he will find it comes from a clodpole"; and
finally, he is abused by Toby's exaggerated report of his adversary: "Why, man, he's a very devil; I have not seen such a firago. . . . They say he has been fencer to the Sophy." The densest
concentration of the Illyrian fog which rolled in from the sea with
Viola here settles about the head of Sir Andrew. Of the total,
infinitely complex situation which the dramatist has spread out
plainly to our view, he sees nothing in its right shape, colour, or
dimension. "So soon as ever thou seest him, draw," Sir Toby has
directed him; "and, as thou draw'st, swear horrible." When the
time comes, Sir Andrew's resolution is shattered by the terrifying
images looming through his wall of fog: "Let him let the matter
slip, and I'll give him my horse, grey Capilet."

If it concerned him alone, the effect of the episode would be
purely comic. But Sir Toby's device makes sport of "Cesario" also:
"This will so fright them both that they will kill one another by

the look, like cockatrices." For the very first time, yoked with a booby as the butt of a joke, Viola is in danger of looking ridiculous. Hitherto our only advantage over her has been our knowledge of Sebastian's survival—an advantage that has provided comforting assurance but given no cause for laughter. Yet again, as in the case of Olivia stricken with passion for "Cesario," though the plight is laughable the victim is not. It bears repeating that Viola is one of the most feminine of Shakespeare's heroines. No other heroine is less suited to brave it in a man's role—unless it were Hero, who would not dare. To Viola, a duel with a warrior such as Sir Toby describes is unthinkable:

> He is knight, dubb'd with unhatch'd rapier and on carpet
> consideration; but he is a devil in private brawl. Souls and
> bodies hath he divorc'd three; and his incensement at this
> moment is so implacable, that satisfaction can be none but
> by pangs of death and sepulchre. Hob, nob, is his word; give
> 't or take 't.

> (III iv 257–63)

Rosalind could manage this Aguecheek; but even if Viola knew the truth about him, duelling would not be for her. "I am one that had rather go with sir priest than sir knight," she tells Fabian; "I care not who knows so much of my mettle." Shakespeare has balanced the scales delicately between laughter and tears, and Viola's exquisite femininity keeps them so; capable Rosalind would destroy the tension. From the outset the trials in which Viola's disguise involves her have been hard; this one frightens her nearly to surrendering her secret: "A little thing would make me tell them how much I lack of a man."

The line prods our awareness at a crucial moment: the grotesque basis of the duel, the blubbering terror of Sir Andrew, and the swaggering, gross humour of Sir Toby would assuredly tip the scales to the side of hilarity if we should momentarily forget what "Cesario" is. Further, this particular line of Viola's, being set just after Sir Toby's loudest exhortation to the reluctant duellists, subtly reminds us that Sir Andrew and Viola are not the only butts of this joke: they are the butts in Sir Toby's perspective, but Sir Toby is the butt in ours. If Sir Andrew is ignorant that "Cesario" is not "a very devil . . . a firago," and if "Cesario" is ignorant that Sir Andrew is all hare and no lion, yet Toby is ignorant that "Cesario" is Viola. This is the cream of the cream: that the boisterous manipulator, perpetrator of multiple practices on Sir Andrew, overpeerer also of "Cesario" by virtue of his better acquaintance with the silly knight's valour, absolute master, in his own perspective, of all elements in the situation, as self-assured as Malvolio in his utterances—should be all the while ignorant of the most important fact in the entire action. "Marry," he tells us confidentially of Aguecheek, "I'll ride your horse as well as I ride you." But Shakespeare has enabled us to ride Sir Toby.

Perhaps, then, Viola gets off free here, when her unawareness invites laughter at her expense. But in the final episode of the scene, though she escapes laughter, she is exposed under an unflattering light. The fault, of course, is not hers, but Antonio's in mistaking her for Sebastian. In a sense, Antonio's level is lower than Illyria's, for Orsino, Olivia, and others have only supposed Viola to be "Cesario," while Antonio, ignorant alike of "Cesario" and Viola, takes her to be Sebastian. Yet in another sense Illyria's error is deeper, for "Cesario" is a fiction, whereas Sebastian is a fact.

For this episode the dramatist has so arranged the awarenesses that they set contradictory responses fighting for supremacy. Here again, also, the initial preparation lies far back, in the scene which first shows us Sebastian. Antonio has saved him from the sea, weeps with him for his drowned sister, is solicitous for his welfare, begs to serve him, and, finally, braving old enemies in Orsino's court, insists on accompanying him: "I do adore thee so/ That danger shall seem sport, and I will go." When next we see the pair, the expression of Antonio's regard for his young friend is emphatic to the point of being conspicuous; what is more, it is backed up by action: "Hold sir, here's my purse."

Perhaps Shakespeare remembered another Antonio, who risked his flesh for his friend Bassanio: had the sense of that Antonio's goodness not been established in our minds, our anxiety for him while danger increased would hardly have been stirred, and the tensions that make the court scene great would have been flabby. Sebastian's magnanimous Antonio is like Bassanio's; hence, when he mistakes "Cesario" for Sebastian, is arrested, asks return of his purse—"It grieves me/Much more for

what I cannot do for you/Than what befalls me"—is stared at and
refused, our knowledge of his kindness compels sympathy for
him—and resentment towards the cause of this sudden shock
given to his nature:

> Will you deny me now?
> Is 't possible that my deserts to you
> Can lack persuasion?

(Ibid. 381-3)

It is a moment shrewdly wrought, which brings into conflict two
urgent awarenesses—of Antonio's selflessness and of Viola's femininity and perfect innocence. Though we know Antonio to be in
error and Viola blameless, yet in the eyes of this kind man she is
terribly guilty. Shakespeare's devotion to such moments of extreme tension sometimes leads him to the edge of psychological
calamity; perhaps here he goes too near, and his heroine, despite
our awareness that she is innocent and despite her eagerness to
do what she can for Antonio—"My having is not much./I'll make
division of my present with you"—is singed by an involuntary
flash of our resentment.

The incident closes the scene. Presenting four interlocked
episodes all the relationships of which are constantly exposed to
our Olympian view; parading forth nearly all the persons of the
play in their relative states of ignorance, none understanding all,
and some—Malvolio, Aguecheek, Olivia, Antonio—understanding nothing that is going on; moving from the hilarious exhibition
of Malvolio's delusion to the painful representation of Antonio's
sudden disillusionment with humankind, it is, from the point of
view of the creation, maintenance, and exploitation of multiple
discrepant awarenesses, the most remarkable achievement in
Shakespearian comedy before *Cymbeline*.

The brief scene which follows is the very cap atop the action
of the play, the tip of the summit. In short space are exploited the
gaps between the several levels—all inferior to ours—of the six
persons who enter. In Shakespeare's comedies, almost infallibly,
two contrasting moments make the great peaks: first, the moment in which, errors having been compounded and various lines
of action brought to a central point, confusion is nearest universal, visibility nearest zero; second, that in which confusion is

dispelled. In the present scene, the first movement is marked by Feste's doubly ironical expostulation with Sebastian:

> No, I do not know you; nor I am not sent to you by my lady, to bid you come speak with her; nor your name is not Master Cesario; nor this is not my nose either. Nothing that is so is so.
>
> (IV i 5-9)

So speaks the Clown, wise enough to *play* the fool, yet lost like the others in the Illyrian fog. He is the first of the five who in quick succession mistake Sebastian for "Cesario." The formula is the same on which the entire action of *The Comedy of Errors* is based, but it is here used with a difference. In the early play, when Adriana mistakes Antipholus of Syracuse for her husband, she is only once removed from the truth apparent to us—for there is indeed an Antipholus of Ephesus. But the "Cesario" for whom Sebastian is mistaken is himself a fiction. All five persons, thus, being twice removed from truth, hold a level even lower than Sebastian's. For Sebastian, though he has come from outside into a situation of which he is totally ignorant—knowing neither that Viola lives nor that she poses as "Cesario," that Olivia loves this "Cesario," or that Sir Andrew is jealous of him—is nevertheless well enough aware that he is himself Sebastian and no other; not seeing the illusion that blinds the others, he is nearer reality than they. Oblivion is a lower level than mystification; they are oblivious, and he is mystified:

> What relish is in this? How runs the stream?
> Or I am mad, or else this is a dream.
>
> (Ibid. 64-5)

His mystification continues through his next scene, when it contrasts with Olivia's blissful error as she draws him home in the company of a priest. In all Shakespeare's comedies, only the twin brothers of *The Comedy of Errors*, masters and servants, remain longer in this precise degree of awareness; indeed, among the enormous number of persons in the comedies shown ignorant of their situations, only a few are truly mystified. For a moment or two in *Love's Labour's Lost*, upon their return to the ladies after posing as Russians, the King and his companions stand in this condition. Briefly also, Bassanio and Gratiano, in *The Merchant of Venice*, are mystified when Portia and Nerissa suddenly show the rings earlier presented to the "doctor" and the "clerk." In *Much Ado About Nothing* Hero is briefly mystified by Claudio's harsh indictment of her honour. In *The Merry Wives of Windsor* Ford is twice mystified by his failure to find Falstaff in his wife's company. In the later comedies, as we shall note, moments in which a participant's mystification is exploited are similarly rare and brief. In both intensity and duration, Sebastian's mystification comes nearest that of Antipholus of Syracuse; thus, after his first meeting with Olivia:

> This is the air, that is the glorious sun,
> This pearl she gave me, I do feel 't and see 't;
> And though 'tis wonder that enwraps me thus,
> Yet 'tis not madness.

> (IV iii 1–4)

His relation to the illusion-ridden city of Illyria differs in one particular from that of Antipholus of Syracuse to Ephesus. Until Antipholus and his Dromio arrived, no illusion existed in Ephesus; what follows is all of their own making. But when Sebastian came out of the sea to Illyria, Viola had preceded him, bringing in the fog that now engulfs everyone. "Madman, thou errest," the Clown tells Malvolio in the continuing practice on this most extreme case of the Illyrian affliction. "I say, there is no darkness but ignorance, in which thou are more puzzl'd than the Egyptians in their fog." Malvolio best represents also the Illyrians' inability to perceive their illusion: "I tell thee, I am as well in my wits as any man in Illyria." In contrast, coming from outside into all this, Sebastian knows enough to be mystified; though he cannot see through the fog, he can see that it is there: "There's something in 't/That is deceivable."

At the opening of Act V the burden of the context which preceding acts have established in our minds is staggering. *During Acts II, III, and IV no fully aware person except Viola has appeared before us*— and during part of this time she too has lacked full vision. At precisely what moment she rejoins us in our omniscience is the final question to be considered; indeed, the question of the state of Viola's awareness during the last two acts is the great question of the play.

At the close of Act IV we saw Olivia and Sebastian go to be married. We therefore hold advantage over Viola and Orsino upon their entrance in Act V. Over Orsino, of course, we hold other advantages also—the same that we have held for three acts. But are we to suppose that we hold any additional advantage over Viola? She is ignorant that her brother—in a state like that of shock—is now repeating the marriage oath before Olivia's priest. But is she still ignorant that he escaped drowning and has arrived in Illyria?

At the end of Act III, when Antonio interrupted her match with Sir Andrew, the cause of his error was as open to her as to us. That she then perceived the truth there can be little doubt:

> Methinks his words do from such passion fly
> That he believes himself; so do not I.
> Prove true, imagination, O, prove true,
> That I, dear brother, be now ta'en for you!
>
> (III iv 407–10)

And again:

> He nam'd Sebastian. I my brother know
> Yet living in my glass; even such and so
> In favour was my brother, and he went
> Still in this fashion, colour, ornament,
> For him I imitate.
>
> (Ibid. 414–18)

But now, at the opening of Act V, with Orsino, again meeting Antonio, she speaks with wide-eyed amazement:

> He did me kindness, sir, drew on my side,
> But in conclusion put strange speech upon me.
> I know not what 'twas but distraction.
>
> (V i 69–71)

"That most ingrateful boy there by your side,/From the rude sea's enrag'd and foamy mouth/did I redeem," asserts Antonio. The sea captain who had saved Viola had told her:

> I saw your brother,
> Most provident in peril, bind himself,
> Courage and hope both teaching him the practice,
> To a strong mast that liv'd upon the sea;
> Where, like Arion on the dolphin's back,

I saw him hold acquaintance with the waves
So long as I could see.

                                                    (I ii 11–17)

And she had replied:

Mine own escape unfoldeth to my hope,
Whereto thy speech serves for authority,
The like of him.

                                                    (Ibid. 19–21)

From the first she had entertained hope; then Antonio had mistaken her and named Sebastian, whom she imitated in her masquerade; and, finally, Antonio describes a sea-rescue that accords
with other evidence of Sebastian's survival. When Antonio has
finished his account of the rescue and his three-months' life with
Sebastian, Viola could, with few words, disabuse the tormented
fellow, whose experience with ingratitude is maddening him.
Instead, wide-eyed as before, she inquires, "How can this be?"

      That is to say, she holds to her masquerade in spite of all at
this crucial moment—and even, in feigning ignorance, grafts a
new practice on the old. Why does she do so? A damning answer
is that Shakespeare is willing to sacrifice plausibility in order to
preserve to the last moment the richly exploitable gap between
Illyria's oblivion and Viola's awareness, so that when all lines have
converged upon that moment, he can achieve a spectacular de-
nouement, with Illyria's awareness shooting up like a rocket
when Sebastian and "Cesario" come face to face. That Shakespeare always set a high rate on exploitable gaps and that he here
forces the situation to yield its utmost effect before he explodes it
is unquestionable. But that he sacrifices plausibility in doing so is
not so sure.

      At the opening of Act V Viola is yet ignorant of one fact: that
Olivia and Sebastian are married. *If she knew that*, she would know
that time, on which she early set her hope—"O time! thou must
untangle this, not I"—has already solved her problem. Not knowing it, and being Viola, feminine as no other, she maintains her
old fiction and compounds a new one of silence and innocence.
Like Portia and Rosalind, Vincentio and Prospero in that she plays
the role of chief practiser and controlling force, she is unlike these
in her attitude toward it. She has found no joy in the role; she has

been tempted to abandon it: "A little thing would make me tell them how much I lack of a man." More significantly, whereas the other controlling forces manipulate persons and contrive practices to bring their ends about, she has contrived nothing beyond her initial disguise. Though her goal—implied in "He was a bachelor then" at her arrival in Illyria and shortly thereafter confirmed in "Whoe'er I woo, myself would be his wife"—has always been to catch this Duke, she has played fair with both him and Olivia, serving faithfully, twisting nothing to her own purpose, striving only to stay out of trouble—and waiting on time. When trouble came, in the form of Olivia's passion and Sir Toby's practice, she rode it out despite embarrassment, pity, and even terror. When at last Antonio's terror advised her of her brother's survival, her hope took ecstatic new life: the end was in sight. Being Viola, she could not then break faith with time, even to save the good Antonio from misanthropy. Feminine in her patient waiting, she is no less so in her persistence: it is not enough that the end is in sight; it must actually be reached. When the Duke berates her, even threatening death, she opposes her patience to his fury:

> And I, most jocund, apt, and willingly,
> To do you rest, a thousand deaths would die.
>
> (V i 135–6)

The final silent moments of her masquerade are the hardest.

So great is her subtlety at the last that it is difficult to identify the instant at which she perceives that time has performed its final chore on her behalf. But she must be fully aware by the time of Olivia's exclamation: "Cesario, husband, stay!" Nevertheless, to the Duke's enraged "Her husband, sirrah!" she replies with a wide-eyed denial that we should perhaps take instead as a victory whoop: "No, my lord, not I." The priest confirms Olivia's word that "Cesario" is her husband. Sir Andrew and Sir Toby berate "Cesario" for hurting them. Still Viola keeps silent, except to deny the charges. Then follow fifty lines of dialogue in the course of which Sebastian enters and astonishes all Illyria except herself. And she speaks never a word. The arrival of Sebastian cannot be a surprise to her; his tender greeting of Olivia can be none. The long, superb silence, more wonderful than the Illyrians' ejaculations of amazement, is almost but not quite the extremest dem-

onstration of her femininity. That demonstration comes only
after Sebastian has subjected her to direct questioning, when she
replies with wide-eyed and incredible incredulity:

> Such a Sebastian was my brother too;
> So went he suited to his watery tomb.
> If spirits can assume both form and suit,
> You come to fright us.

> (Ibid. 241-3)

In this last instant before giving over her long masquerade, she
thus devises a final fiction: neither husband, brother, nor sister-
in-law will ever learn from her lips anything other than she had
been ignorant, *until this instant*, of her brother's survival, his arrival
in Illyria, and his marriage. This shred of a great secret she will
never give up, that she had ridden her masquerade to the very
end, biding time—"O time! thou must untangle this, not I"—until
it took Olivia off her hands and gave her Orsino.

Harry Levin

The Underplot of *Twelfth Night*

The kind of comedy that was practiced by Shakespeare has
repeatedly challenged definition. Though his last comedies have
been retrospectively classified as romances, most of their compo-
nents are equally characteristic of his earlier ones: love, adventure, coincidence, recognition, and occasional pathos. The problem is not simplified by the circumstance that his greatest comic
character, Falstaff, was far more impressive in two histories than
he is in *The Merry Wives of Windsor*. Traditional definitions of the
comic somehow fail to hit the Shakespearean mark, perhaps
because they tend to emphasize the spectatorial attitude of ridicule. Shakespeare's attitude is more participatory; its emphasis
falls upon playfulness, man at play, the esthetic principle that
Johan Huizinga has so brilliantly illuminated in his historico-
cultural study, *Homo Ludens*. Whereas we may laugh at Ben Jonson's characters, we generally laugh with Shakespeare's; indeed, if
we begin by laughing at Falstaff or the clowns, we end by laughing with them at ourselves; semantically speaking, they are therefore not ridiculous but ludicrous. The critical approach that best
succeeds in catching this spirit, it would seem to me, is that of
C. L. Barber in *Shakespeare's Festive Comedy*. That the same approach
can be applied to Plautus, as Erich Segal has convincingly demonstrated in his book *Roman Laughter*, suggests that "the Saturnalian
pattern" may well be universal. *Twelfth Night* very appropriately
marks the culmination of Professor Barber's argument. Since the
play is so rich and the argument so fertile, I am tempted to add a

few notes here, encouraged by his gracious recollection that our personal dialogue on comedy has extended over many years.

Any speculation about *Twelfth Night* might start with its alternative title, which has no counterpart among the other plays in the First Folio. The subtitle *What You Will* echoes the common and casual phrase that Olivia uses at one point in addressing Malvolio (I.v.109); it would later be used as a title by John Marston; and the German version is simply entitled *Was ihn wollt*. It is not equivalent to *As You Like It*, Bernard Shaw would argue; the latter means "this is the sort of play you would like"; the former means "it doesn't really matter what you call this play." To designate it by the seasonal dating would have touched off some associations, especially since *Twelfth Night* signalized the grand finale to the Christmas entertainment at Queen Elizabeth's court, and sometimes featured a performance by Shakespeare's company. But the English term seems relatively vague, when contrasted with the overtones of the French and Italian translations. *La Nuit des Rois* almost seems to promise a visitation of the Magi; Shakespeare anticlimatically gives us, instead, the iconological joke about "We Three" and a clownish snatch of song from Sir Toby, "Three merry men be we" (II.iii.17, 76-7). *La Notte dell'Epifania* may also hold theological—or at least, in Joycean terms, psychological—connotations. Shakespeare merely seems concerned to promise his audience a pleasant surprise by evoking a winter holiday, even as he did with the opposite season in *A Midsummer Night's Dream*. Festivals are the matrices of drama, after all, and that "holiday humor" in which the transvested Rosalind invites Orlando to rehearse his wooing sets the prevalent mood for Shakespearean comedy (*As You Like It*, IV.i.69).

Some of Shakespeare's other comedies have titles so broadly general that they could be interchanged without much loss of meaning: *The Comedy of Errors*, *Much Ado About Nothing*, *All's Well That Ends Well*. *Twelfth Night*, which has figured more prominently in the repertory than most of the others, has frequently been cited by concrete reference to its most memorable characterization. Thus Charles I entitled it "Malvolio" in his inscribed copy of the Second Folio, and a court production for James I was entered into the records under that name. As it happens, five of the other parts in the play are actually longer than Malvolio's: in order of

length, Sir Toby's, Viola's, Olivia's, Feste's, and even Sir Andrew's. Yet stage history has gradually made it clear that, with
slightly less than ten per cent of the lines, this has come to be
regarded as the stellar role. The other roles I have listed offer
varied opportunities to actors and actresses, and Viola's embodies
the special attraction of the hoydenish heroine in tights. That
advantage is somewhat lessened by the complication of having to
be passed off as identical with her unexpected twin brother
Sebastian. Hence the plot "wants credibility," as Dr. Johnson put
it, though our incredulity is all but disarmed by the Pirandellian
comment of Fabian: "If this were play'd upon a stage now, I could
condemn it as an improbable fiction" (III.iv.127–8). Henry Irving,
Herbert Beerbohm Tree, and many other stars have absurdly
twinkled in the part of Malvolio. There may be a latent significance in the fact that the leading actor of the Restoration,
Thomas Betterton, played the adversary role of Sir Toby Belch.

The impression registered in the diary of John Manningham,
who had attended a performance at the Middle Temple in 1602, is
particularly significant:

> At our feast wee had a play called "Twelue Night, or What
> You Will", much like the Commedy of Errores, or Menechmi
> in Plautus, but most like and neere to that in Italian called
> *Inganni*. A good practise in it to make the Steward beleeve his
> Lady widdowe was in love with him, by counterfeyting a
> letter as from his Lady in generall termes, telling him what
> shee liked best in him, and prescribing his gesture in smiling,
> his aparaile, &c., and then when he came to practise making
> him beleeue they tooke him to be mad.

It is true that Shakespeare's adaptation from Plautus had likewise
dealt with a pair of twins divided by shipwreck and reunited after
the *contretemps* of mistaken identity. Manningham might also have
mentioned *The Two Gentlemen of Verona*, where the heroine disguises
herself as a page so that she may serve the man she loves. And
Manningham's Italian cross-reference has led the source-hunters
to various plays and *novelle* which are quite analogous to the main
plot. But the episode he singles out for praise does not figure in
any of them. Malvolio, with no established source behind him,
must be reckoned as one of Shakespeare's originals. Efforts to
discern an actual prototype in the court gossip about Sir William

Knollys, who was Comptroller to Her Majesty's Household, have carried little conviction. Nor is there much topical implication in Maria's qualified epithet, "a kind of puritan," which she herself immediately rejects in favor of "timepleaser" and "affectioned ass" (II.iii.140, 148). There is not very much in common between Jonson's Ananias or Zeal-of-the-Land Busy and this Italianate upstart who aspires to "be proud" and "read politic authors" (II.v.161). He is undoubtedly puritanical in the psychological sense; as Professor Barber perceptively comments, "he is like a Puritan because he is hostile to holiday." William Archer considered him more of a Philistine than a Puritan, more to be approached as a sequence of "comic effects" than as "a consistent, closely-observed type," and therefore somewhat opaquely presented as a personality. "He has no sense of humour," so Archer summed it up, "—that is the head and front of his offending."

In a formal as well as a functional manner, he is thus an intruder into the play. Shakespeare's plot, as its forerunners had shown, could have got along without him. Olivia already had two suitors to be rejected, plus the masculine twin who was ready to replace his sister as the object of Olivia's choice. The lovesick Duke Orsino, after the fiasco of his vicarious courtship, could submit no less quickly and rather more gracefully than she to this sudden change of partners. The odd-man out, Sir Andrew, might have weakly borne the full onus of the underplot, insofar as it burlesques the main plot and has its *agon* in the reluctant duel. Music sets the keynote at the beginning, at the conclusion, and throughout. Illyria would almost seem to be the idyllic setting for an operetta. Yet, despite the roistering-snorts of melody and the high-kicking capers of the roisterers, the cadence often has a dying fall. "O mistress mine" is balanced against "Come away, death," and the singer Feste—whom G. L. Kittredge called "the merriest of Shakespeare's fools"—shares his concluding refrain with the tragic Fool of *King Lear*: "For the rain it raineth every day" (II.iii.39ff; iv.51ff.; V.i.392; cf. *King Lear*, III.ii.77). Even in the sunniest of Shakespeare's comedies, there are shadows now and then, and it is worth remembering that *Twelfth Night* was probably conceived in the same year as *Hamlet*. The aura of melancholy emanates from Olivia's household, but it extends to Orsino's palace because of his unwelcome suit. Widow-like, the veiled

Olivia mourns her dead brother; Viola, the go-between, though she depicts herself as the mourning figure of "Patience on a monument," cherishes justified hopes for her own brother lost at sea (II.iv.114).

Together, these adventurous siblings are destined to dispel the shade that has overcast the Illyrian horizon. Olivia's house of mourning should have been, and will again become, a house of mirth—to reverse the language of Ecclesiastes. Toward the end her kinsman, Sir Toby Belch, and his gregarious crew of what Malvolio will term "the lighter people" have been doing their damnedest to turn the kitchen into a tavern and to obliterate the differences between night and day (V.i.339). Over their eructations the hard-drinking Sir Toby fitly presides as a sort of miniature Falstaff, the local agent of revelry and misrule. "Th'art a scholar," he tells his eager gull Sir Andrew Aguecheek, the carpet knight whose linguistic accomplishments are as limited as his skills at fencing and dancing. "Let us therefore eat and drink" (II.iii.13–4). Sir Andrew's surname bespeaks his pallid face and quivering figure; all his claims to wit and gallantry and bravado only exist in order to be put down. When Feste asks "Would you have a love-song, or a song of good life?" and Toby responds, "A love-song, a love-song," Andrew gives himself away by blurting out, "Ay, ay, I care not for good life" (35–8). Akin to Justice Shallow and Master Slender, he is the ancestor of those witless foplings who will strive so vainly to cut a caper in Restoration comedy. And yet this ninny is not without his touch of Shakespearean poignance. When his mentor Toby—who is, if nothing else, a genuine *bon vivant*—complacently avows himself to be adored by Maria, Andrew sighs, "I was adored once too" (181). Behind that sigh lies some namby-pamby case history, about which we are relieved to hear no more.

Maria, the classic soubrette, is the most effectual of the plotters against Malvolio, and her recompense for forging the letter is marriage with Sir Toby. This provides a comic parallel for the two romantic betrothals, and it is announced by Fabian in the absence of the less-than-joyful couple, Toby having been discomfited along with Andrew by Sebastian. Since Andrew has essentially been a figure of fun, not a funster, he is gradually supplanted among the merrymakers by Fabian. It is Fabian who faces Olivia in the final disentanglement, backed by the festive exultations of the fool. Feste's maxim—"Better a witty fool than a foolish wit"— underlines the implicit contrast between himself and Andrew (I.v.36). One of the jester's assumed *personae* is that of the Vice, the principal mischief-maker in the old-fashioned morality plays (IV.ii.124). As "an allow'd fool," he has the privilege of raillery, which we hear that Olivia's father "took much delight in" (I.v.94; II.iv.12). Her father's death, which cannot have happened very long before, has presumably added to her brother's in deepening the gloom of the abode where she now finds herself mistress. Shakespeare has gone out of his way to darken the background of the conventional situation among the lovers, possibly reflecting the widespread preoccupation with the theme of melancholia during the early years of the seventeenth century. If so, his ultimate concern was to lift the clouds, to brighten the effect of the picture as a whole by the deft use of *chiaroscuro*, to heighten the triumph of the comic spirit by presenting it under attack. And, of course, with the rise of Puritanism, it was increasingly subject to attackers.

Such considerations may help to explain why Shakespeare went even farther by introducing the character of Malvolio—a superimposition so marked that one of the commentators, F. G. Fleay, has argued that the two plots are separable and may have been composed at different times. That seems too mechanical an inference, since Shakespeare has taken pains to unify them; since Olivia is "addicted to a melancholy," it follows that she should employ a majordomo who is "sad and civil," as she says, "And suits well for a servant with my fortunes" (II.v.202; III.iv.5–6). Though she tolerates Feste, her first impulse is to dismiss him from her company. His response is both a catechism and a syllogism, demonstrating that she should not mourn because her brother is better off in heaven and proving the fool's dialectical point that his interlocutor must be still more foolish than he: "Take away the fool, gentlemen" (I.v.71–2). She is mildly cheered by the nimbleness of the repartee; but Malvolio is distinctly not amused; and his hostile and humorless reaction is our introduction to him. Gleefully and ironically recalling this exchange, Feste will reveal the natural antipathy that was bound to operate between himself and Malvolio: "'Madam, why laugh you at such a

barren rascal? An you smile not, he's gagg'd.' And thus the
whirligig of time brings in his revenges" (V.i.374-7). Malvolio and
Feste are brought together and kept at odds by a certain comple-
mentarity, like that between the melancholy Jaques and the festive Touchstone in *As You Like It* or the clowns and the "humorous
men" of Jonson and Marston. The pretensions of the Alazon are
thus laid open to the exposures of the Eiron.

The issue is sharply drawn by Sir Toby's entrance speech:
"What a plague means my niece to take the death of her brother
thus? I am sure care's an enemy to life" (I.iii.1-2). As a master of
the revels, he and his fellow revelers embody the forces of life,
on the one hand. On the other, the interloping Malvolio represents the force of care, which has usurped a temporary control
over once-carefree Illyria. It is not for nothing that his name
signifies "ill-wisher." He is the perennial spoilsport, fighting an
aggressive rearguard action against a crapulous playboy and his
Bacchanalian cohorts. As Olivia's steward, Malvolio's functions
are more than ceremonial; he can not only cut off the daily
bounties of existence; he can threaten, and he does, to expel the
incumbent devotees of good living. After Toby's rhetorical question on behalf of cakes and ale, seconded by Feste's plea for
ginger, their prodigal levity takes the offensive against his false
dignity. By a convention which is not less amusing because it is
artificial, the practical jokers overhear—and react to—the soliloquy expressing Malvolio's fantasies and delusions of grandeur:
"To be Count Malvolio! . ." (II.v.35). It brings home the self-love
and the ambition to regulate the lives of others that they have
resented all along. And it plays into the trap that Maria has
baited, the letter that he is obliging enough to read aloud. To act
out its malevolent instructions is to betray his solemn and pompous nature. Not only must this non-laugher—this agelast, as
Meredith would classify him—doff his somber black for yellow
stockings and cross-garters, but he must force his atrabilious
features into an unremitting smile.

The romance of the main plot is ordered, or disordered, by the
workings of chance: Viola has been saved "perchance," and so
may Sebastian be (I.ii.6, 7). The satire of the underplot is managed
by human contrivance, which motivates the duel and fabricates
the letter. Malvolio ascribes his prospective elevation to a wise

providence ("it is Jove's doing"), but we know that it is a hoax on the part of Maria and her tosspot companions (III.iv.74-5). He is thereby prompted to strut through his grand scene of *hubris*, all the more ironic in its deliberate reduction of self-importance to silliness. Instead of having greatness thrust upon him, he is thereupon thrust down into a dark room, where he is bound and treated like a madman—like the Ephesian Antipholus in *The Comedy of Errors*, whose questioners look for symptoms of derangement in his answers. Malvolio's most pertinacious visitor and inquisitor is Feste, who has thrown himself into the *persona* of the neighboring curate Sir Topas. When the prisoner complains that the house is dark as hell, the pseudocurate replies in Feste's vein of Rabelaisian nonsense: "Why, it hath bay windows transparent as barricadoes, and the clerestories toward the south north are as lustrous as ebony; and yet complainest thou of obstruction" (IV.ii.36-9). At the height of his vainglory, Malvolio has admitted that his sartorial alteration had caused "some obstruction in the blood;" but this was nothing, if the result pleased Olivia; and to her inquiry about the state of his health he has answered, "Not black in my mind, though yellow in my legs" (III.iv.21, 26-7). The trouble was that so black a mind could never have become accustomed to bright colors.

It is therefore fitting that he be plunged into literal darkness, although Feste's paradoxes seem to suggest that brightness may have something to do with the eye of the beholder. Maria had begun by requesting Sir Toby to "confine" himself "within the modest limits of order," and he had blustered back with a pun: "Confine? I'll confine myself no finer than I am" (I.iii.8-11). When we see Malvolio confined, we may be weak enough to feel sorry for him; Charles Lamb, with Romantic perversity, has even worked up "a kind of tragic interest", and some of those leading actors who have appeared in the part have made the most of that potentiality. However, though Shakespeare's laughingstocks have a way of enlisting our sympathies, though we may be torn by Prince Hal's repudiation of Falstaff, though Shylock and Jaques may take with them some measure of respect when they make their solitary departures, we should be glad to get rid of Malvolio. Poetic justice prevails in comedy if not in tragedy, and it requires that he be finally "baffled" (V.i.369). Olivia can charitably speak, as his patron, of his having been "notoriously abused" (379). But his parting vow of revenge has been neutralized by Fabian's wish that "sportful malice"—a combination of the ludicrous and the ridiculous—"May rather pluck on laughter than revenge" (365-6). Nor, having witnessed his threat of expulsion to Sir Toby and his crew, should we repine at seeing this gloomy interloper expelled. As a sycophant, a social climber, and an officious snob, he well deserves to be put back in his place—or, as Jonson would have it, in his humor, for Malvolio seems to have a Jonsonian rather than a Shakespearean temperament.

What we have been watching is a reenactment of a timeless ritual, whose theatrical manifestation takes the obvious form of the villain foiled, and whose deeper roots in folklore go back to the scapegoat cast into the outer darkness. The business of baiting him is not a sadistic gesture but a cathartic impulse of *Schadenfreude*: an affirmation of Life against Care, if we allow Sir Toby to lay down the terms of our allegory. We could point to an illustration so rich in detail and so panoramic in design that it might prove distracting, if it were not so sharply focused on the conflict before us, Pieter Breughel's *Battle between Carnival and Lent*. There the jolly corpulent personification of *Mardi Gras*, astride a cask of wine and armed with a spit impaling a roasted pig, jousts against a grim penitential hag carted by a monk and a nun, and flourishing a paddle replete with two herrings. Beggars and buffoons and many others, the highly variegated proponents of revelry and of self-mortification, intermingle in the teeming crowd. Which of the antagonists will gain the upper hand? Each of them, in due season. J. G. Frazer has instanced many analogues for the observance, both in the Burial of the Carnival and in the mock-sacrifice of Jack o' Lent. Shakespeare loaded his dice on the side of carnival, in that hungover hanger-on, Sir Toby, as against the lenten Malvolio, that prince of wet-blankets. But Shakespeare was writing a comedy—and, what is more, a comedy written in defense of the comic spirit. He could commit himself, in this case, to the wisdom of folly and to the ultimate foolishness of the conventional wisdom. But, in his dramaturgy, he was moving onward to care, to death, to mourning, and toward tragedy.

Harold Jenkins

Shakespeare's *Twelfth Night*

What I shall try to do in this lecture is to examine some features of Shakespeare's comic art in one particular example. It may seem temerity enough to have chosen *Twelfth Night*; but since a dramatist, after all, even Shakespeare, is made as well as born, and it is interesting to see, if indeed one ever can, how his art perfects itself, I shall also venture from time to time some comparison between *Twelfth Night* and one of the earlier comedies of Shakespeare which led up to it.

In a book on *Twelfth Night* published four years ago Dr. Leslie Hotson suggested that the play was written to compliment an Italian nobleman, Virginio Orsino, Duke of Bracciano, in a court entertainment given for him on Twelfth Night, 1601, and that it was after this Orsino that one of the principal characters was named. I am not sure that the Italian Orsino would have felt complimented by seeing himself portrayed as a handsome and poetical but ineffective lover, and I do not think that Queen Elizabeth would have witnessed the play with delight if she had agreed with Dr. Hotson that the lady Olivia in the play was intended to represent her. But even if *Twelfth Night* were the play with which the Queen entertained the Italian Duke, it would not be necessary to suppose with Dr. Hotson that Shakespeare wrote it in ten or eleven days.[1] It is true that the Lord Chamberlain made a memorandum to arrange with the players "to make choice of" a play that would be "most pleasing to her Majesty" on this occasion,[2] but "to make choice of a play" is not quite the same thing as instructing the players to get up a new one.

Reprinted by permission of The Rice Institute, Rice University, from Rice Institute pamphlet 45, no. 4, January 1959.

The most interesting thing of course is that in however short a time Shakespeare ultimately wrote this play, he had in a sense been composing it during most of the previous decade. It was several years before the Twelfth Night entertainment of 1601—certainly not later than 1594—that Shakespeare first wrote a play about identical twins who were separated from one another in a shipwreck and afterwards mistaken for one another even by the wife of one of them; and it was at a similarly early stage in his career that Shakespeare wrote another play about a woman who served her lover as a page, and who in her page's disguise carried messages of love from her lover to another woman. When Shakespeare makes these things happen in *Twelfth Night* he is, in fact, combining the plots of *The Comedy of Errors* and *The Two Gentlemen of Verona*. He does not, however, combine them in equal degree. The heartsick heroine who in page's disguise takes messages of love to another woman provided little more than an episode in the complicated relations of the two gentlemen of Verona; but in *Twelfth Night* this episode has grown into the central situation from which the play draws its life. On the other hand, the confusion of twins which entertained us for five acts of *The Comedy of Errors* appears now as little more than an adroit device to bring about a happy ending. These shifts of emphasis show clearly enough the direction that Shakespeare's art of comedy has taken. When Sebastian appears in *Twelfth Night* we see that Shakespeare can still delight in the jolly mix-up of mistaken identities, not to mention their consequence of broken pates, but his plot now gives chief attention to the delineation of romantic love. This is more than just a preference for one situation rather than another: it means that a plot which turns on external appearances—a resemblance between men's faces—gives way to an action which involves their feelings. In *The Comedy of Errors*, though the physical resemblance between twins is no doubt a fact of nature, the confusion is really the result of accidental circumstances and is as accidentally cleared up. But in *Twelfth Night* the confusion is in the emotions and no *dénouement* is possible until the characters have grown in insight to the point where they can acknowledge the feelings that nature has planted in them. Thus *Twelfth Night* exhibits in its action one of the fundamental motifs of comedy: the education of a man or woman. For a comedy, as everyone knows, is a play in which the situation holds some threat of disaster but issues in the achievement of happiness; and those comedies may satisfy us most deeply in which danger is averted and happiness achieved through something that takes place within the characters. Orsino and Olivia come to their happy ending when they have learnt a new attitude to others and to themselves.

This, I take it, is what is also meant to happen in *The Two Gentlemen of Verona* in the much misunderstood conclusion of that play. Proteus, significantly named for his fickle nature, has vexed the critics by coming into a happiness he seems to have done nothing to deserve. But the point is that when his best friend has denounced him as a "treacherous man" and his mistress has rebuked him for his changeableness, he can penitently say, "O heaven, were man but constant he were perfect." This has struck some as complacent; but it is not to be taken lightly. For it means that Proteus has now learned the value of constancy, the very virtue he conspicuously lacked. This is what the play set out to teach him and it is only when he has learned it that he can say, "Bear witness, Heaven, I have my wish for ever," expressing simultaneously a sense of the happiness he is granted and a vow of constancy in future. It is true that in *The Two Gentlemen of Verona* Shakespeare did not allow himself scope to develop all the implications of Proteus's fickleness and reform; but such a story of treachery, if fully explored, might strike too deep for comedy. *Twelfth Night* has no unfaithful lover. But it cannot escape notice that Orsino's love is repeatedly compared to the sea—vast, hungry, but unstable, while his mind appears to Feste like an opal, a jewel of magical but ever-changing colors. The changeable man is there, but he has undergone a subtle transformation, and to notice that is, I think, of far more importance than to object, as Charlotte Lennox did in the eighteenth century, that Shakespeare in *Twelfth Night* has ruined the story of Bandello which she regarded as "undoubtedly" Shakespeare's source.[3] Shakespeare, she objects, deprives the story of probability because he neglects to provide his characters with acceptable motives. Viola, she says, "all of a sudden takes up an unaccountable resolution to serve the young bachelor-duke in the habit of a man." And since Viola has not even the excuse of being in love with the duke to start with, this goes "greatly beyond the bounds of decency." But if Shake-

speare had wanted to make Viola assume her man's disguise
because she was already in love with Orsino, he did not need
Bandello to teach him; he had already tried that situation with
Julia and Proteus, and it had necessarily involved Proteus in that
heartless infidelity from which Orsino is to be spared. The emotional situation of *Twelfth Night* is of a much less obvious kind.

The most important source for *Twelfth Night*, one might therefore say, is *The Two Gentlemen of Verona*. For it is only by a paradox of
scholarship that the word *source* is usually restricted to material
that an author draws on from someone else's work. But that
there were other sources for *Twelfth Night* I readily admit.[4] Charlotte Lennox knew of one in Bandello. And long before that one
of Shakespeare's own contemporaries had pointed to another.
When John Manningham saw *Twelfth Night* in 1602, he said in his
Diary that it reminded him of an Italian play called *Gl'Inganni* (or
The Mistakes). There were at least two plays of this title that
Shakespeare might have used, and in one of them the heroine, on
disguising herself as a page, assumed the name Cesare, which
may well be why Shakespeare's Viola elects to call herself Cesario. There was also another Italian play called *Gl'Ingannati* (or *The
Mistaken*), in which the master told the page, "You are a child, you
do not know the force of love," and Shakespeare's Orsino of
course is always similarly reminding Cesario of his uninitiated
youth. So the nineteenth-century scholar, Joseph Hunter, perhaps influenced by the fact that he discovered it, found in this
play *Gl'Ingannati* "the true origin" of Shakespeare's. Collier, however, asserted that it was from an English tale by Barnabe Riche,
called *Apolonius and Silla*, that Shakespeare drew his plot. Furness
was equally certain that he did not, but as he hoped that Shakespeare had never looked in Riche's "coarse, repulsive novel,"[5]
perhaps this also was not quite an impartial judgment.

For my part I find no difficulty in agreeing with those modern
scholars who assume that Shakespeare was familiar with all these
versions of a story in which a woman disguised as a page pleads
her lover's suit with another woman, who then falls in love with
the page. But that Shakespeare read up these plays and novels for
the express purpose of writing his own play is perhaps another
matter. The similarities between Shakespeare and these others

are certainly interesting; yet to point out similarities will usually end in drawing attention to their difference. For instance, *Twelfth Night* seems to echo Riche's tale when Olivia, declaring her unrequited love for Cesario, says she has "laid" her "honor too unchary out."[6] But in Riche the lady said that she had "charity preserved" her "honor." The phrasing is reminiscent; but Riche's lady boasts of her honor after she has sacrificed her chastity, while Shakespeare's Olivia reproaches herself for being careless of her honor when her chastity of course is not in question. Riche's lady is anxious lest she has lost her reputation in the eyes of the world, Olivia lest she has fallen from her own high ideal of conduct. Without accepting Furness's view that any reference to the act of sex is coarse and repulsive, we may easily find it significant that Shakespeare leaves it out. His delineation of Olivia's love for the page, in contrast to most of the earlier versions, omits all the physical demonstrations. The usual way when the lady falls in love with the page is for her to astonish him by falling on his neck and kissing him. In Secchi's play of *Gl'Inganni* the relations between them reach the point where the woman page is expected to play the man's part in an actual assignation and she gets out of it by the cunning substitution of her brother. In the play of *Gl'Ingannati*, which comes closer to Shakespeare, the lady takes the brother by mistake, but he goes to bed with her just the same. In Riche's story this incident has consequences, which force the lady so chary of her honor to demand marriage of the page, who can only establish innocence by the disclosure of *her* sex. Shakespeare appropriates this convenient brother as a husband for Olivia, but since he could easily have invented Viola's twin, and in *The Comedy of Errors* had, one might say, already tried him out, this debt is not a profound one. What is more remarkable, the similarity as usual embracing a contrast, is that when Olivia mistakes Sebastian for Cesario she takes him not to bed but to a priest. Olivia no less than Orsino is kept free of moral taint. And this is no mere matter of prudishness. The reckless abandonment of scruple shown by all these earlier lovers—both by the gentlemen who desert their mistresses and the ladies who fling themselves upon the page-boys—cannot coexist with the more delicate sentiment which gives *Twelfth Night* its character. In Shakespeare, even the twin brother, prop to the plot as he may be, shares in this refinement. When Olivia takes charge of Sebastian's person, what he gives her is less his body than his imagination. He is enwrapped, he says, in "wonder." And it is his capacity to experience this wonder that lifts him to the level of the other lovers in the play, so that he becomes a worthy partner for Orsino's adored one and Viola's adorer.

Now if *Twelfth Night* is the greatest of Shakespeare's romantic comedies, it is partly because of its success in embodying these feelings of wonder in the principal persons of the play. Stories of romantic love owe something of their perennial appeal, we need not be ashamed to admit, to the taste for tales of pursuit and mysterious adventure, as well as to what psychologists no doubt explain as the sublimation of the natural impulses of sex. But the devotion which the romantic lover bestows upon a woman as pure as she is unattainable may also symbolize the mind's aspiration towards some ever alluring but ever elusive ideal. In the traditional romantic stories the course of true love does not run smooth because of obstacles presented by refractory parents or inconvenient rivals, who have to be overcome or made to change. This is the case in *A Midsummer-Night's Dream*. There are perhaps subtler situations, where the obstacles exist in the very nature of the protagonists, who must themselves be made to change. This is variously the case in *The Taming of the Shrew* and *Love's Labour's Lost*, where in their very different ways Katherina and the young gentlemen of Navarre are, to begin with, recalcitrant to love. But a still subtler situation may arise with characters who are from the beginning full of devotion to an ideal of love while mistaking the direction in which it should be sought. This, I take it, is the case with Orsino and Olivia. Orsino, with whom *Twelfth Night* begins and who draws us from the start into the aura of his imagination, is in some ways the most perfect of Shakespeare's romantic lovers simply because he is so much more. This is easily appreciated if we compare him with his earlier prototypes in *The Two Gentlemen of Verona*. He is, as I have suggested, the inconstant Proteus transformed. But he is also the other gentleman, the constant Valentine. He is

> Unstaid and skittish in all motions else
> Save in the constant image of the creature
> That is beloved.

So, simultaneously volatile and steadfast, he combines in a single figure those aspects of man's nature which in the earlier comedy had been systematically contrasted and opposed.

In Valentine, of course, we recognize the typical victim of the passion of courtly love. He tells us himself how he suffers

> With bitter fasts, with penitential groans,
> With nightly tears and daily heartsore sighs.

That these groans and sighs survive in Orsino is clear when Olivia asks "How does he love me?" and the messenger replies,

> With adorations, with[7] fertile tears,
> With groans that thunder love, with sighs of fire.

The danger of such a hero is, as Professor Charlton has remarked, that, in fulfilling his conventional role, he may to the quizzical eye seem a fool. Shakespeare guards against this danger by anticipating our ridicule; but his mockery of Valentine and Orsino is quite different in kind. The romantic Valentine is given an unromantic servant who pokes broad fun at his conduct: "to sigh like a schoolboy that has lost his A.B.C.; to weep like a young wench that had buried her grandam; to fast like one that takes diet," and so forth. But Orsino, instead of a servant who laughs at him for loving, has a page who can show him how to do it. "If I did love you in my master's flame," says Cesario, I would

> Make me a willow-cabin at your gate
> And call upon my soul within the house

till all the hills reverberated with the name of the beloved. This famous willow-cabin speech, often praised for its lyricism, is of course no less a parody of romantic love than are Speed's gibes at Valentine. The willow is the emblem of forsaken love and those songs that issue from it in the dead of night apostrophizing the mistress as her lover's "soul"—they are easily recognizable as the traditional love-laments. But the parody, though it has its hint of laughter, is of the kind that does not belittle but transfigures its original. So it comes as no surprise when Olivia, hitherto heedless of sighs and groans, suddenly starts to listen. To the page she says, "*You* might do much," and these words are her first acknowledgement of love's power. Orsino, content to woo by proxy a woman who immures herself in a seven-year mourning for a

dead brother, may have the glamor of a knight of romance but he
is *not* quite free from the risk of absurdity. He seems, they tell us
with some justice, in love not so much with a woman as with his
own idea of love. But what they do not so often tell us is how
splendid an idea this is. His very groans go beyond Valentine's;
they were said, it will have been noticed, to *thunder*, and his sighs
were *fire*. If he indulges his own emotions, this is in no mere
dilettantism but with the avidity of hunger.

> If music be the *food* of love, play on,
> Give me *excess* of it, that *surfeiting*,
> The *appetite* may sicken and so die.

This wonderful opening speech suggests no doubt the changeableness of human emotion. "Play on . . . that strain again! It had
a dying fall. . . . Enough, no more! 'Tis not so sweet now as it was
before." But if the spirit of love is as transitory as music and as
unstable as the sea, it is also as living and capacious. New waves
form as often as waves break; the shapes of fancy, insubstantial as
they are, make a splendor in the mind, and renew themselves as
quickly as they fade. So Orsino's repeated rejections by his mistress do not throw him into despair. Instead he recognizes, in her
equally fantastic devotion, a nature of surpassingly "fine frame"
and he reflects on how she *will* love when the throne of her heart
shall find its "king." How too will *he* love, we are entitled to infer,
when his inexhaustible but as yet deluded fancy shall also find the
true sovereign it seeks. This of course it does at the end of the
play when he exchanges all his dreams of passion for the love of
someone he has come to know. In the play's last line before the
final song he is able to greet Viola as "Orsino's mistress and his
fancy's queen."

Before this consummation Orsino and Viola have only one big
scene together, and in view of all that depends on it it will need to
be a powerful one. Again it finds a model in *The Two Gentlemen of
Verona*, where already there is a scene in which a man declares his
love for one woman in the hearing of another woman who loves
him. The technique is in each case that of a scene that centers
upon a song, which makes a varying impact upon the different
characters who hear it. In *The Two Gentlemen of Verona* a song of
adoration to a mistress is presented by a faithless lover and is

overheard by the woman he has deserted, while her heartbreak goes undetected by her escort, who calmly falls asleep. This is admirably dramatic, but its irony may seem a trifle obvious when set beside the comparable scene in *Twelfth Night*. The song here is one of forsaken love and it is sung to two constant lovers. Most artfully introduced, it is called for by Orsino, whose request for music sustains the role in which he began the play; and the way in which he calls for the song characterizes both him and it before its opening notes are heard. It is to be an old and antique song, belonging to some primitive age, the kind of song chanted by women at their weaving or their knitting in the sun. It will appeal to Orsino in its simple innocence, or, we may say if we wish, by its ideal immunity from fact. So the rational mind can disengage itself from the sentiment in advance, and as soon as the song is ended its effect is counteracted by the jests of the clown who has sung it and the practical necessity of paying him. Yet the sentiment of the song remains to float back and forth over the dialogue which surrounds it as Orsino and Viola tell us of their love. The contrast here is not, as in *The Two Gentlemen of Verona*, between the faithful and the faithless, the heartbroken and the heart-whole. It is between one who is eloquent about an imaginary passion and one who suffers a real grief in concealment. Orsino appropriates the song to himself, yet it is Viola who hears in it

> a very echo to the seat
> Where Love is throned.

Orsino is still sending messages to one he calls his "sovereign," but *his* throne, we may say, is still unoccupied. For his splendid fantasies are as yet self-regarding. When Viola objects, "But if she cannot love you, sir?" he dismisses this with "I cannot be so answered." Yet when she simply retorts, "Sooth, but you must," he receives his first instruction in the necessity of accommodating his fantasies to practical realities. And soon he begins, however unwittingly, to learn. As Viola tells the history of her father's daughter, though he does not see that she is speaking of herself, he finds himself for the first time giving attention to a sorrow not his own. "But died thy sister of her love, my boy?" he asks. To this Viola can only reply, "I know not"; for at this stage in the drama the issue is still in the balance, though Orsino's new absorption in another's plight will provide us with a clue to the outcome. In the very act of sending a fresh embassy to his mistress his thoughts are momentarily distracted from his own affair. When it is necessary for Viola to prompt him—"Sir, shall I to this lady?"—though he rapidly collects himself, we know that his development has begun.

In the emotional pattern of the play Viola represents a genuineness of feeling against which the illusory can be measured. As the go-between she is of course also at the center of the plot. It is her role to draw Orsino and Olivia from their insubstantial passions and win them to reality. But her impact upon each of them is inevitably different. Orsino, whom she loves but cannot tell her love, responds to her womanly constancy and sentiment; Olivia, whom she cannot love but has to woo, is to be fascinated by her page-boy effrontery and wit.

Now in all the stories of the woman-page who woos for her master and supplants him, the transference of the mistress's affections must be the pivot of the action. In *The Two Gentlemen of Verona*, of course, the lady fails to fall in love with the page at all, which is really a little surprising of her, since she had done so in Shakespeare's source. It is almost as though Shakespeare were reserving this crowning situation, in which the mistress loves the woman-page, for treatment in some later play. At any rate, in *Twelfth Night* he takes care to throw the emphasis upon it from the first. Viola is got into her page-boy clothes before we are halfway through the first act. The plausibility of this, notwithstanding Mrs. Lennox and Dr. Johnson, is not the question. What matters is that the encounter of the lady and the page, upon which the plot is to turn, shall be momentous. And there is no encounter in Shakespeare, not even that of Hamlet with the ghost, which is more elaborately prepared for. Olivia's situation is referred to in each of the first four scenes before she herself appears in the fifth. Out of her love for her dead brother she had abjured the sight of men. This is the plain fact as a plain sea captain tells it to Viola and us. But in the more embroidered description of one of Orsino's gentlemen we may detect perhaps a hint of the preposterous:

> like a cloistress she will veiled walk
> And water once a day her chamber round
> With eye-offending brine.

In the fanciful Orsino this inspires adoration; but how it may appear to a less poetical nature we may gather from the first words of Sir Toby Belch: "What a plague means my niece to take the death of her brother thus?" All these varied views are insinuated naturally into the dialogue, but their cumulative effect is to give Olivia's situation in the round and to make us curious to see her for ourselves. When after all this she appears, curiosity is not satisfied but intensified; she is not, I think, what we expected. Instead of the veiled lady sprinkling her chamber with tears there enters a mistress commanding her household, and her first words are, "Take the fool away." Equally unexpected is the fool's retort, "Do you not hear, fellows? Take away the lady." This great dame is called a fool by one of her own attendants, who then goes on to prove it:

> *Clown.* Good madonna, why mourn'st thou?
> *Olivia.* Good fool, for my brother's death.
> *Clown.* I think his soul is in hell, madonna.
> *Olivia.* I know his soul is in heaven, fool.
> *Clown.* The more fool, madonna, to mourn for your brother's
>   soul being in heaven. Take away the fool, gentlemen.

Now this is excellent fooling, but Shakespeare's incidental gaieties have a way of illuminating important matters and our conception of Olivia is one of them. It is only a fool who calls her a fool, but, as the fool himself has suggested, a fool "may pass for a wise man," while those who think they have wit "do very oft prove fools." The question of Olivia's folly remains open. It is kept alive below the surface of the quipping dialogue which entertains us while Olivia defends the fool and is thanked by the fool in characteristically equivocal terms. "Thou hast spoke for us, madonna, as if thy eldest son should be a fool." One could hardly say more than that. Yet the suggestion that her eldest son might be a fool is at best a left-handed compliment. The fool is quick to right it with a prayer that Jove may cram his skull with brains, but it seems that Jove's intervention may be necessary, for—as Sir Toby enters—"one of thy kin has a most weak pia mater." The chances of brains or folly in the skull of any son of Olivia seem then to be about equal. But what is surely most remarkable is the notion of Olivia's ever having a son at all. We have been made to associate her not with birth but death. The weeping cloistress, as Orsino's gentleman put it, was seasoning a "dead love," and what plagued Sir Toby about this was that care was "an enemy to life." Yet the fool seems to see her as available for motherhood. The remarks of a fool—again—strike as deep as you choose to let them—that is the dramatic use of fools—but Olivia interests us more and more.

By now the page is at the gate. Indeed three different messengers announce him. Sir Toby of the weak pia mater is too drunk to do more than keep us in suspense, but Malvolio precisely catalogues the young man's strange behavior, till we are as curious to see him as is Olivia herself. "Tell him he shall not speak with me," she has insisted; but when this changes to "Let him approach," the first of her defences is down. Our interest in each of them is now at such a height that the moment of their meeting cannot fail to be electric.

How different all this is from what happened in *The Two Gentlemen of Verona*, where only a single soliloquy prepared us before the page and Sylvia just came together pat. But it is interesting to see how the seeds strewn in the earlier play now germinate in Shakespeare's mature inventiveness. When the page came upon Sylvia, he did not know who she was and actually asked her to direct him to herself. This confusion gave a momentary amusement and the dramatic importance of the encounter was faintly underlined. But as Sylvia at once disclosed her identity, this little gambit came to nothing. In *Twelfth Night*, however, Cesario only pretends not to recognize Olivia so as to confound her with his raillery. "Most radiant, exquisite and unmatchable beauty," he begins and then breaks off to enquire whether the lady before him is the radiant unmatchable or not. As he has never seen her, how can he possibly tell? This opens up a brilliant series of exchanges in the course of which the familiar moves of the conventional courtship are all similarly transformed. In *The Two Gentlemen of Verona* Proteus was simply following the usual pattern of suitors when he instructed the page,

> Give her that ring and therewithal
> This letter . . . Tell my lady
> I claim the promise for her heavenly picture.

To be fair, even in this early play the conventional properties, the ring, the letter, and the picture, each made a dramatic point: for

Sylvia recognized the ring as that of her rival and so refused to accept it, while she tore the letter up; and if she compliantly handed over her portrait, she was careful to add the comment that a picture was only a shadow and might appropriately be given for a fickle lover to worship. But in *Twelfth Night* the letter, the picture, and the ring are changed almost out of recognition. Shakespeare's superbly original invention allows Orsino to dispense with them; yet they are all vestigially present. Instead of bearing missives, the page is given the task of acting out his master's woes, and so instead of the lover's own letter we are to have the page's speech. This cunningly diverts attention from the message to the messenger, and the effect is still further enhanced when even the speech never gets delivered apart from its opening words. Instead there is talk about the speech—how "excellently well penn'd," how "poetical" it is—and are you really the right lady so that I may not waste the praise I have taken such pains to compose? Olivia in turn delights us by matching Cesario's mockery, but as we watch them finesse about how and even whether the speech shall be delivered, their mocking dialogue says more than any formal speech could say. In fact the very circumventing of the speech brings them to the heart of its forbidden theme. And so we come to the picture. There is of course no picture, any more than there was a letter; but the convention whereby the lover asks for a picture of his mistress is made to provide a metaphor through which the witty duel may proceed. Olivia draws back the curtain and reveals a picture, they talk of the colors that the artist's "cunning hand laid on," and Cesario asks for a copy. But the curtain Olivia draws back is her own veil, the artist is Nature, and the copy of Nature's handiwork will come as the fruit of marriage. Again the suggestion that Olivia could have a child. The cloistress who dedicates herself to the dead is reminded of the claims of life. She waves them aside for the moment by deftly changing the application of the metaphor. Certainly there shall be a copy of her beauty; why not an inventory of its items? As she catalogues them—"two lips, indifferent red . . . two grey eyes, with lids to them"—she ridicules the wooer's praises; but at the same time, it may not be too much to suggest, she robs her womanhood of its incipient animation. Yet the cloistress has removed her veil and presently there is the ring.

Orsino again sent no ring, but that need not prevent Olivia from returning it. And with this ruse the ring no less than the picture takes on a new significance. By means of it Olivia rejects Orsino's love but at the same time declares her own. And as Malvolio flings the ring upon the stage it makes its little dramatic *éclat*.

Shakespeare's portrait of Olivia has usually, I think, been underrated. The critics who used to talk about Shakespeare's heroines fell in love with Viola, and actresses have naturally preferred the bravura of her essentially easier role. Besides there is the risk of the ridiculous about a woman who mistakenly loves one of her own sex. But the delicacy of Shakespeare's handling, once more in contrast with that of his predecessors, steers the situation right away from farce and contrives to show, through her potentially absurd and undisguisedly pathetic plight, the gradual awakening of that noble nature which Orsino detected from the first. We have still permission to laugh at her. The fool, reminding us that foolery like the sun shines everywhere, flits between Orsino's house and hers. But when he is called the Lady Olivia's fool he makes one of his astonishing replies. "No indeed, sir. The Lady Olivia has no folly." It is true that his remark is as usual double-edged. "She will keep no fool, sir, till she be married." Her present exemption, it would seem, lies in her not having yet secured the husband she is seeking. But when the fool now tells us that the Lady Olivia has no folly, we are forcibly reminded that he began by proving her a fool. It seems clear she is making progress. The comic artist only hints this with a lightness which the heavy hand of the critic inevitably destroys; but is there not the suggestion that when Olivia ceases to mourn the dead and gives herself to the pursuit of the living, she has advanced some small way towards wisdom?

There is one character in the play who, unlike Olivia and Orsino, is unable to make this journey. And that brings me to the subplot. For it will already be apparent that I do not agree with a recent paper in the *Shakespeare Quarterly* which makes Malvolio the central figure of the play.[8] The mistake is not a new one. The record of a court performance in the year of the First Folio actually calls the play *Malvolio* and there are other seventeenth-century references, beginning with Manningham in 1602, which go to show that the sublime swagger with which Malvolio walks into the box-hedge trap to emerge in yellow stockings was largely responsible, then as now, for the play's theatrical popularity. The distortion of emphasis this implies is a tribute to Shakespeare's invention of the most novel situation in the play, but if I venture to suggest that it does no great credit to his audience, no doubt some one will rise up like Sir Toby and ask me, "Dost thou think because thou art virtuous there shall be no more cakes and ale?" All I think is that the cake-and-ale jollifications are very jolly indeed so long as they stay, whether in criticism or performance, within the bounds of a subplot, which the whole technique of the dramatic exposition marks them out to be. These more hilarious goings-on make an admirable counterweight to the more fragile wit and sentiment of which the main plot is woven; but attention is firmly directed to the love story of Orsino, Olivia, and Viola before Sir Toby and Malvolio are heard of, and the courtships are well in progress by the time we come to the midnight caterwaulings. So the love-delusions of Malvolio, brilliant as they are, fall into perspective as a parody of the more delicate aberrations of his mistress and her suitor. Like them Malvolio aspires towards an illusory ideal of love, but his mistake is a grosser one than theirs, his posturings more extravagant and grotesque. So *his* illusion enlarges the suggestions of the main plot about the mind's capacity for self-deception and if, as Lamb maintained,[9] it gives Malvolio a glory such as no mere reason can attain to, still "lunacy" was one of Lamb's words for it and it is to the madman's dungeon that it leads.

Malvolio's fate, like Falstaff's, has been much resented by the critics. But drama, as Aristotle indicated and Shakespeare evidently perceived, is not quite the same as life, and punishments that in life would seem excessive have their place in the more ideal world of art. In the ethical scheme of comedy, it may be the doom of those who cannot correct themselves to be imprisoned or suppressed. Olivia and Prince Hal, within their vastly different realms, have shown themselves capable of learning, as Malvolio and Falstaff have not.

The comparison between Olivia and Malvolio is one that the play specifically invites. He is the trusted steward of her household, and he suits her, she says, by being "sad and civil." This reminds us that it was with her authority that he descended on the midnight revels to quell that "uncivil rule." Have you no manners, he demands of Sir Toby and his crew; and his rebuke is one that Olivia herself will echo later when she calls Sir Toby a barbarian fit to dwell in "caves Where manners ne'er were preached." But if Olivia and Malvolio are united in seeking to impose an ordered regimen on these unruly elements, that does not mean, though I have found it said, that they share a doctrine of austerity.[10] Indeed the resemblance between them serves to bring out a distinction that is fundamental to the play. It is clearly marked for us on their first appearance. Significantly enough, they are brought on the stage together and placed in the same situation, as if to attract our attention to their contrasting reactions. The first remark of each of them is one of dissatisfaction with the fool, and the fool's retaliation is first to prove Olivia a fool and then to call Malvolio one. But Olivia is amused and Malvolio is not. "I marvel your ladyship takes delight in such a barren rascal." What Olivia delights in, Malvolio finds barren. "Doth he not mend?" she says, suggesting that the fool is getting wittier. But Malvolio rejoins, Yes, he is mending by becoming a more perfect fool—"and shall do till the pangs of death shake him." Olivia too has given her thoughts to death, but whereas she mourns the dead, prettily if absurdly, Malvolio threatens the living in words which betray a cruel relish. This is his first speech in the play and it carries a corresponding emphasis. There are already signs that Olivia may be won from death to life, but the spirit of Malvolio can only be destructive. To say this is again to put it more portentously than it is the nature of comedy to do, but it is Olivia, not Malvolio, whom the comic dialogue invites to have a son, with brains in his skull or otherwise.

The difference in their natures appears in various subtle ways, and I will cite just one example. When Olivia sends after Cesario with the ring, the message that she sends is,

> If that the youth will come this way tomorrow,
> I'll give him reasons for't.

But Malvolio, who bears the message, translates it thus:

> Be never so hardy to come again in his affairs, unless it
> be to report your lord's taking of this.

It is true that Malvolio cannot know, as we do, the secret meaning of the ring, but that hardly leaves him guiltless when he replaces "if" by "unless" and a positive by a negative: "If that the youth will come . . . ," "Be never so hardy to come . . . unless. . . ." An invitation has become a warning off.

As the action proceeds, Olivia opens her heart to the new love that is being born within her, but Malvolio is only confirmed in that sickness of self-love of which she has accused him. At the height of his love-dream, his imaginings are all of his own advancement—"sitting in my state," "in my branched velvet gown," "calling my officers about me" as I "wind up my watch or play with my—some rich jewel."[11] When he showed resentment at the fool, Olivia reproached Malvolio for his lack of generosity and now his very words freeze every generous impulse—"I frown the while," "quenching my familiar smile with an austere regard of control."[12] This is not the language of Olivia. She speaks of the impossibility of quenching those natural feelings which rise up within her, and which we are made to recognize even in the comicality of her predicament:

> Cesario, by the roses of the spring,
> By maidhood, honour, truth and everything,
> I love thee so that maugre all thy pride,
> No wit nor reason can my passion hide.

So Olivia, notwithstanding her mistakes, is allowed to find a husband while Malvolio is shut up in the dark.

The ironic fitness of Malvolio's downfall is dramatically underscored in every detail of his situation. When he dreamed of his own greatness he pictured Sir Toby coming to him with a curtsey and he told Sir Toby to amend his drunkenness: it is now his bitterest complaint that this drunken cousin has been given rule over him. When he rebuked the tipsy revellers, he began, "My masters, are you mad?" and their revenge upon him is to make it seem that he is mad himself. Particularly instructive is the leading part taken in his torment by the fool he began the play by spurning. The fool taunts him in the darkness of the dungeon and he begs the fool to help him to some light. It is to the fool that the man contemptuous of fools is now made to plead his own sanity. But his insistence on his sanity—"I am as well in my wits, fool, as thou art"—leaves the matter in some ambiguity, as the fool very promptly retorts: "Then you are mad indeed, if you be no better in your wits than a fool." And Malvolio ends the play as he began by being called a fool. And if at first it was only the fool who called him so, now it is his mistress herself. Even as she pities him for the trick that has been played on him, "Alas, poor fool" are the words that Shakespeare puts into her mouth.

What then is folly and what wisdom, the comedy seems to ask. The question first appeared in that early cross-talk with the fool which brought Olivia into contrast with Malvolio even while we were awaiting her reception of Cesario. So that the manner in which Malvolio's story is begun clearly puts it into relation with the main plot of the wooing. And of course it is only appropriate that scenes of romantic love should be surrounded by a comic dialogue which gaily tosses off its hints about whether these characters are fools. For the pursuit of the ideal life is not quite compatible with reason. And, as another of Shakespeare's comedies puts it, those who in imagination see more than "reason ever comprehends" are the lover, the poet, and the lunatic. So where does the noble vision end and the madman's dream begin? The greatness and the folly that lie in the mind of man are inextricably entangled and the characters in *Twelfth Night* have each their share of both. Malvolio's moment of lunacy may be, as Lamb suggests, the moment of his glory. Yet Malvolio, so scornful of the follies of others, would persuade us that his own are sane. His sanity is indeed established, but only to leave us wondering whether sanity may not sometimes be the greater folly. What the comedy *may* suggest is that he who in his egotism seeks to fit the world to the procrustean bed of his own reason deserves his own discomfiture. But Olivia, who self-confessedly abandons reason, and Orsino, who avidly gives his mind to all the shapes of fancy, are permitted to pass through whatever folly there may be in this to a greater illumination. Although what they sought has inevitably eluded them, it has nevertheless been vouchsafed to them in another form.

Yet it is the art of Shakespeare's comedy, and perhaps also its wisdom, to make no final judgments. The spirit of the piece, after all, is that of Twelfth Night and it is in the ideal world of Twelfth Night that Malvolio may be justly punished. Perhaps we should also remember, as even the Twelfth Night lovers do, to pause, if only for a moment, to recognize his precisian virtues. Olivia agrees with him that he has been "notoriously abused" and the poet-lover Orsino sends after him to "entreat him to a peace," before they finally enter into the happiness to which "golden time" will summon them. "Golden time"—the epithet is characteristically Orsino's. It is only the wise fool who stays to sing to us about the rain that raineth every day.

NOTES

1. *The First Night of "Twelfth Night,"* 1954, p. 97.
2. *Ibid.*, p. 15.
3. *Shakespeare Illustrated*, 1753, I, 237 ff.
4. For a survey and discussion of them, see Kenneth Muir, *Shakespeare's Sources*, 1957, pp. 66 ff. The more important ones are now assembled in *Narrative and Dramatic Sources of Shakespeare*, ed. Geoffrey Bullough, Vol. 2, 1958.
5. *Twelfth Night*, Variorum Edition, p. xvii.
6. I follow the emendation of Theobald, adopted by most editors, for the Folio *on't*.
7. Folio omits *with*.
8. Milton Crane, "*Twelfth Night* and Shakespearean Comedy," *Shakespeare Quarterly*, VI (1955). Cf. also Mark Van Doren, *Shakespeare*, 1939, p. 169: "The center is Malvolio."
9. In his account of Bensley's Malvolio in the essay "On Some of the Old Actors."
10. See especially M. P. Tilley, "The Organic Unity of *Twelfth Night*," *PMLA*, XXIX (1914).
11. Cf. John Russell Brown, *Shakespeare and his Comedies*, 1957, p. 167.
12. On the style of Malvolio's speeches, see Mark Van Doren, *Shakespeare*, 1939, p. 167.

L. G. Salingar

The Design of *Twelfth Night*

Most readers of *Twelfth Night* would probably agree that this is the most delightful, harmonious and accomplished of Shakespeare's romantic comedies, in many ways his crowning achievement in one branch of his art. They would probably agree, too, that it has a prevailing atmosphere of happiness, or at least of "tempests dissolved in music." Yet there are striking differences of opinion over the design of *Twelfth Night*. Is it, for example, a vindication of romance, or a depreciation of romance?[1] Is it mainly a love-story or a comedy of humours; a "poem of escape" or a realistic comment on economic security and prudential marriage?[2] And there are further variations. The principal character, according to choice, is Viola, Olivia, Malvolio, or Feste.

To some extent, the play itself seems to invite such varying reactions: *Twelfth Night; or, What You Will.* Shakespeare here is both polishing his craftsmanship and exploring new facets of his experience,[3] so that the play has the buoyancy of a mind exhilarated by discovery, testing one human impulse against another, and satisfied with a momentary state of balance which seems all the more trustworthy because its limits have been felt and recognized. But in consequence, Shakespeare's attitude towards his people comes near to humorous detachment, to a kind of Socratic irony. He refrains from emphasizing any one of his themes at the expense of the rest. He carefully plays down and transforms the crisis of sentiment in his main plot, while giving unusual prominence to his comic sub-plot. He distributes the interest more evenly among his characters than in *As You Like It* or the other

Reprinted from *Shakespeare Quarterly*, no. 9 (1958), by permission of Shakespeare Quarterly.

comedies, providing more numerous (and more unexpected) points of contact between them, not only in the action but on the plane of psychology. And the whole manner of *Twelfth Night* is light and mercurial. The prose is full of ideas, but playful, not discursive. The poetry, for all its lyrical glow, gives a sense of restraint and ease, of keenly perceptive and yet relaxed enjoyment, rather than of any compelling pressure of emotion.

Perhaps this attitude on Shakespeare's part is responsible for the inconsistency of his interpreters. Those who dwell on the romantic side of the play seem uncertain about its connection with the comic realism; while those who concentrate on the elements of realism have to meet the kind of objection gravely stated by Dr. Johnson—that "the marriage of Olivia, and the succeeding perplexity, though well enough contrived to divert on the stage, wants credibility, and fails to produce the proper instruction required in the drama, as it exhibits no just picture of life." The question to be interpreted, then, is how Shakespeare is using the instrument of theatrical contrivance, which is present, of course, in all his comedies, but which he uses here with exceptional delicacy and freedom.

Briefly, Shakespeare has taken a familiar kind of love-story and transformed it so as to extend the interest from the heroine to a group of characters who reveal varying responses to the power of love. He has modified the main situation further, and brought home his comments on it, by using methods of construction he had mastered previously in his *Comedy of Errors*. And he has added a sub-plot based on the customary jokes and revels of a feast of misrule, when normal restraints and relationships were overthrown. As the main title implies, the idea of a time of misrule gives the underlying constructive principle of the whole play.

In *Twelfth Night*, as Miss Welsford puts it, Shakespeare "transmutes into poetry the quintessence of the Saturnalia."[4] The sub-plot shows a prolonged season of misrule, or "uncivil rule," in Olivia's household, with Sir Toby turning night into day; there are drinking, dancing, and singing, scenes of mock wooing, a mock sword fight, and the gulling of an unpopular member of the household, with Feste mumming it as a priest and attempting a mock exorcism in the manner of the Feast of Fools. Sir Andrew and Malvolio resemble Ben Jonson's social pretenders[5]; but Shakespeare goes beyond Jonson in ringing the changes on the theme of Folly and in making his speakers turn logic and courtesy on their heads. A girl and a coward are given out to be ferocious duellists; a steward imagines that he can marry his lady; and finally a fool pretends to assure a wise man that darkness is light. In Feste, Shakespeare creates his most finished portrait of a professional fool; he is superfluous to the plot, but affects the mood of the play more than any other of Shakespeare's clowns.

Moreover, this saturnalian spirit invades the whole play. In the main plot, sister is mistaken for brother, and brother for sister. Viola tells Olivia "That you do think you are not what you are"—and admits that the same holds true of herself. The women take the initiative in wooing, both in appearance and in fact; the heroine performs love-service for the lover. The Duke makes his servant "your master's mistress" and the lady who has withdrawn from the sight of men embraces a stranger. The four main actors all reverse their desires or break their vows before the comedy is over; while Antonio, the one singleminded representative of romantic devotion, is also the only character in the main plot who tries to establish a false identity and fails (III.iv.341–343); and he is left unrewarded and almost disregarded. Such reversals are, as Johnson says, devices peculiar to the stage, but Shakespeare makes them spring, or seem to spring, from the very nature of love. In *The Comedy of Errors* the confusions of identity are due to external circumstances; in *A Midsummer Night's Dream* Shakespeare begins to connect them with the capricious, illusory factor in subjective "fancy" that is common to the madman, the lover, and the creative poet. In *Twelfth Night*, he takes this similitude further. Love here will "be clamorous, and leap all civil bounds," like a lord of misrule; "love's night is noon," like Sir Toby's carousals. Love seems as powerful as the sea, tempestuous, indifferent, and changeable as the sea. And fortune, or fate, reveals the same paradoxical benevolence in this imbroglio of mistakes and disguises: "Tempests are kind, and salt waves fresh in love."

The analysis of love as a kind of folly was a common theme of Renaissance moralists, who delighted in contrasting it with the wisdom of the stoic or the man of affairs. Shakespeare's treatment of the theme in *Twelfth Night* is a natural development from his own previous work, but he could have found strong hints of it in the possible sources of his Viola-Orsino story. Bandello remarks, for instance, that it arouses wonder to hear of a gentleman disguising himself as a servant, and still more in the case of a girl: but when you realize that love is the cause, "the wonder ceases at once, because this passion of love is much too potent and causes actions much more amazing and excessive than that"; a person in love has "lost his liberty, and . . . no miracle if he commits a thousand errors."⁶ And Barnabe Riche tells his readers that in his story of *Apolonius and Silla*, "you shall see Dame Error so play her part with a leash of lovers, a male and two females, as shall work a wonder to your wise judgement."⁷ In effect, then, what Shakespeare could take for granted in his audience was not simply a readiness to be interested in romance, but a sense of the opposition between romance and reason.

On this basis, Shakespeare can unite his main action with his sub-plot, bending a romantic story in the direction of farce. By the same contrivances, he can disclose the follies surrounding love and celebrate its life-giving power. And he can do this without sacrificing emotional reality—which is not exactly the same as Dr. Johnson's "just picture of life"—because he takes his stage machinery from the traditions of a feast of misrule, where social custom has already begun to transform normal behavior into the material of comic art.⁸ The whole play is a festivity, where reality and play-acting meet. By presenting his main story on these lines, Shakespeare can develop his insight into the protean, contradictory nature of love with more economy and force than by keeping to the lines of an ordinary stage narrative. At the same time he can extend this theme through his realistic images of "uncivil rule" in the sub-plot, disclosing the conflicting impulses of an aristocratic community in a period of social change, and touching on the potentially tragic problems of the place of time and order in human affairs.

Shakespeare's intentions may stand out more clearly when one compares his treatment of the Viola story with its possible or probable sources.⁹ The ultimate source is held to be the anonymous Sienese comedy, *Gl'Ingannati* (*The Deceived*), first performed at a carnival of 1531 and frequently reprinted, translated, or imitated in the course of the sixteenth century. Shakespeare may

also have known Bandello's story, which follows the plot of Gl'Ingannati closely, omitting the subordinate comic parts; and he probably knew Riche's *Apolonius and Silla* (1581), derived indirectly and
with variations from Bandello. Another source of the main plot
must have been the *Menaechmi* of Plautus, which presumably had
already contributed something to Gl'Ingannati, but affects the composition of *Twelfth Night* more directly by way of *The Comedy of
Errors*. In any case, Shakespeare's situations were part of the common stock of classical and medieval romance, as Manningham
saw at one of the first performances of *Twelfth Night*, when he
noted in his diary that it was "much like the Commedy of Errores,
or Menechmi in Plautus, but most like and neere to that in Italian
called *Inganni*" (one of the offshoots of Gl'Ingannati).

There are four essential characters common to Gl'Ingannati,
Bandello, Riche, and Shakespeare; namely, a lover, a heroine in
his service disguised as a page, her twin brother (who at first has
disappeared), and a second heroine. The basic elements common
to all four plots are: the heroine's secret love for her master; her
employment as go-between, leading to the complication of a
cross-wooing; and a final solution by means of the unforeseen
arrival of the missing twin.

If Shakespeare knew Bandello or Gl'Ingannati, he altered their
material radically. The Italians both take the romance motif of a
heroine's constancy and love-service, set it in a realistic bourgeois
environment, and rationalize it with respectful irony. In Bandello,
the irony is severely rational—because it is a tale of love, "the
wonder ceases at once." In Gl'Ingannati, the tone is whimsical.
"Two lessons above all you will extract from this play," says the
Prologue: "how much chance and good fortune can do in matters
of love; and how much long patience is worth in such cases,
accompanied by good advice."[10] Both Italian authors give the
heroine a strong motive for assuming her disguise, in that the
lover has previously returned her affection, but has now forgotten her and turned elsewhere. Both provide her with a formidable
father in the background and a foster-mother like Juliet's Nurse,
who admonishes and helps her; and both credit her with the
intention of bilking her rival if she can. On the other side, they
both respect the code of courtly love to the extent of stressing the
lover's penitence at the end, and his recognition that he must

repay the heroine for her devotion. "I believe," he says in the play, "that this is certainly the will of God, who must have taken pity on this virtuous maiden and on my soul, that it should not go to perdition. . . ."[11]

Riche keeps this framework of sentiment, vulgarizes the narrative, and changes some of the material circumstances, generally in the direction of an Arcadian romance.

Shakespeare, for his part, changes the story fundamentally, broadening the interest and at the same time making the whole situation more romantically improbable, more melancholy at some points, more fantastic at others. He stiffens the heroine's loyalty, but deprives her of her original motive, her initiative, and her family. In place of these, he gives her the background of a vague "Messaline" and a romantic shipwreck, for which he may have taken a hint, but no more, from the episode of the shipwreck in Riche. Shakespeare's Viola, then, is a more romantic heroine than the rest, and the only one to fall in love *after* assuming her disguise. At the same time, however, Shakespeare enlarges the role of her twin brother and gives unprecedented weight to coincidence in the dénouement, which in both Italian stories is brought about more rationally, by the deliberate action of the heroine and her nurse; so that Shakespeare's Viola is also unique in that her happiness is due to "good fortune" more than "long patience," and to "good advice" not at all.

In his exposition, therefore, Shakespeare sketches a situation from romance in place of a logical intrigue. But the purpose, or at any rate, the effect, of his plan is to shift attention at the outset from the circumstances of the love story to the sentiments as such, especially in their more mysterious and irrational aspects. Shakespeare may have taken hints, for Orsino and Olivia, from his predecessors' comments on the "error" of "following them that fly from us." But however that may be, his comedy now consists in the triumph of natural love over affectation and melancholy. And, taken together, the leading characters in *Twelfth Night* form the most subtle portrayal of the psychology of love that Shakespeare had yet drawn.

Viola's love is fresh and direct, and gathers strength as the play advances. When she first appears, Viola mourns her brother, like Olivia, and by choice would join Olivia in her seclusion:

> O, that I serv'd that lady,
> And might not be deliver'd to the world,
> Till I had made mine own occasion mellow,
> What my estate is.
>
> (I.ii.40)

Shakespeare makes the most here of the vagueness surrounding
Viola; she seems the child of the sea, and of time. But even when
her feelings and her problem have become distinct she still commits herself to "time" with a gentle air of detachment:

> What will become of this? As I am a man,
> My state is desperate for my master's love;
> As I am a woman,—now alas the day!—
> What thriftless sighs shall poor Olivia breathe!
> O time, thou must untangle this, not I,
> It is too hard a knot for me t'untie.
>
> (II.ii.37)

She has none of the vehement determination of the Italian
heroines,[12] and, though nimble-witted, she is less resourceful and
high-spirited than Rosalind. She foreshadows Perdita and Miranda in the romantically adolescent quality of her part.

There are stronger colors than this in Viola, admittedly. Before she appears on the stage, Orsino has spoken of the capacity
for love inherent in a woman's devoted sorrow for her brother;
and in two scenes in the middle of the play Viola herself speaks in
more passionate terms. But in both cases her own feeling seems
muffled or distorted, since she is acting a part, and in both cases
her tone is distinctly theatrical. She tells Olivia how, if she were
Orsino, she would

> Write loyal cantons of contemned love,
> And sing them loud even in the dead of night;
> Holla your name to the reverberate hills,
> And make the babbling gossip of the air
> Cry out "Olivia";
>
> (I.v.279)

she tells Orsino, on the other hand, that her imaginary sister

> never told her love,
> But let concealment, like a worm i'the bud
> Feed on her damask cheek;—
>
> (II.iv.III)

—in each case, with an overtone of romantic excess. She does not speak out in her own voice, therefore, until the later scenes, when the more vigorous (and more artificial) emotions of the older pair have had full play. Meanwhile, the hints of excess in her two fictitious declarations of love reflect on the others as well as herself: she speaks for Orsino in the spirit of his injunction to "be clamorous, and leap all civil bounds"; while her image of repressed desire could apply to Olivia. Her own development in the comedy is closely attuned to the others'.

Shakespeare begins the play with Orsino. He follows Riche in making the lover in his comedy a duke (not, as with the Italians, a citizen), who has been a warrior but has now "become a scholar in love's school."[13] Orsino suffers from the melancholy proper to courtly and "heroical" love; and Shakespeare fixes attention on his passion, which is more violent and "fantastical" than in the other versions of the story, by keeping Orsino inactive in his court to dramatize his own feelings like Richard II. Unlike the Italian lovers, he has not been fickle, yet changefulness is the very essence of his condition. He twice calls for music in the play, but there is no harmony in himself. Within a few lines, he countermands the first order, to apostrophize the spirit of love:

> Enough, no more!
> 'Tis not so sweet now as it was before.
> O spirit of love, how quick and fresh art thou,
> That, notwithstanding thy capacity
> Receiveth as the sea, nought enters there,
> Of what validity and pitch soe'er,
> But falls into abatement and low price,
> Even in a minute: so full of shapes is fancy
> That it alone is high fantastical.
>
> (I.i.7)

This apostrophe carries opposing meanings. "Quick" and "fresh," coming after "sicken" a few lines before, imply the vigor of life, but they also prolong the grosser sense of "appetite" and "surfeiting." The sea image glorifies Orsino's "spirit of love" and, in relation to the drama as a whole, it prepares the way for the sea-change that comes to Viola and Sebastian; but it also leads on to the image of Sir Toby "drowned" in drink (I.v.135). And Orsino's most striking metaphors here, those of sinking and "low price," suggest that what the speaker largely feels is chill and dismay. Nothing has any value by comparison with love; but also, nothing has any lasting, intrinsic value for a lover. Later, referring to the sea-fight, Orsino utters a similar paradox when he describes the "fame and honour" Antonio had won in "a bawbling vessel . . . For shallow draught and bulk unprizable" (V.i.52). But there, the paradox enhances Antonio's courage; here, it is depressing.[14] For Orsino, the only constant feature of love is instability. He tells Viola (II.iv.17) that all true lovers are

> Unstaid and skittish in all motions else
> Save in the constant image of the creature
> That is beloved;

a moment later, it is the "image" that changes—

> For, boy, however we do praise ourselves,
> Our fancies are more giddy and unfirm,
> More longing, wavering, sooner lost and worn
> Than women's are;—

and then, as he thinks of Olivia, it is the woman's "appetite," not the man's, that can "suffer surfeit, cloyment, and revolt" (II.iv.98). Feste sketches the life of such a lover with fitting ambiguity: "I would have men of such constancy put to sea, that their business might be every thing and their intent every where; for that's it that always makes a good voyage of nothing" (II.iv.75); they dissipate their advantages and can be satisfied with illusions. By its very nature, then, Orsino's love for Olivia is self-destructive, subject to time and change. Although, or rather, because, it is "all as hungry as the sea," it is impossible to satisfy. And it seems almost without an object, or incommensurate with any object, a "monstrosity" in the same sense as Troilus' love for Cressida, in its grasping after the infinite.

Moreover, Orsino's "spirit of love" seems something outside the rest of his personality, a tyrant from whom he longs to escape. His desires pursue him "like fell and cruel hounds." He wants music to diminish his passion, to relieve it with the thought of death. And when at last he confronts Olivia, something like hatred bursts through his conventional phrases of love-homage: "yond same sovereign cruelty" (II.iv) is now (V.i) a "perverse," "uncivil lady," "ingrate and unauspicious," "the marble-breasted tyrant." In his jealous rage he feels himself "at point of death":

Why should I not, had I the heart to do it,
Like to the Egyptian thief at point of death,
Kill what I love? a savage jealousy
That sometime savours nobly.

(V.i.115)

In all this, however, there is as much injured vanity as anything
else. His "fancy" is at the point of dying, not his heart; and it is
fully consistent with his character that he can swerve almost at
once to Viola, gratified and relieved by the surprise of her identity
and the full disclosure of her devotion to himself. His emotions,
then, give a powerful upsurge to the play, but they are kept
within the bounds of comedy. His real "error," in Shakespeare, is
that he only imagines himself to be pursuing love. Olivia's, correspondingly, is that she only imagines herself to be flying from it.

With Olivia, even more than with Orsino, Shakespeare di-
verges from his possible sources, making her a much more prominent and interesting character than her prototypes. In the Italian
stories, the second heroine is heiress to a wealthy old dotard, is
kept out of sight most of the time, and is treated with ribald irony
for her amorous forwardness. In *Apolonius and Silla*, she is a
wealthy widow. In all three, she is considered only as rival and
pendant to the Viola-heroine. Shakespeare, however, makes her a
virgin, psychologically an elder sister to Viola, and better able to
sustain the comedy of awakening desire. At the same time, she is
the mistress of a noble household, and hence the focus of the sub-
plot as well as the main plot.[15] When she first appears, she can
rebuke Malvolio with aristocratic courtesy (I.v.94): "To be generous, guiltless, and of free disposition, is to take those things for
bird-bolts that you deem cannon-bullets." But Olivia, like Orsino—like Malvolio, even—suffers from ignorance of herself, and
must be cured of affectation; as Sebastian says (V.i.262), "nature
to her bias drew in that."

Her vow of mourning has a tinge of the same aristocratic
extravagance as Orsino's "spirit of love." Orsino compares her to
an angry Diana; but then there follows at once the account of her
vow, which already begins to disclose the comic, unseasonable
side of her assumed coldness:

The element itself, till seven years' heat,
Shall not behold her face at ample view;

> But, like a cloistress, she will veiled walk,
> And water once a day her chamber round
> With eye-offending brine: all this to season
> A brother's dead love, which she would keep fresh
> And lasting in her sad remembrance.
>
> (I.i.25)

Olivia is to be rescued from her cloister (like Diana's priestess in *The Comedy of Errors* or Hermia in *A Midsummer Night's Dream*[16]) and exposed to the sunshine. Feste warns her, in gentle mockery, that she is a "fool"; the hood does not make the monk, and "as there is no true cuckold but calamity, so beauty's a flower" (I.v). She is obliged to unveil her beauty, and has natural vanity enough to claim that "'twill endure wind and weather" (I.v.246); and Viola's speech, which stirs her heart, is also a form of comic retribution, hollaing her name to "the reverberate hills" and "the babling gossip of the air"—

> O, you should not rest
> Between the elements of air and earth,
> But you should pity me.
>
> (I.v.281)

"Element" is made one of the comic catchwords of the play.[17]

The comic reversal of Olivia's attitude culminates in her declaration of love to Viola, the most delicate and yet impressive speech in the play (III.i.150). It is now Olivia's turn to plead against "scorn," to "unclasp the book of her secret soul" to Viola[18]—and, equally, to herself. After two lines, she turns to the same verse form of impersonal, or extra-personal, "sentences" in rhyme that Shakespeare gives to other heroines at their moment of truth:

> O, what a deal of scorn looks beautiful
> In the contempt and anger of his lip!
> A murd'rous guilt shows not itself more soon
> Than love that would seem hid: love's night is noon.
> Cesario, by the roses of the spring,
> By maidhood, honour, truth, and every thing,
> I love thee so, that, maugre all thy pride,
> Nor wit nor reason can my passion hide.
> Do not extort thy reasons from this clause,
> For that I woo, thou therefore hast no cause;

> But rather reason thus with reason fetter,
> Love sought is good, but given unsought is better.

Having already thrown off her original veil, Olivia now breaks
through the concealments of her pride, her modesty, and her
feminine "wit." Her speech is mainly a vehement persuasion to
love, urged "by the roses of the spring."[19] Yet she keeps her
dignity, and keeps it all the more in view of the secondary meaning latent in her words, her timid fear that Cesario's scorn is not
the disdain of rejection at all but the scorn of conquest. Logically,
indeed, her first rhyming couplet implies just this, implies that his
cruel looks are the signs of a guilty lust rising to the surface; and
this implication is carried on as she speaks of his "pride" (with its
hint of sexual desire[20]), and into her last lines, with their covert
pleading not to "extort" a callous advantage from her confession.
But in either case—whatever Cesario's intentions—love now appears to Olivia as a startling paradox: guilty, even murderous, an
irruption of misrule; and at the same time irrepressible, fettering
reason, and creating its own light out of darkness. And, in either
case, the conclusion to her perplexities is a plain one—"Love
sought is good, but given unsought is better." This is Shakespeare's departure from the moral argument of his predecessors,[21] and it marks the turning-point of *Twelfth Night*.

There is still a trace of irony attaching to Olivia, in that her
wooing is addressed to another woman and has been parodied
beforehand in Maria's forged love-letter (II.v). And this irony
pursues her to the end, even in her marriage, when once again
she tries, and fails, "To keep in darkness what occasion now
Reveals before 'tis ripe" (V.i.151). But from the point of her
declaration to Viola, the way is clear for the resolution of the
whole comedy on the plane of sentiment. In terms of sentiment,
she has justified her gift of love to a stranger. She is soon
completely sure of herself, and in the later scenes she handles Sir
Toby, Orsino, and Cesario-Sebastian with brusque decision;
while her demon of austerity is cast out through Malvolio. The
main action of *Twelfth Night*, then, is planned with a suggestive
likeness to a revel, in which Olivia is masked, Orsino's part
is "giddy" and "fantastical," Viola-Sebastian is the mysterious
stranger—less of a character and more of a poetic symbol than

the others—and in the end, as Feste says of his own "interlude" with Malvolio, "the whirligig of time brings in his revenges."

Although Olivia's declaration forms the crisis of the main action, the resolution of the plot has still to be worked out. And here Shakespeare departs in a new way from his predecessors. Shakespeare's Sebastian, by character and adventures, has little in common with the brother in *Gl'Ingannati*, and still less with Silla's brother in Riche; but nearly everything in common—as Manningham presumably noticed—with the visiting brother in Plautus, Menaechmus of Syracuse. And Antonio's part in the plot (though not his character) is largely that of Menaechmus' slave in Plautus, while his emotional role stems from the Aegeon story that Shakespeare himself had already added to *Menaechmi* in *The Comedy of Errors*. These Plautine elements in the brother's story have been altered in *Gl'Ingannati* and dropped from, or camouflaged in, *Apolonius and Silla*. Whichever of the latter Shakespeare used for Viola, therefore, he deliberately reverted to Plautus for Sebastian, sometimes drawing on his own elaborations in *The Comedy of Errors*, but mainly going back directly to the original.[22]

Hence the second half of *Twelfth Night* is largely more farcical than its predecessors, whereas the first half had been, in a sense, more romantic. Shakespeare thus provides a telling finale, proper, as Dr. Johnson observes, to the stage. But he does much more than this. His farcical dénouement gives tangible shape to the notion of misrule inherent in his romantic exposition. Faults of judgment in the first part of *Twelfth Night* are answered with mistakes of identity in the second, while the action swirls to a joyful ending through a crescendo of errors. And by the same manoeuvre, Shakespeare charges his romance with a new emotional significance, bringing it nearer to tragedy.

How are Viola and Olivia to be freed? In *Apolonius and Silla*, the widow, pregnant after her welcome to Silla's brother, demands justice of the disguised heroine, thus forcing her to reveal herself and clearing the way for her marriage to the duke. Only when the rumor of this wedding has spread abroad does the wandering brother return to the scene and espouse the widow. In the Italian stories, the heroine reaches an understanding with her master by her own devices and the aid of her nurse, without any kind of help from the arrival of her brother; and this is a logical solution, since the heroine's love-service is the clear center of interest. But Shakespeare has been more broadly concerned with love as a force in life as a whole. He has shifted the emphasis to the two older lovers, keeping Viola's share of passion in reserve. And even after the crisis, he continues to withhold the initiative the Italians had given her. Shakespeare is alone in making the heroine reveal herself *after* her brother's marriage with the second heroine, as a consequence of it. And the whole Plautine sequence in *Twelfth Night* is designed to lead to this conclusion. Hence, while the first half of Shakespeare's comedy dwells on self-deception in love, the second half stresses the benevolent irony of fate.

In the early scenes, fate appears to the speakers as an overriding power which is nevertheless obscurely rooted in their own desires (the obverse, that is, to Orsino's "spirit of love," which springs from himself, yet seems to dominate him from without).[23] Thus, Viola trusts herself to "time"; Olivia, falling in love, cries, "Fate, show thy force: ourselves we do not owe"; and the letter forged in her name yields an echo to her words: "Thy Fates open their hands; let thy blood and spirit embrace them."[24] Antonio and Sebastian strengthen this motif and clarify it.

Antonio stands for an absolute devotion that is ultimately grounded on fate; he is the embodiment of Olivia's discovery, and his speeches on this theme are interwoven with hers. Shortly after her first lines about fate—and chiming with them—comes his declaration to Sebastian (II.i.47):

> But, come what may, I do adore thee so,
> That danger shall seem sport, and I will go;

and after her cry that love should be a gift, he tells Sebastian in more positive terms:

> I could not stay behind you: my desire,
> More sharp than filed steel, did spur me forth.

> > (III.iii.4)

In the last scene, again, he proclaims to Orsino—

> A witchcraft drew me hither:
> That most ingrateful boy there by your side,
> From the rude sea's enrag'd and foamy mouth
> Did I redeem.

> > (V.i.74)

The resonant sea-image of destiny here dominates the bewildered tone still appropriate, at this point, to a comedy of errors.[25]

Sebastian's part runs parallel with this. When he first appears (II.i), he feels the same melancholy as his sister, and shows a similar vague self-abandonment in his aims: "My determinate voyage is mere extravagancy." But a stronger impression of him has been given already by the Captain, in the outstanding speech of Viola's first scene:

> I saw your brother,
> Most provident in peril, bind himself,
> Courage and hope both teaching him the practice,
> To a strong mast that lived upon the sea;
> Where, like Arion on the dolphin's back,
> I saw him hold acquaintance with the waves
> So long as I could see.

The Captain has told Viola to "comfort [herself] with chance"; Sebastian is "provident in peril," on friendly terms with destiny. When he bobs up resurrected at the end, accordingly, he does precisely what Malvolio had been advised to do, grasps the hands of the Fates and lets himself float with "the stream," with "this accident and flood of fortune" (IV.i.62, IV.iii.11).[26] By the same turn of mind, moreover, he imparts to the dénouement a tone as of clarity following illusion, of an awakening like the end of *A Midsummer Night's Dream*:

> Or I am mad, or else this is a dream. . . .
>
> (IV.i.63)

> This is the air; that is the glorious sun;
> This pearl she gave me, I do feel't and see't;
> And though 'tis wonder that enwraps me thus,
> Yet 'tis not madness. . . .
>
> (IV.iii.1)

"Mad" the lady may appear; but Sebastian—like Olivia before him, except that he does it in all coolness—is ready to "wrangle with his reason" and welcome the gift of love. The comedy of errors in which he figures is thus both counterpart and solution to the initial comedy of sentiment. Riche had called his love-story the work of "Dame Error"; Shakespeare, in effect, takes the hint, and goes back to Plautus.

Having planned his dénouement on these lines, moreover, Shakespeare goes further, adding a superb variation on his Plautine theme in the farcical scene leading up to Viola's meeting with Antonio (II.iv). This scene as a whole, with its rapid changes of mood and action, from Olivia to the sub-plot and back towards Sebastian, braces together the whole comic design. It brings to a climax the misrule, farcical humours, and simulated emotions of the play—with Olivia confessing "madness," Sir Toby triumphant, Malvolio *in excelsis* ("Jove, not I, is the doer of this . . ."), Sir Andrew allegedly "bloody as the hunter,"[27] and Viola, after her unavoidable coldness to Olivia, submitted for the first time to the laughable consequences of her change of sex. And the duel with its sequel perfect this comic catharsis. This duel, or what Sir Toby and Fabian make of it, bears a strong affinity to the sword dances and Mummers' play combats of a season of misrule; it becomes another encounter between St. George and Captain Slasher, the Turkish Knight. One champion is "a devil in private brawl: souls and bodies hath he divorced three"; the other is "a very devil, . . . a firago. . . . He gives me the stuck-in with such a mortal motion that it is inevitable"—and "they say he has been fencer to the Sophy." Now in one sense the duel and what follows are superfluous to the main action, since it is not strictly necessary for Viola to meet Antonio, or to meet him in this way. But in effect this episode of misrule[28] contains the principal conflict between the serious and the ludicrous forces in the play; it prepares emotionally for the resurrection of Sebastian; and, by a further swerve of constructive irony, the additional, gratuitous comedy of errors involving Antonio gives new force to the main theme of the romance.

As it concerns Viola, the dialogue here restores the balance in favor of her character, in that her generosity and her lines against "ingratitude" prepare the audience for her culminating gesture of self-sacrifice in the last act. But, more than this, Antonio's speeches stress the paradox of love that has been gathering force through the play:

> *Antonio:* Let me speak a little. This youth that you see here
> I snatch'd one half out of the jaws of death,
> Reliev'd him with such sanctity of love,

> And to his image, which methought did promise
> Most venerable worth, did I devotion.
> *Officer:* What's that to us? The time goes by: away!
> *Antonio:* But, O, how vile an idol proves this god.
> Thou hast, Sebastian, done good feature shame.
> In nature there's no blemish but the mind;
> None can be call'd deform'd but the unkind:
> Virtue is beauty, but the beauteous evil
> Are empty trunks o'erflourished by the devil.
> *Officer:* The man grows mad: away with him! . . .
>
> (III.iv.372)

It is in keeping with the comedy of errors that Antonio here has mistaken his man, to the point of seeming "mad," that Viola, happy to hear of her brother again, promptly forgets him—as Sir Toby notices (III.iv.400)—and that Antonio, as it turns out, should help Sebastian most effectively by so being forgotten. But this same quirk of fate brings the mood of the play dangerously near the confines of tragedy. The comedy has no answer to his problem of sincere devotion given to a false idol.[29]

Antonio stands outside the main sphere of the comedy. He belongs to the world of merchants, law, and sea-battles, not the world of courtly love. His love for Sebastian is irrational, or beyond reason, and his danger in Orsino's domains is due, similarly, to irrational persistence in an old dispute (III.iii.30–37). But he gives himself completely to his principles, more seriously than anyone else in the play, and tries to live them out as rationally as he can. In contrast to the lovers (except possibly Viola), he is not satisfied with truth of feeling, but demands some more objective standard of values; in his world, law and "time" mean something external, and harder than the unfolding of natural instinct. His problems are appropriate to *Troilus* or *Hamlet*. In one way, therefore, he marks a limit to festivity. Nevertheless, precisely because he takes himself so seriously, he helps to keep the comic balance of the play.

The comedy of errors in the main plot, the element of mummery and misrule, implies a comment on the serious follies of love, and brings a corrective to them. In the sub-plot (or-plots)—his addition to the Viola story—Shakespeare makes this corrective explicit and prepares for the festive atmosphere at the end.

"What a plague means my niece, to take the death of her brother thus? I am sure care's an enemy to life. . . ." "Does not our lives consist of the four elements?—Faith, so they say; but I think it rather consists of eating and drinking." Sir Toby, Maria, Feste, Fabian stand for conviviality and the enjoyment of life, as opposed to the melancholy of romance.

At the same time, however, the sub-plot action reproduces the main action like a comic mirror-image, and the two of them are joined to form a single symmetrical pattern of errors in criss-cross. Shakespeare had attempted a similar pattern before, in *The Comedy of Errors, A Midsummer Night's Dream*, and *Much Ado*, for example, but nowhere else does he bring it off so lightly and ingeniously.

In the main plot there is a lover who pursues love and a lady who tries to hide from it. In the sub-plot there is Malvolio, who pursues love, and Sir Toby, who prefers drinking. Olivia and Sir Toby are "consanguineous" but of opposite tempers; the other two disturb both of them. On their side, Orsino and Malvolio are both self-centered, but one neglects "state" and the other affects it; however, one is a lover who likes solitude, the other a solitary who turns to love. Both imagine they are in love with Olivia, while one is really fired by a forged letter, and the other is blind to the wife in front of his eyes. In the upshot, Orsino unwittingly helps to find a husband for Olivia, and Malvolio, a wife for Sir Toby. At the beginning of the comedy, Olivia had mourned a brother, while Orsino resented it; at the end, she finds a brother again, in Orsino himself.

Between Orsino and Olivia come the twins, Viola-Sebastian, opposite and indistinguishable. Between Malvolio and Sir Toby comes Maria, the "Penthesilia" who forges a false identity. The twins are heirs to fortune, unsuspecting and unambitious; Maria is an intriguer, who signs herself "The Fortunate-Unhappy." In their first scene together, Sir Andrew "accosts," "woos" and "assails" Maria, who drops his hand; Antonio likewise accosts, woos, and assails Viola and Sebastian, who lose or ignore him. The symmetrical pattern is completed at the mid-point of the play, when Sir Andrew and Antonio confront each other with drawn swords. This encounter between the romantic and the comic figures is twice repeated, and on the last occasion it seems to be

Viola's double who is the aggressor (V.i.178–180). Hence, although Sir Andrew and Antonio do not know each other or why
they are quarrelling, they co-operate to bring about an unexpected result; Sir Andrew, to provide a wife for Sebastian, and
Antonio, to provide a husband for Maria.

This dance of changed partners and reversed fortunes is much
more complicated than anything in *Gl'Ingannati*. Shakespeare devises it partly by carrying the Plautine themes of twinship and of
the lost being found again, or brought back to life, much farther
than the Italian had gone; and partly by pursuing his own allied
and festive theme of a Twelfth Night mask of misrule. By this
means, he laces sub-plot and main plot together in a single intri-
cate design.

The interest of the sub-plot is more varied, moreover, and its
links with the main plot are more complex, than a bare summary
of the action can indicate. In relation to the main plot, the comic
figures are somewhat like scapegoats; they reflect the humours of
Orsino and Olivia in caricature and through them these humours
are purged away. Secondly, the sub-plot is a Feast of Fools,[30]
containing its own satire of humours in Malvolio and Sir Andrew.
And, from another point of view, Sir Toby's "uncivil rule" is
complementary to the problem of "time" in the main plot.

Besides Malvolio, Sir Toby and Sir Andrew are to some extent
parodies of Orsino. One will drink Olivia's health till he is
"drowned" or "his brains turn o' the toe like a parish-top"; the
other is a model of gentlemanly indecision, hopes to woo Olivia
without speaking to her, and attacks Viola from jealousy. The
strains of unconscious parody in the sub-plot help to amplify the
general theme of delusion and error.

On Olivia's side, moreover, the disorder in her household is a
direct reaction to her attitude at the beginning of the play.[31]
Malvolio affects a grave austerity to please her, but the instincts
are in revolt. Sir Toby redoubles the clamor of love for her and
personifies her neglect of time and the reproach of the clock
(III.i.135). Sir Andrew, a fool, helps to find her a husband. In
Malvolio's "madness" she comes to see a reflection of her own
(III.iv.15), and at the end he takes her place in cloistered darkness.

In addition, the comic dialogue echoes the thought of the
serious characters and twists it into fantastic shapes. To the

serious actors, life is a sea-voyage: the comic actors deal with journeys more specific, bizarre, and adventurous than theirs, ranging in time from when "Noah was a sailor" to the publishing of "the new map with the augmentation of the Indies," and from the Barents Sea to the gates of Tartar or the equinoctial of Queubus. The serious actors scrutinize a fate which might be pagan in its religious coloring: the comic speakers, for their part, are orthodox Christians, and their dialogue is peppered with biblical and ecclesiastical references. Sir Toby, for instance, "defies lechery" and counts on "faith"; Sir Andrew plumes himself on having "no more wit than a Christian or an ordinary man has," and would beat Malvolio for no "exquisite reason" save that of thinking him a puritan,[32] the duel scene and the madness scenes are full of "devils." In part, these ecclesiastical jokes reinforce the suggestion of Twelfth Night foolery and of mock sermons like Erasmus' sermon of Folly; from this aspect, they lead up to Feste's interlude of Sir Topas. But in part, too, their tone of moral security to the degree of smugness gives a counterweight to the emotions of the serious actors.

Moreover, Sir Andrew and Sir Toby are both alike in feeling very sure of their ideal place in the scheme of things. They are contrasted as shrewd and fatuous, parasite and gull, Carnival and Lent; but they are both, in their differing ways, "sots," and both gentlemen.[33] Their conversation is a handbook to courtesy. And while Sir Andrew is an oafish squire, who will "have but a year in all these ducats," Sir Toby is a degenerate knight, who will not "confine himself within the modest limits of order" and, possessed of the rudiments of good breeding, delights in turning them upside-down. He is repeatedly called "uncivil" (II.iii.125, III.iv.265, Iv.i.55), and his merry-making is out of time and season. He tells Malvolio, "We did keep time, sir, in our catches"; but when at the end he leaves the stage with a broken head, driving Sir Andrew off before him, he is abusing the surgeon, on the lines of the same pun, for "a drunken rogue" whose eyes are "set at eight." Despite his resemblance to Falstaff, Sir Toby has a smaller mind, and this shows itself in his complacency with his position in Olivia's household.

Malvolio is a more complex and formidable character. Evidently Maria's "good practise" on this overweening steward was the distinctive attraction of *Twelfth Night* to Stuart audiences; but that does not mean (as some critics would have it, reacting against Lamb[34]) that Malvolio is presented as a contemptible butt. An audience is more likely to enjoy and remember the humiliation of someone who in real life would be feared than the humiliation of a mere impostor like Parolles. Malvolio is neither a puritan nor an upstart, though he has qualities in common with both. Olivia and Viola call him a "gentleman" (V.i.279,282), as the steward of a countess's household no doubt would be, and in seeking to repress disorders he is simply carrying out the duties of his office:

> Have you no wit, manners, nor honesty, but to gabble like tinkers at this time of night? Do ye make an alehouse of my lady's house, that ye squeak out your coziers' catches without any mitigation or remorse of voice? Is there no respect of place, persons, nor time in you?
>
> (II.iii.89)

These early speeches to Sir Toby have a firm ring about them that explains Olivia's confidence in Malvolio, without as yet disclosing the "politic" affectation that Maria sees in him. On the other hand, his principle of degree and order is simply a mask for his pride. He is "sick of self-love," unable to live spontaneously as one of a community, as is hinted from the outset by his recoil from the sociable side of the jester's art—an office that also requires the understanding of place, persons, and time. And even before finding Maria's letter, he shows the self-ignorance of a divided personality in the day-dream he weaves about himself and Olivia, indulging his "humour of state." Nevertheless, when his humour has been mocked to the full, Shakespeare still makes him protest that he "thinks nobly of the soul," and he remains a force to be reckoned with right to the end. With his unconscious hypocrisy in the exercise of power and his rankling sense of injustice, he comes midway between Shylock and the Angelo of *Measure for Measure*.

Sir Toby, Sir Andrew and Malvolio—all three—are striving to be something false, whether novel or antiquated, which is out of place in a healthy community; they are a would-be retainer, a would-be gallant, a would-be "politician." But the conflict over revelry between Malvolio and Sir Toby is a conflict of two opposed reactions towards changing social and economic conditions.

In Malvolio's eyes, Sir Toby "wastes the treasure of his time." So he does; and so, in their ways, do Olivia and Orsino. A natural way of living, Shakespeare seems to imply, must observe impersonal factors such as time as well as the healthy gratification of instinct—and in the last resort, the two may be incompatible with each other. Hence Malvolio in the end is neither crushed nor pacified. He belongs, like Antonio, to the world of law and business, outside the festive circle of the play. Both are imprisoned for a while by the others. They stand for two extremes of self-sacrifice and self-love, but they share a rigid belief in principle. And neither can be fully assimilated into the comedy.

There are discordant strains, then, in the harmony of *Twelfth Night*—strains of melancholy and of something harsher. As far as any one actor can resolve them, this task falls to Feste.

Feste is not only the most fully portrayed of Shakespeare's clowns, he is also the most agile-minded of them. He has fewer set pieces than Touchstone and fewer proverbs than the Fool in *Lear*. He is proud of his professional skill—"better a witty fool than a foolish wit"—but he wields it lightly, in darting paradoxes; he is a "corrupter of words." Yet, besides being exceptionally imaginative and sophisticated, he is exceptionally given to scrounging for tips. This trait is consistent with the traditional aspect of his role, especially as the fool in a feast of misrule, but it helps to make him more like a real character and less like a stage type.

This money-sense of Feste and his awareness of his social status bring him within the conflict of ideas affecting the other actors. Although he depends for his living on other people's pleasure, and can sing to any tune—"a love-song or a song of good life"—Feste is neither a servile entertainer nor an advocate of go-as-you-please. On the contrary, he is a moralist with a strong bent towards scepticism. "As there is no true cuckold but calamity, so beauty's a flower. . . . Truly, sir, and pleasure will be paid, one time or another. . . . The whirligig of time brings in his revenges:" one factor will always cancel another. As against Malvolio, he belittles the soul; but he shows hardly any more confidence in the survival-value of folly, and marriage is the only form of it he recommends. For Feste himself could very easily belong to the ship of fools he designates for Orsino, having his business and intent everywhere and making "a good voyage of nothing." (The same thought is present when he tells Viola that foolery "does walk about the orb like the sun; it shines every where.") There is a persistent hint, then, that his enigmas glance at himself as well as others, and that he feels his own position to be insecure. And it is consistent with this that he should be the only character in Shakespeare to take pleasure, or refuge, in fantasies of pure nonsense: "as the old hermit of Prague, that never saw pen and ink, very wittily said to a niece of King Gorboduc, 'That that is is.'" It is impossible to go further than a non-existent hermit of Prague.

Feste is not the ringleader in *Twelfth Night*, nor is he exactly the play's philosopher. He is cut off from an independent life of his own by his traditional role in reality and on the stage, and what he sees at the bottom of the well is "nothing." He knows that without festivity he is nothing; and he knows, in his epilogue, that misrule does not last, and that men shut their gates against toss-pots, lechers, knaves, and fools. A play is only a play, and no more. Yet it is precisely on this finely-poised balance of his that the whole play comes to rest. Orsino, Olivia, Viola, Sebastian, Sir Toby, Maria, Malvolio, Feste himself—nearly everyone in *Twelfth Night* acts a part in some sense, but Feste is the only one who takes this aspect of life for granted. The others commit errors and have divided emotions; but Feste can have no real emotions of his own, and may only live in his quibbles. Yet by virtue of this very disability, he sees the element of misrule in life more clearly than the rest, appreciating its value because he knows its limitations. A play to Feste may be only a play, but it is also the breath of life.

Feste is the principal link between the other characters in *Twelfth Night*. Unless Puck is counted, he is the only clown for whom Shakespeare provides an epilogue. And as it happens, his is the epilogue to the whole group of Shakespeare's romantic comedies.

APPENDIX

Shakespeare and Plautus: The Plautine motif of confused identities is present in *Gl'Ingannati*, and possibly in Riche. But a comparison of *TN* with *Menaechmi* and *CE* on one side, and with *Gl'Ingannati*, Bandello, and

Riche on the other makes it seem certain that Shakespeare was consciously borrowing from Plautus in planning Sebastian's role, at the same time, however, enlarging this borrowed material on the lines of *CE:*

(a) *Background:* In *Men.*, there are twin brothers, long separated and unknown to each other; their father is dead. In *CE*, they have been separated by a tempest; their father is alive. In both, one of the "lost" brothers hopes to find the other in the course of his travels. In *Gl'Ingannati* and Bandello, the twin brother has been lost since the sack of Rome in 1527; he comes expecting to find his father, still alive, and his sister. In Riche, the brother sets off in pursuit of his sister, who has followed the duke and has suffered shipwreck; their father is still alive. So far, *TN* might be a compound of all the others.

(b) *Sebastian:* In *Men.*, Menaechmus of Syracuse, searching for his brother, lands at Epidamnus with his slave. He is hot-tempered (Loeb ed., II.i.269)—a trait only emphasized here and in *TN*. Leaving his slave, he meets in turn a cook, a courtesan, and a parasite, who mistake him for his twin. He thinks them mad, or drunk, or dreaming (II.iii.373,395), but sleeps with the courtesan, accepts her gifts—a mantle and a bracelet—and makes off "while time and circumstance permit," thanking the gods for his unexpected luck (III.iii.551-3). He misses his slave, and gets involved in a squabble with his sister-in-law and her father, feigning madness to frighten them off. His doings react on his brother. Finally, the brothers meet, compare notes about their father, and recognize each other with the help of the slave.

Sebastian's actions follow exactly the same pattern. He appears in Illyria with a companion, then leaves him; he is going to the court, but has no definite goal since his twin sister has apparently died (II.i). Meeting his companion again, he says he wants to view "the reliques of this town"; they separate a second time, after making an appointment (III.iii). He then meets in turn a clown, a parasite (Sir Toby) and his friend, and a lady, who mistake him for his twin. He thinks they are mad, or that he is mad or else dreaming, fights the parasite and his friend, but accepts the lady's invitation to accompany her (IV.i). He has missed his companion, but accepts the lady's gift of a pearl, welcomes "this accident and flood of fortune," and agrees to marry her (IV.iii). Off-stage, he fights the parasite a second time (V.i.178-80). Meanwhile, his doings have reacted on his twin, partly through the agency of his companion. Finally, the twins meet, compare notes about their father, and recognize each other.

In *Gl'Ingannati*, the brother comes to Modena with a servant and a tutor, a pedant who describes the sights of the town in detail (III.i). He leaves them to go sight-seeing, meets the second heroine's maid, and agrees to visit the mistress, supposing her to be some courtesan (III.v). Then he meets her father and his own father, who take him to be his twin sister, dressed as a man; he calls them mad, and they lock him up with the second heroine (III.vii), whereupon he seduces her. He does not meet his twin sister until she is married.

In Bandello the only characters the brother meets at first are the second heroine and her maid; in Riche, only the second heroine.

With Sebastian, then, Shakespeare ignores Gl'Ingannati (except conceivably for the sight-seeing), and follows Plautus in detail. He had used much of this material before, in CE. But there he had introduced variations (e.g., the "lost" brother's business affairs and the character of Luciana); here he goes back directly to his source.

(c) *Messaline*. Apparently no editor of TN has explained satisfactorily why Shakespeare makes Sebastian come from "Messaline," "a town unknown to geography." Perhaps this is because they have concentrated unduly on the Italian background of TN; (cp. Draper, who suggests Manzolino, or "Mensoline," near Modena, pp. 262–263). But reference to Plautus offers a very likely solution. In *Men.*, II.i the slave asks Menaechmus of Syracuse how long he means to go on searching for his twin: "Istrians, Spaniards, *Massilians, Illyrians* (*Massiliensis, Hilurios*), the entire Adriatic, and foreign Greece and the whole coast of Italy—every section the sea washes—we've visited in our travels . . ." (Loeb ed., pp. 235–238). This scene corresponds to TN, II.i, where Sebastian mentions "Messaline," telling Antonio that his "determinate voyage is mere extravagancy" because his sister is drowned. Hence it seems almost certain that Shakespeare invented the name "Messaline," in connexion with Illyria, from a reminiscence of these lines of Plautus (where, in addition, the speaker's name is Messenio); (cp. *Times Lit. Supp.*, June 3, 1955). This suggests that the parallel between Sebastian and Menaechmus was clearly present to Shakespeare's mind from the beginning.

(d) *Antonio*. In *Men.*, the slave is a purse-bearer, warns Menaechmus against the dangers of Epidamnus, intervenes to save his master's twin from danger, is promised his liberty, has the promise withdrawn, and then has it renewed. Antonio's part corresponds to this closely. There is nothing like this in Gl'Ingannati, nor much in the Dromio of CE. On the other hand, Shakespeare seems to have taken some traits in Antonio from Aegeon in CE (cp. note 28, above).

(e) The *Captain* who comes on with Viola in TN, I.ii has only a minimal part as her confidant. In this, his only scene, his main speech concerns Sebastian; while the later news of his arrest at Malvolio's suit (V.i.276–278) recalls the legal business in CE, like the arrest of Antonio. He therefore belongs to Sebastian's part in the composition of TN, rather than Viola's. (There is a captain in *Apolonius and Silla*, but he tries to rape the heroine, and then disappears.)

(f) *Illyria*. The assumption that Shakespeare's knowledge of *Men.* played a large—and not merely an incidental—part in the composition of *TN* throws some further light on Shakespeare's methods of construction. In particular, it suggests why he set the play in "Illyria." On the face of it, there is no special reason for this choice of a setting, unless perhaps Viola's pun on "Elysium" when the place is first mentioned. Although the name has since acquired a romantic aura from the play itself, there is nothing specially Arcadian or Ruritanian about "Illyria" in *TN*, and no strong local color, as there is for Modena in *Gl'Ingannati*, or for Venice in Shakespeare's other plays. What there is, moreover, is slightly inconsistent; for Antonio's warning to Sebastian about the dangers of "these parts," which he says are "rough and inhospitable" (III.iii.8–11), is not exactly borne out by the rest of the play, and is vague in any case, so that it seems to belong to Antonio, not to Illyria. This speech can be traced back, however, to the more specific warning of the slave in *Men.* II.i.258–264, to the effect that Epidamnus is a town of "rakes, drinkers, sycophants and alluring harlots," owing its very name to the tricks it plays on strangers—and this (together with the way the warning is falsified) does correspond very closely to Illyria as Sebastian finds it. Further, Hotson points out that the real Illyria of Shakespeare's day was known for riotous behavior, drinking and piracy (p. 151). These touches account for the sea-fighting in *TN* (but not the tricks of fortune), and otherwise they match with Epidamnus; so that Epidamnus and the real country together furnish the sketchy local color of "Illyria" in *TN*. It looks, therefore, as if Shakespeare, having planned to modify the Viola story with the aid of Plautus, looked for a place-name that would fit the attributes he wanted, and chose "Illyria" accordingly. If so, his memory could have prompted him from the same line of *Men.* that yields the source of "Messaline."

(g) *Olivia's household*. Assuming that Shakespeare founded Illyria from Epidamnus, he would have looked to the mother-town for some of the inhabitants and their customs. There is a good deal of banqueting in Epidamnus, and some talk of law-suits. And there is one important character whom Shakespeare had not used already in *CE*. This is the parasite, Peniculus or "Brush," a greedy drinker and a schemer. He pushes himself on the courtesan's house, urges his patron to dance at one point (*Men.*, I.iii.197—cp. *TN*, I.iii.143), and elsewhere provokes Menaechmus of Syracuse. And he seems to be reincarnated in the person of Sir Toby.

Secondly, there are the episodes of feigned inspiration, or frenzy, in

Men., V, with a comic doctor and a scuffle over the wrong twin. Shakespeare had used these already in *CE*, IV.iv (cp. note 28, above), but there was no reason why he should not use them again. They could well have furnished hints for the duel scene with its "devils" in *TN* and the scene of Malvolio and Sir Topas.

Moreover, anyone approaching the Viola story by way of Plautus would be inclined to give more prominence to the second heroine (the supposed "courtesan" of the Italian tales) and her companions. And in fact, Olivia and her household, in their actions towards Sebastian, reproduce very closely the actions of the courtesan, her servants, and the parasite in *Men.*, without any hint of indebtedness to *Gl'Ingannati*, Riche, or the transformed Plautine incidents of *CE*. These considerations need not imply that Shakespeare imagined Olivia and her household simply as afterthoughts to the Plautine twin; but they do seem to suggest how, once he had begun thinking about the material in Plautus, the whole of his composition could have fallen into shape.

Finally, (h) *Errors and misrule*. The circumstances of the performance of *CE* at the Gray's Inn revels in 1594 could well have suggested to Shakespeare the plan of introducing a Plautine comedy of mistaken identity into a larger framework of misrule (cp. note 8, above). He had done something like this already in *The Shrew*, where the sub-plot is a comedy of changed identities borrowed from Ariosto, and the Framework story of Sly as a lord is an episode of misrule.

To sum up, it is plausible to reconstruct the composition of *TN* somewhat as follows. Reading the Viola story, in Riche or elsewhere, Shakespeare was struck by the notion of "error" implicit in "following them that fly from us," and this gave him the hint for Orsino and Olivia. Secondly, "error" suggested the role of Sebastian, with its Plautine farce and its romantic overtones of sea-adventure prolonged from *CE*. And the same notion of "error" also suggested the stage devices of misrule, prominent in the sub-plot of *TN* and latent in the whole play. Though it leaves much of the emotional content of *TN* untouched, this conjecture does seem to account for the way the whole stage design of the play holds so beautifully together.

NOTES

1. Karl F. Thompson, "Shakespeare's Romantic Comedies," *PMLA*, LXVII (1952); E. C. Pettet, *Shakespeare and the Romance Tradition* (1949), 122–132. "Tempests dissolved in music" in the phrase of G. Wilson Knight, *The Shakespearian Tempest* (1953 ed.), pp. 121–127.

2. This is the interpretation of John W. Draper, *The Twelfth Night of Shakespeare's Audience* (Stanford Univ. Press, 1950).

3. "Shakespearian comedy . . . speculates imaginatively on modes, not of preserving a good already reached, but of enlarging and extending the possibilities of this and other kinds of good." H. B. Charlton, *Shakespearian Comedy* (1938), pp. 277–278.

4. Enid Welsford, *The Fool* (1935), p. 251; cp. E. K. Chambers, *Mediaeval Stage* (1903), I, 403 n. Leslie Hotson gives further details connecting the play with the Feast of Mis-rule in *The First Night of Twelfth Night* (1954), ch. vii. To the various possible meanings of Malvolio's yellow stockings (Hotson, p. 113) it is worth adding that, according to Stubbes, yellow or green "or some other light wanton colour" was the livery of "my Lord of Mis-rule" in the parishes (*Anatomy of Abuses*, 1583: ed. Furnivall, p. 147). Stubbes is speaking of summer games, but misrule was not confined to Christmas—cp. *TN* (Arden edn.), III.iv.148: "More matter for a May morning."

5. P. Mueschke and J. Fleisher, "Jonsonian Elements in the Comic Underplot of *TN*," *PMLA*, XLVIII (1933).

6. "Ma come si dice che egli era innamorato, subito cessa l'ammirazione, perciò che questa passione amorosa è di troppo gran potere e fa far cose assai piú meravigliose e strabocchevoli di questa. Né crediate che per altro la fabulosa Grecia finga i dèi innamorati aver fatte tante pazzie vituperose . . . , se non per darci ad intendere che come l'uomo si lascia soggiogar ad amore . . . , egli può dir d'aver giocata e perduta la sua libertà, e che miracolo non è se poi fa mille errori!" Bandello, *Le Novelle*, II, xxxvi (ed. G. Brognoligo, Bari, 1911, III, 252).

7. Riche's *Apolonius and Silla* (ed. Morton Luce, The Shakespeare Classics, 1912), p. 53; cp. p. 52: "in all other things, wherein we show ourselves to be most drunken with this poisoned cup [of error], it is in our action of love; for the lover is so estranged from that is right, and wandereth so wide from the bounds of reason, that he is not able to deem white from black . . . ; but only led by the appetite of his own affections, and grounding them on the foolishness of his own fancies, will so settle his liking on such a one, as either by desert or unworthiness will merit rather to be loathed than loved." Contrasts between love and reason are prominent, again, in Erasmus' *In Praise of Folly* and Sidney's *Arcadia*, two likely sources of the general themes of *TN*. Bacon's essay "Of Love" comes nearer still to the subject-matter of Shakespeare's play, illustrating the tension of ideas there from a point of view almost directly opposite: "The stage is more beholding to love than the life of man; for as to the stage, love is ever matter of comedies, and now and then of tragedies; but

in life it doth much mischief, sometimes like a Siren, sometimes like a Fury. . . . Great spirits and great business do keep out this weak passion . . . ; for whosoever esteemeth too much of amorous affection, quitteth both riches and wisdom. This passion hath his floods in the very times of weakness, which are, great prosperity and great adversity . . . ; both which times kindle love, and make it more fervent, and therefore show it to be the child of folly." This essay could almost be a commentary on Malvolio, Orsino, Viola and Sebastian.

8. The idea of representing life as a festival of misrule was already implicit, of course, in the common notion that "all the world's a stage," and in the general Renaissance tradition of Folly, especially in Erasmus (cp. Welsford, pp. 236–242). Robert Armin, who acted Feste, may have helped to give point to the idea; in his *Neste of Ninnies* (1600–08; ed. J. P. Collier, 1842), he represents the World, sick of a surfeit of drink and revelling, being shown a pageant of fools, who are partly endearing and partly symbols of the World's vices (cp. Welsford, pp. 162–165, 284). Armin does not treat of love, but John Heywood's *Play of Love* (–1533) is a Christmas interlude consisting of debates on the "reasons" of love between Lover not Loved, Loved not Loving (the woman), Lover Loved, and Neither Lover nor Loved (the Vice). And much nearer to *TN* comes Jonson's *Cynthia's Revels; or, the Fountain of Self-Love* (1600). Moreover, Shakespeare himself is very likely to have remembered the suggestive episode of December 28, 1594, when the *Comedy of Errors* was performed in the "disordered" revels of Gray's Inn; "So that Night was begun, and continued to the end, in nothing but Confusion and Errors; whereupon, it was ever afterwards called, *The Night of Errors*. . . . We preferred Judgments . . . against a Sorcerer or Conjuror that was supposed to be the cause of that confused Inconvenience. . . . And Lastly, that he had foisted a Company of base and common Fellows, to make up our Disorders with a Play of Errors and Confusions; and that that Night had gained to us Discredit, and itself a Nickname of Errors" (*Gesta Grayorum*; E. K. Chambers, *Shakespeare*, Appendix, "Performances"). Lastly, Shakespeare uses the metaphor of life as a mask of misrule directly in *Troilus*, a play linked in several ways with *TN:* "Degree being vizarded,/The unworthiest shows as fairly in the mask" (I.iii.83).

9. This paragraph is based on Morton Luce's Arden ed. of *TN* (1906) and his ed. of Riche. Luce assembles parallels between *TN* and Riche, Bandello, and *Gl'Ingannati*, from which it seems very possible, though not certain, that Shakespeare knew any or all of the latter. Luce mentions, but does not examine, Shakespeare's debt to Plautus.

10. "Due ammaestramenti sopra tutto ne cavarete: quanto possa il caso e la buona fortuna nelle cosa d'amore; e quanto, in quella, vaglia una longa pazienzia accompagnata da buon consiglio" (ed. I. Sanesi, *Commedie del Cinquecento*, Bari, 1912, I, 316).

11. "Io credo che questa sia certamente volontá di Dio che abbia avuto pietá di questa virtuosa giovane e dell'anima mia; ch'ella non vada in perdizione. E però, madonna Lelia, . . . io non voglio altra moglie che vio . . ." (V, iii; ed. Sanesi, p. 393). Cp. Bandello, pp. 273–275; Richie, p. 82.

12. Cp. Lelia, in *Gl'Ingannati:* "O what a fate is mine! I love him who hates me, . . . I serve him who knows me not; and, worse still, I help him to love another . . . only in the hope of gratifying these eyes with seeing him, one day, in my own way." About her rival, she says: "I pretend not to want to love her, unless she makes Flamminio withdraw from his love to her; and I have already brought the affair to a conclusion . . ." (I.iii; pp. 322, 328). Bandello's heroine says: "I have done so much that I want to see the end of it, come what may. . . . Then God will help me, who knows my heart and knows I have only taken pains so as to have Lattanzio for a husband" (p. 262).

13. Riche, p. 64. Draper (ch. vi) argues that Orsino is meant as a wholly admirable or sympathetic character, and that *TN* is "a genial satire on the vulgar love of Malvolio and Sir Andrew in contrast to the refined passion of Orsino, Olivia, and Viola-Sebastian" (p. 131). As regards Orsino, Riche's mildly scoffing attitude to his ducal lover hardly bears this out; nor do the quotations that Draper brings forward from the psychologists, e.g., his apt quotation from Burton: "Love . . . rageth with all sorts and conditions of men, yet is most evident among such as are young and lusty, in the flower of their years, nobly descended, high fed, such as live idly, and at ease; and for that cause (which our Divines call burning lust) . . . this mad and beastly passion . . . is named by our Physicians *Heroical* Love, and a more honorable title put upon it, *amor nobilis*, . . . because Noble men and women make a common practice of it, and are so ordinarily affected with it" (Burton, pt.III.ii.I.2; Draper, p. 122). For similar reasons, it is difficult to accept Hotson's conjecture (ch. vi) that Orsino is meant for the visiting Virginio Orsino, Duke of Bracciano, and Olivia for the Virgin Queen; if Shakespeare intended flattery, it seems unlikely that he would have presented both characters in an ironic light.

14. Cp. Julina's speech in Riche, p. 66: ". . . men be of this condition, rather to desire those things which they cannot come by, than to

esteem or value of that which . . . liberally is offered unto them; but if the liberality of my proffer hath made to seem less the value of the thing that I meant to present, it is but in your own conceit. . . ." Shakespeare returns to the problems of value and the self-destruction of desire in *Hamlet* and *Troilus*. Orsino's "shapes" and "fancy" recall Theseus' lines in *MND*, V.i.4–22; and in *Henry IV, pt. 2*, Falstaff connects them with drink: "A good sherris-sack . . . ascends me into the brain; . . . makes it apprehensive, quick, forgetive, full of nimble, fiery, and delectable shapes . . ." (IV.iii.107). These are points of contact between Orsino and Sir Toby.

15. Cp. Draper, pp. 215–219.

16. Cp. *MND*, I.i.65–78 (". . . For aye to be in shady cloister mew'd"), and Portia, in *MV*, I.ii.112–114. In *The Comedy of Errors*, Shakespeare moves the scene from the Epidamnus of *Menaechmi* to Ephesus so as to make Aemilia the priestess, or "abbess," of Diana's temple there. Possibly he was turning to account the passage in *Miles Gloriosus*, where the courtesan pretends to give thanks to Diana of Ephesus for rescuing her from Neptune's blustering realm (Loeb ed., II.v.411ff; cp. Aegeon's narrative of the storm in *C.E.*, I.i, which has no equivalent in *Menaechmi*). But in any case, the motif of a woman rescued from imposed celibacy after a sea-adventure is an important part of what could be called Shakespeare's mythology—Wilson Knight's "tempest" theme; cp. Portia again, (*MV*, III.ii. 53–57), and, of course, Marina, Perdita and Miranda. (There are satiric references to a convent from which the heroine runs away in Bandello and *Gl'Ingannati*).

17. Cp. II.iii.10, III.i.62, III.iv.130. There are other echoes, mainly comic, of the theme of Olivia-cloister-moon at: I.ii.32 (gossip); I.iii.126–128 (Mistress Mall's curtained picture); I.v.20 (". . . let summer bear it out"); I.v.206 ("'tis not that time of moon with me"); II.iii.59, etc. ("rouse the night-owl in a catch"); II.iv.44 ("the knitters in the sun"); II.v.164 ("Daylight and champain discovers not more"); III.i.41 ("Foolry . . . does walk about the orb like the sun"); III.i.89 ("the heavens rain odours on you"); III.iv.58 ("midsummer madness'); IV.ii (Malvolio in darkness); IV.iii.I ("that is the glorious sun"); IV.iii.28–35 ("conceal it . . . heavens so shine"); V.i.151 ("To keep in darkness . . ."); V.i.295–9 (Feste shouting); V.i.346 ("Kept in a dark house, visited by the priest"); and "the wind and the rain" in Feste's epilogue.

18. Cp. Orsino, I.iv.13–14. For Olivia's use of rhyme here, cp. Beatrice (*Much Ado*, III.i.107), Helena (*All's Well*, I.i.223) and Cressida (*Troilus*, I.ii.307).

19. Cp. I.v.53 (". . . so beauty's a flower"), II.iv.38 ("For women are as roses . . ."), II.iv.112 ("concealment, like a worm i' the bud . . .").

20. Cp. Tarquin, in *Lucrece*, 432, and the setting there. It is worth noting that Olivia's seal is a "Lucrece" (II.v.96).

21. There is no real equivalent to this interview, or Olivia's share of it, in Shakespeare's likely sources, unless partly in Riche, p. 66 (quoted above, note 14. But cp. Pasquella, in *Gl'Ingannati*, II.iii, p. 339; and Luce, *TN*, p. 184, cites verbal parallels from Bandello for III.i.117 and 149). As to the moral argument of the tale, both the Italians and Riche dwell on the justice and reason of exchanging love for love— e.g., *Gl'Ingannati*, I.iii (quoted above, note 12), IV.ii (p. 349), V.ii (p. 390; the lover here decries "ingratitude," as in *TN*, III.iv.367), V.ii (quoted above, note 11); Bandello, 273–275. Further, Bandello's heroine tells her master that his sufferings in his second love are a just retribution for ingratitude in his first: "you have received the return (*contracambio*) you deserved, because if you had been so much loved by a girl as beautiful as you say, you have done endlessly wrong to leave her for this one, who is avenging her without knowing it. A lover wants to be loved, not to follow someone in flight (*Egli si vuol amar chi ama e non seguir chi se ne fugge*). Who knows if this beautiful girl is not still in love with you and living in the greatest misery for you?" (Bandello, pp. 265–266). As Luce points out (*TN*, p. 184), this dialogue as a whole may have suggested Viola's dialogue with Orsino in II.vi.90–120; but the notion of love is still an exchange, not a gift. Similarly, Riche, p. 53, stresses "desert," or reciprocity, as "the ground of reasonable love," and he echoes Bandello: "for to love them that hate us, to follow them that fly from us, . . . who will not confess this to be an erroneous love, neither grounded upon wit nor reason?" Olivia's speech could almost be a reply to this.

22. See appendix to this article in its original printing.

23. Cp. Paul Reyher, *Essai sur les Idées dans l'Oeuvre de Shakespeare* (Paris, 1947) pp. 374–378.

24. *TN*, I.ii.60; II.ii.41; I.v.310; II.v.149.

25. Cp the theme of "witchcraft" (not present in *Menaechmi*) in *CE*, I.ii.100; II.ii.189; III.ii.45–52, 153; IV.iii.11, 66; and IV.iv.146. Antonio's "witchcraft," however, also harks back to the "enchantment" Cesario has worked on Olivia (III.i.117).

26. CP. the sailors in the storm in *CE*, I.i.75–95; and the speeches of Menaechmus of Syracuse, where, after receiving the courtesan's gifts, he thanks the gods and hurries off "while time and circumstance permit" ("dum datur mi occasio/tempusque"; *Menaechmi*, Loeb ed., III.ii.473–474, 551–553). Bandello's young man, at a similar point

in the story, also decides to "try his luck" ("Lasciami andar a provar la mia fortuna," p. 267), but Sebastian comes nearer to Plautus; cp. note 23. The Italians virtually ignore the Plautine motif of resurrection, which Shakespeare develops; cp. note 29.

27. III.iv.231; cp. Orsino's "desires, like fell and cruel hounds" (I.i.21) and Olivia's metaphor at III.i.123–125.

28. Cp. Chambers, *Mediaeval Stage*, I, 190–198 (Christmas sword-dances), 206–227 (Mummers' plays), and *The English Folk-Play* (1933), pp. 3–9, 23–33 (the champions). Besides the rodomontade quoted above and the comic fighting, the following details of contact or resemblance between the duel episode and the Mummers' plays seem worth noting: two of the main actors here are a fool and a woman dressed as a man; there is a lady in the background, like St. George's Sabra (*EFP*, pp. 25, 175), and the duel is a kind of wooing contest (*EFP*, pp. 99–104); "cockatrices" and "firago" suggest the Dragon (*EFP*, pp. 30, 156, 177, 204); the deliberate nonsense and Fabian's "bear" (III.iv. 307–308) recall the clowning in *Mucedorus* (which has Mummers' play associations—cp. R. J. E. Tiddy, *The Mummers' Play*, pp. 84–85, 129–133); Sir Andrew's offer of a reward for sparing his life has some resemblance to Jack of Lent's offer in the processional game described by Machyn (Chambers, *EFP*, pp. 155–156), while Antonio's entry corresponds to the entry of a Mummers' play Doctor; and finally, like the Mummers' play combats (*EFP*, p. 194), the duel is followed by a kind of resurrection—the resurrection of one of the fighters' second self.

On the other hand (apart from a desire to satirize the duello), there is a possible source for this episode in the episode of feigned madness and demonic possession in *Menaechmi*, V.ii (which Shakespeare had already used in *CE*, IV.iv). Antonio's part resembles the sequel in *Men.*, V.vii–viii, where the slave rushes in to rescue his master's twin from a scuffle, is promised his liberty, and then loses it again; and there, too, the episode of "devils" leads on to a resurrection. In addition, Antonio's part here recalls the passages in *CE* where Aegeon is arrested on a journey of love (I.i.124–139) and where the Officer arrests Angelo for debt (IV.i); and this indirectly strengthens the case for attributing this part of *TN* to a borrowing from Plautus. It is quite plausible, however, to suppose that Shakespeare noted the likeness between the resurrection motif and the folk-plays and the resurrection motif in Plautus, and decided to exploit it.

29. Antonio's lines about "empty trunks" hark back to Viola's speeches earlier (at. I.ii.46–50 and II.ii.28–29) and to speeches in the previous

comedies, e.g. Bassanio in the casket scene (*MV*, III.ii.73ff.). But the tone of his "idolatry" metaphor rather points forward to the debate between Troilus and Hector in *Troilus*, II.ii. Cp. Bacon's comments on love as the worship of an "idol," "and how it braves the nature and value of things," in his essay "Of Love."

30. The first offspring of Folly, according to Erasmus, are Drunkenness, Ignorance and Self-Love.

31. Cp. Morris P. Tilley, "The Organic Unity of *TN*," *PMLA*, XXIX (1914).

32. *TN*, I.v.129–133; I.iii.85 and II.iii.145–150. There are many other instances, e.g.: I.iii.129 ("go to church in a galliard"); I.v.9–15 ("a good lenten answer . . ."); I.v.28 (Maria "as witty a piece of Eve's flesh . . ."); I.v.57 ("cucullus non facit monachum"); I.v.70–3 (Olivia's brother's soul in "hell"); II.iii.119 ("by Saint Anne"; cp. Hotson, p. 101); II.vv.43 ("Fie on him, Jezebel!"); III.i.3–7 (Feste lives "by the church"); III,ii,16 ("Noah"); III.ii.31 ("a Brownist"); III.ii.71–74 ("Malvolio is turned heathen, a very renegado; for there is no Christian, that means to be saved by believing rightly, can ever believe such impossible passages of grossness"); III.ii.78; III.iv.89–131 ("all the devils in hell . . . the fiend is rough . . . 'tis not for gravity to play at cherry-pit with Satan . . . Get him to say his prayers," etc.); III.iv.245–306 ("devil," repeated; "souls and bodies hath he divorced three . . . death and sepulchre . . . perdition of souls"); IV.ii.1–63 (Sir Topas, "the old hermit of Prague," "Satan," "the Egyptians in their fog," Pythagoras and the soul, etc.); III.iv.126–137 ("Like to the old Vice . . . Adieu, goodman devil"); V.i.35–38 (Christmas dicing—cp. Hotson, p. 164,—and "the bells of Saint Bennet"); V.i.45 ("the sin of covetousness"); V.i.178–180 ("For the love of God . . . the very devil incardinate"); V.i.286 ("Beelzebub"); V.i.289–299 ("gospels"—cp. J. Dover Wilson, *TN*, Cambridge ed., p. 168); V.i.381 (the whirligig—cp. Hotson, p. 164). In addition, Sir Toby anticipates Sebastian's reference to astrology (I.iii.139, II.i.3). By contrast with these numerous comic references to religion, the serious actors cite mythology; and, apart from Olivia's Priest, also a little comic, they hardly refer to orthodox religion at all (unless Antonio's words at III.iv.327 and 363 contain such a reference implicitly—"I take the fault upon me," and "Do not . . . make me so unsound a man"; cp. Wilson, p. 156). Among the sub-plot actors, however, Malvolio is notable for his references to "Jove" (II.v.177, 183; II.iv.79, 87). Wilson, p. 97, argues that these are a sign of alterations in the text, to satisfy the statute of 1606 against blasphemy; but they seem more

likely to be a comic sign that Malvolio is coming within the orbit of romance.

33. Draper, chs. ii-iii, gives much illuminating material on the social background of Sir Toby and Sir Andrew. But he introduces the very questionable assumption that Sir Andrew is meant to be a social climber of nouveau-riche parentage. Draper bases his argument on Sir Andrew's "carpet"-knighthood and his boorishness. But the son of an ambitious self-made man would have been quite likely to be sent to a university (like Yellowhammer junior in *A Chaste Maid in Cheapside*); and, on the other side, a gentleman might buy a knighthood (if that is in fact what "carpet consideration" implies—Draper, p. 48). Sir Andrew's follies are simply those of a wealthy heir. He admires his horse, has no sense of humor, is quarrelsome, frowns or capers without reason, has no languages, dresses absurdly, and gets drunk—and this is the catalogue of follies in Portia's noble suitors in *MV*, I.iii. He is thin, vain, and insignificant, like Justice Shallow in his youth, and has grown up a similar ignoramus (*2 H. IV*, III.ii, V.i.65-80); precisely as Orlando, too, fears to grow up if he, a "gentleman" by birth, is kept "rustically at home" for his education (*AYLI*, I.i). Some of Shakespeare's contemporaries comment scornfully on the English custom of keeping a wealthy heir "like a mome" on his estate, while his younger brother must fend for himself (T. Wilson, *The State of England, 1600*, ed. F. J. Fisher, pp. 23-24; cp. *Cyvile and Uncyvile Life*, 1579, Roxburghe Library ed., p. 24; Fynes Moryson, *Itinerary*, 1617, ed. MacLehose, IV, 61). Sir Andrew, with his self-esteem, seems just such an heir, now converting himself into an Improvident Gallant. In short (apart from his ambitions on Olivia, which are really very faint), the point of the satire is not that Sir Andrew is trying to climb above his class, but that he is a gentleman born, adjusting himself foolishly to changing manners and conditions. The same could be said of the comparable characters in Ben Jonson, e.g., Master Stephen or Kastril, the angry boy.

34. E.g. O. J. Campbell, *Shakespeare's Satire* (New York, 1943), pp. 84-88; Draper, ch. v, The Countess's Steward in *All's Well* is apparently a gentleman by rank; Antonio in *The Duchess of Malfi* is certainly one; and the historical characters who have been suggested as possible originals for Malvolio have been of the rank of knights or above (cp. Luce, *Apolonius and Silla*, p. 95; Draper, pp. 110-111; Hoston, ch. v). The argument that Malvolio must be plebian because he is presumptuous seems to rest on a false assumption about Elizabethan satire.

A.S. Leggatt

Twelfth Night

As You Like It and *Twelfth Night* are often seen as the twin peaks of Shakespeare's achievement in romantic comedy, yet within the conventions of the genre they could hardly be more different. It is as though the later play was created by taking the major impulses behind its predecessor and throwing them into reverse. While *As You Like It* was almost without conventional comic intrigue, *Twelfth Night* bristles with plot complications. Instead of enjoying the freedom of the forest, with the organic cycles of nature in the background, the characters are enclosed in houses and formal gardens, and in the background is not the familiar countryside but the implacable, mysterious sea. Instead of the swift, decisive matings and friendly courtship games of the earlier play, we have unrequited love (a minor motif in *As You Like It*) expressing itself through unreliable messengers. Not since *The Two Gentlemen of Verona* has there been such emphasis on the pains rather than the pleasures of love; not since *Love's Labour's Lost* have we been so aware that love's means of expression are unreliable. It is as though the ground won in the intervening plays—and most notably in *As You Like It*—has been deliberately surrendered.

A civilized liberty was the keynote of the earlier play. *Twelfth Night* is, by comparison, strictly divided into compartments. In the earlier play, prose and verse mingled freely, and both could be used for moments of casual naturalism, or moments of formality. Here there is a stricter division, and a tighter logic—prose for comic or naturalistic effects, verse for formal and romantic ones. This reflects a firmer separation of romantic and comic figures:

Reprinted by permission of Methuen and Company, Ltd., from *Shakespeare's Comedies of Love* (1974), by A. S. Leggatt.

the plotlessness of *As You Like It* allowed a casual mingling; in *Twelfth Night* each set of characters has a plot to tend to, and is largely kept within the confines of that plot. When a character from one plot becomes involved in the other, the effect is not so much to unify the play as to create a comic shock. Viola among the clowns, and Malvolio trying to be a lover, are both laughably out of their depth. There is also a sharp division between the two households that dominate the play. Orsino's is dramatically simple—a single figure surrounded by attendants, who except for Viola are functional and characterless—and even Viola is utterly dedicated to her master. Olivia's household is dramatically more open and complex: there is a fully developed life below stairs, largely unconcerned with Olivia's problems, and even the attendants who appear with their mistress, Malvolio and Maria, spend most of the action engaged in their own affairs.

The "dykes that separate man from man," upon which, according to W. B. Yeats, "comedy keeps house,"[1] are nowhere more apparent in Shakespeare's comedies than they are in *Twelfth Night*. In plays like *A Midsummer Night's Dream* and *As You Like It* the confrontation of different minds was mostly stimulating and entertaining—a celebration of human variety. In *Twelfth Night*, however, we see the other side of this vision: each individual is locked in his own private understanding, and his ability to escape from himself and share experiences with others is limited. That did not matter so much in *A Midsummer Night's Dream* and *As You Like It*, where the comedy created a broad, secure community, and our delight sprang from watching each individual take his place in that community, all of them contributing to a larger vision. But here the sense of community is weaker. Instead, we are aware of each character as an individual, out on his own, the lovers trying to make contact but with limited success, and the comic figures either openly hostile or forming relationships based on temporary expediency. If the frequent comparisons between *Twelfth Night* and Jonsonian comedy have any basis,[2] it may be in this sense of sharply distinguishing individuals adrift in a fragmented world, each with his own obsession. Certainly individual characters come more clearly into focus than in any previous comedy of Shakespeare's, and the sense that they can be bound together in a common experience is weaker. The play ends not with a dance or a procession of couples trooping off to bed, but with a solitary figure of Feste, singing of the wind and the rain. And this image of solitude echoes and reverberates throughout the play.

The solitude of the lovers results from their experience of unrequited love, an experience that leaves them frustrated and restless. Our first impression of Orsino is of a character in search of an attitude, full of emotion but with no satisfactory outlet for emotion, nothing around which to shape it. He calls for music, savours it, then suddenly finds it tiresome. His unrequited love for Olivia may appear to be the centre of his life, but even in the first scene his attitude to that love shifts uneasily:

> O spirit of love, how quick and fresh art thou!
> That, notwithstanding thy capacity
> Receiveth as the sea, naught enters there,
> Of what validity and pitch soe'er,
> But falls into abatement and low price
> Even in a minute.
>
> (I.i.9–14)

The life-giving suggestions of "quick and fresh" are suddenly replaced by an image of annihilation. Here as throughout Shakespeare, the sea suggests both destruction and new life; in Orsino's mind, however, the ideas are held not in balance but in confusion. This shifting quality persists throughout the first scene:

> O, when mine eyes did see Olivia first,
> Methought she purg'd the air of pestilence!
> That instant was I turn'd into a hart,
> And my desires, like fell and cruel hounds,
> E'er since pursue me.
>
> (I.i.19–23)

An image of cleansing is succeeded by images of guilt and danger; again, the shift is rapid and illogical, with no coherent attitude behind it. When he hears of Olivia's vow he seizes on it, surprisingly, as a source of hope:

> How will she love when the rich golden shaft
> Hath kill'd the flock of all affections else
> That live in her; when liver, brain, and heart,
> These sovereign thrones, are all supplied and fill'd,
> Her sweet perfections, with one self king!
>
> (I.i.35–9)

For a moment he seems confident and self-assertive, in the role of the dominant, masculine lover; but then he cries "Away before me to sweet beds of flow'rs:/Love-thoughts lie rich when canopied with bow'rs' (I.i.40–1)—and once more his love collapses into passive self-indulgence. The love of Olivia dominates his life, or so he thinks. But no clear image of that love, or of Olivia herself, emerges from this scene. There may be some point in Viola's question, "Is he inconstant, sir, in his favours?" (I.iv.6). The speed with which "Cesario" becomes a favourite suggests that the impulse of love, seeking an outlet, has fixed on the nearest thing that looks like a woman (for that is how Orsino describes his new servant—I.iv.29–33). When Feste sums him up the sea is invoked once again, this time to suggest a restless, pointless wandering:

> Now the melancholy god protect thee; and the tailor make thy doublet of changeable taffeta, for thy mind is a very opal. I would have men of such constancy put to sea, that their business might be everything, and their intent everywhere; for that's it that always makes a good voyage of nothing.
>
> (II.iv.72–7)

What we see in Orsino is an unfulfilled nature—to add another image to Feste's—prowling to and fro like a caged animal.

He and Olivia are both locked up in their respective houses. At first she is dedicated to the self-punishing routine of mourning for her brother:

> But like a cloistress she will veiled walk,
> And water once a day her chamber round
> With eye-offending brine
>
> (I.i.28–30)

Again, we notice the sense of enclosure, with the suggestion this time of circles traced out in a prison yard. But Olivia, no less than Orsino, is restless, and will not settle to a routine. If her mourning were serious, she would not accept Feste's daring joke about her brother's soul so easily as she does. And while she has vowed not to accept Orsino's messages, Malvolio's description of the messenger, laying insulting emphasis on his youth, is enough to make her change her mind. But while she finds an object for her love, it is an unresponsive one, and Olivia becomes trapped in a situation beyond her control, one in which there is no right course of action. In III.i, we see her trying various approaches to Cesario, dropping broad hints but urging him to speak first:

> To one of your receiving
> Enough is shown; a cypress, not a bosom,
> Hides my heart. So, let me hear you speak.
>
> (III.i.117–19)

—then pretending indifference: "Be not afraid, good youth; I will not have you" (III.i.128); then pathetically trying to turn the conversation round again: "I prithee tell me what thou think'st of me" (III.i.135). Finally, her reserve collapses in a frank and passionate declaration (III.i.146–53). She knows she has compromised herself and betrayed her dignity by offering love so frankly to an inferior, and one who is unwilling to accept her; but she is powerless to control her feelings:

> I have said too much unto a heart of stone,
> And laid mine honour too unchary out;
> There's something in me that reproves my fault;
> But such a headstrong potent fault it is
> That it but mocks reproof.
>
> (III.iv.191–5)

By the normal standards of courtship, a woman who is the active wooer is in a false position, and she makes embarrassing mistakes. In her first meeting with Cesario she offers him money, which he indignantly rejects, yet we see her later, prepared to make the same mistake again: "How shall I feast him? What bestow of him?/For youth is bought more oft than begg'd or borrow'd" (III.iv.2–3). Her dependence on Malvolio to deliver what is in effect her first message of love is symptomatic of her dilemma: he makes the message as insulting as he can, adding the unnecessary touch of hurling the ring to the ground, and claiming (falsely) that this was part of Olivia's orders. Olivia's love can find no satisfactory outlet, no reliable means of expression. It is, like Orsino's, a passion that leaves her trapped and unfulfilled.

The lovers are confined by circumstance as much as by their own natures: so long as their love is misdirected, they find no relief or satisfaction. The figures of the comic plot are trapped in another way—by limited, clearly defined comic personalities. In Sir Toby Belch's opening pun, "Confine? I'll confine myself no finer than I am" (I.iii.9), there may be an extra significance of which he is not aware. To be occasionally drunk may be the sign of a free spirit; to be consistently drunk is not. Sir Toby may challenge the restrictions of Olivia's household, but he is too bound by his addiction to the bottle to put genuine liberty in their place. Even his respect for his niece finds alcoholic expression: "I'll drink to her as long as there is a passage in my throat and drink in Illyria. He's a coward and a coystrill that will not drink to my niece till his brains turn o'th' toe like a parish-top" (I.iii.35–8). Sir Andrew , with the fuddled good sense of which he is occasionally capable, sees how their lives have been restricted:

> *Sir Toby:* . . .Does not our lives consist of the four elements?
> *Sir Andrew:* Faith, so they say; but I think it rather consists of
>   eating and drinking.
> *Sir Toby:* Th'art a scholar; let us therefore eat and drink.
>   (II.iii. 9–12)

Sir Toby's only answer is to accept the charge and open another bottle. Sir Andrew yearns for better things: he imagines for himself the full life of the courtier, soldier and scholar: dancing, dueling, masques and revels. He envies the fool's singing voice, and Cesario's gift with words; and he will, if goaded, try almost anything once. But the aspirations of Sir Philip Sidney are wedded to the capacities of Sir Andrew Aguecheek. However earnestly he may try to improve himself, he suffers a comic paralysis of will; his weakness ties him to the more decisive character of Sir Toby, and he is confined in Sir Toby's narrow world of eating and drinking. He is occasionally let out on his chain—as when Sir Toby encourages his efforts at dancing or wooing—but only for his companion's amusement.[3] Sir Toby has the capacities of a gentleman—he is shrewd, witty and not afraid of swordplay; but his talents have no outlet. He has come to terms with life, but in a way that belittles and restricts him. Sir Andrew has the ambition but not the capacity; both are trapped by their own natures— comically, but, the more we look at them, pathetically too.

It is more difficult to see pathos in Malvolio—in his early

scenes, at least. He too is in the prison of his ego, but for him it is a gorgeous palace. His egotism kills his capacity for ordinary pleasure: 'O, you are sick of self-love, Malvolio, and taste with a distemper'd appetite' (I.v.85–6). He takes no pleasure, that is, if it is provided by anyone else—by Feste, for example. But he is an endless source of pleasure to himself. Like Orsino, he leads a fantasy life, "practising behaviour to his own shadow" (II.v.15). In the long soliloquy of the letter scene the stiff constraint of his ordinary manner disappears, and he becomes urbane and expansive, revelling in the details of his dream. In fact Malvolio is fully happy only when he is alone; his prickly manner at other times is his reaction to the presence of other people, whose very existence is an irritating intrusion: "Go off; I discard you. Let me enjoy my private" (III.iv.84–5). Malvolio is the most obviously solitary figure in Illyria; but his solitude is also a striking comic variant on the confinement suffered by Orsino and Olivia, indulging fantasies of love that cannot be gratified, and the restriction of personality that lies behind the gregariousness of the drunken knights.

The fascination with the power—and the dangers—of language that runs through Shakespeare's comedies appears again in *Twelfth Night*. Here, as in *Love's Labour's Lost*, the emphasis is on the dangers. The foibles of the characters are shown through the way they misuse words, and are trapped by words.[4] Orsino turns everything into verbal fantasies, to feed his desire for sensation. Even an invitation to healthy activity produces a pun:

> *Curio:* Will you go hunt, my lord?
> *Orsino:* What, Curio?
> *Curio:* The hart.
> *Orsino:* Why, so I do, the noblest that I have.
>
> > (I.i.16–18)

Instead of hunting, he develops an elaborate conceit of himself as Actaeon. For Orsino, all activities (including love itself) are swallowed up by the language that expresses them, and the result is a life of words alone, with no hope of action. Sir Toby plays tricks with such simple terms as "late" and "early" in order to give himself an excuse to keep on drinking:

> *Sir Toby:* . . . Not to be abed after midnight is to be up betimes; and 'diluculo surgere' thou know'st—

> *Sir Andrew:* Nay, by my troth, I know not; but I know to be
> up late is to be up late.
> *Sir Toby:* A false conclusion! I hate it as an unfill'd can. To be
> up after midnight and to go to bed then is early; so that to
> go to bed after midnight is to go to bed betimes.
>
> (II.iii.1–8)

Sir Andrew sees the truth of the matter—one imagines him picking his way, slowly and carefully, to the conclusion that to be up late is to be up late. But Sir Toby can talk rings around him, and create a fantasy world where the cry of "Time, gentlemen, please" is never heard. Malvolio also creates a fantasy world, and bends language to this purpose. The one point in Maria's letter that does not seem to co-operate must be made to co-operate: "M, O, A, I. This simulation is not as the former; and yet, to crush this a little it would bow to me, for every one of these letters are in my name" (II.v.125–7). When convinced of Olivia's love, he takes even "fellow" as a term of endearment (III.iv.72–73). Sir Andrew's futile aspirations include a desire to be eloquent, and he anxiously connects words that he thinks will help: " 'Odours,' 'pregnant,' and 'vouchsafed'—I'll get 'em all three all ready" (III.i.87–8). He does not notice the irony with which Viola used the words. His problem is not so much that he creates his own private world from language—rather, that his feelings of verbal inadequacy make him susceptible to the fantasies of others, Sir Toby in particular. He is always trying to catch up—"Is that the meaning of 'accost'?," "What's your metaphor?," "What is 'pourquoi'—do or not do?" (I.iii.55, 67, 86). For all these characters, language is not a means of escaping from the private self, and making contact with others; it is rather a means of defining the self and confirming its privateness—one more barrier erected against the realities of the world outside.

It is not so much that words are inherently unreliable, as in *Love's Labour's Lost*. It is more that words, honest enough if let alone, can be made corrupt by those who use them. Feste and Viola, who both depend on words—one as a professional wit, the other as a messenger of love—see the dangers of the medium on which they rely:

> *Feste:* . . . To see this age! A sentence is but a chev'ril glove to
> a good wit. How quickly the wrong side may be turn'd
> outward!

> *Viola:* Nay, that's certain; they that dally nicely with words
> may quickly make them wanton.
> *Feste:* I would, therefore, my sister had no name, sir.
> *Viola:* Why, man?
> *Feste:* Why, sir, her name's a word, and to dally with that
> word might make my sister wanton. But indeed words are
> very rascals since bonds disgrac'd them.
> *Viola:* Thy reason, man?
> *Feste:* Troth, sir, I can yield you none without words, and
> words are grown so false I am loath to prove reason with
> them.
>
> (III.i.10–23)

This special awareness of language sets Feste and Viola somewhat apart, as characters with an extra measure of insight. And
to some extent they are free from the constraints of circumstance
and personality that afflict the others. They can move, as no one
else can, from one household to another; and they can extend
their natures by playing roles, while keeping the role and the
inner personality distinct: "I am not that I play" (I.v.173); "I wear
not motley in my brain' (I.v.51–2).

Both characters show, in their different ways, a sensitivity to
the people they deal with. Feste in his role as commentator and
entertainer has to understand the minds of his audience, and tune
his speech to their moods—as Viola also does in a less calculating
way, when she speaks of love to Olivia and Orsino. It is Viola, in
fact, who sees most clearly this aspect of the fool's art:

> He must observe their mood on whom he jests,
> The quality of persons, and the time;
> And, like the haggard, check at every feather
> That comes before his eye.
>
> (III.i.59–62)

He knows already what amateurs like Berowne must learn—the
importance of his audience. We see him, before risking his satire
on Olivia's mourning, testing the air: "I must catechize you for it,
madonna. Good my mouse of virtue, answer me" (I.v.57–8). From
this point of view, Malvolio is the sort of audience every comedian
dreads, for he knows just how much depends on him, and he
refuses to co-operate: "Look you now, he's out of his guard
already; unless you laugh and minister occasion to him, he is

gagg'd" (I.v.81–2). But the others, at one time or another, fall under Feste's spell, and in this respect he goes some way towards drawing together the broken world of Illyria. He can unite Sir Toby and Sir Andrew into a silent, appreciative audience by singing to them of love; he can rouse Olivia and Orsino to laughter. On the rare occasions when he takes a direct part in the action, it is to bring people together: he fetches Olivia to her first meeting with Sebastian, and he delivers the letter that clears up the confusion surrounding Malvolio. But these direct interventions are rare. If his role as entertainer gives him freedom of movement, it also gives him a certain detachment. One reason for his absence in the early stages of the trick against Malvolio may be that he cannot be part of a team, taking sides with one faction against another. Foolery—which "does walk about the orb like the sun" (III.i.36)—is too universal for that. When he does join in the trick, impersonating Sir Topas, he plays for both sides, taking instructions from Malvolio as well as Sir Toby. An important condition of his professional freedom is that he does not become too closely involved with any member of his audience. His role, in the end, is both liberating and confining.

In Viola we see an intuitive, outgoing sympathy, an ability to share in the predicaments of others: her involvement is greater than Feste's, for she lacks his professional detachment. Like Olivia, she begins by mourning for a brother, and when she hears of the Countess's grief, she exclaims "O that I serv'd that lady" (I.iii.41). But her sympathy for both Olivia and Orsino finally depends on a shared experience of unrequited love. When Orsino tells her "It shall become thee well to act my woes" (I.iv.25), he is speaking more truly than he knows, for she feels for him what he feels for Olivia—and what, ironically, Olivia feels for her. E. K. Chambers writes of Viola, "With the specific of simple truth she purges the pestilence of artifice and rhetoric."[5] On the contrary, she uses the rhetoric of love for all it is worth. She makes her first serious contact with Orsino by demonstrating that she can speak his language:

> *Orsino:* . . . How dost thou like this tune?
> *Viola:* It gives a very echo to the seat
>   Where Love is thron'd.
> *Orsino:* Thou dost speak masterly.

> My life upon't, young though thou art, thine eye
> Hath stray'd upon some favour that it loves.
>
> (II.iv.19–23)

He takes her eloquence as a sign of love, and whatever we may
feel about this as a general principle, he is right in this case. But
despite her eloquence, her outgoing sympathy and the freedom
created by her role as Cesario, that role (like Feste's) finally
imposes limits on her. We see her power, and the restrictions on
that power, in two crucial interviews—one with Olivia and one
with Orsino.

When Viola comes to Olivia's house as the messenger of
Orsino's love, barrier after barrier falls. Sir Toby is ordered away
from the gate, and replaced by the more formidable Malvolio; but
when Malvolio reports his attempt to keep Viola out, the messenger sounds so interesting that she is admitted after all. In the
interview itself the process continues: Viola is left alone with
Olivia; and then Olivia unveils. Step by step, but rapidly, Viola is
allowed to take liberties that would have seemed unthinkable at
the beginning of the scene. This progressive removal of inhibition
is reflected in the way language is used. At first we may wonder
how seriously Viola is taking her own mission:

> Most radiant, exquisite, and unmatchable beauty—I pray
> you tell me if this be the lady of the house, for I never saw
> her. I would be loath to cast away my speech; for, besides
> that it is excellently well penn'd, I have taken great pains to
> con it.
>
> (I.v.160–4)

She emphasizes that she is putting on an act, and thus calls into
question the sincerity of her words; she denies the reality of
Orsino's love, for reasons we can guess—"Whoe'er I woo, myself
would be his wife" (I.iv.41). Olivia responds in the same spirit,
asking "Are you a comedian?" (I.v.171). Like the ladies of *Love's
Labour's Lost*, she mistrusts the conventional words of love, and
Viola's emphasis on the theatrical nature of her mission makes
this mistrust greater—as it is presumably intended to:

> *Olivia:* Come to what is important in't. I forgive you the
> praise.

> *Viola:* Alas, I took great pains to study it, and 'tis poetical.
> *Olivia:* It is the more like to be feigned; I pray you keep it in.
>   (I.v.180–5)

When they are left alone the joking continues in the same vein for a while; but Viola cannot restrain her curiosity about her rival, and asks to see her face. Her first reaction is a little catty— "Excellently done, if God did all" (I.v.221)—but she is deeply impressed all the same. She can now see Olivia from Orsino's point of view, and with the generosity that is part of her nature she urges his suit with a new seriousness. Olivia's readiness to unveil, and her comic but touching anxiety that the result be appreciated—"Is't not well done?" (I.v.220)—suggest that she is succumbing herself, but she keeps her defences up with conventional anti-Petrarchan jokes. Viola will have none of this, and persists now that she has seen it in taking Olivia's beauty seriously:

> *Viola:* 'Tis beauty truly blent, whose red and white
>   Nature's own sweet and cunning hand laid on.
>   Lady, you are the cruell'st she alive
>   If you will lead these graces to the grave,
>   And leave the world no copy.
> *Olivia:* O, sir, I will not be so hard-hearted: I will give out
>   divers schedules of my beauty. It shall be inventoried, and
>   every particle and utensil labell'd to my will: as—item, two
>   lips indifferent red; item, two grey eyes with lids to them;
>   item, one neck, one chin, and so forth. Were you sent
>   hither to praise me?
> *Viola:* I see you what you are: you are too proud;
>   But, if you were the devil, you are fair.
>   My lord and master loves you—O, such love
>   Could but be recompens'd though you were crown'd
>   The nonpareil of beauty!
> *Olivia:* How does he love me?
>   (I.v.223–39)

The last question suggests that, for all her joking about the conventional language of love, Olivia has become fascinated by Viola's eloquence and wants to hear more.

   She does indeed hear more. When Viola creates an image of yearning, unrequited love ("Make me a willow cabin at your gate

. . .") she fuses her understanding of Orsino's love with he
experience of passion, and the conventional posture of ado. ....
expresses the truth of her own situation. As it was in *As You Like
It*—but this time more swiftly and directly—the satiric view is
swept aside, and we see that through convention love can find its
truest expression. Moreover, the sheer ambiguity of the speech—
does it refer to Orsino, or Viola, or both?—cuts it loose from any
specific love affair, and makes it a general image of unrequited
love, conventional, recognizable, and therefore available to anyone. It clarifies Olivia's growing interest in Cesario, for her
reaction to it is "You might do much./What is your parentage?"
(I.v.260–1). In creating this image of her own feelings, Viola has
unwittingly helped Olivia to acknowledge hers. And like Phebe,
Olivia is forced to admit the reality behind the conventions:

> Even so quickly may one catch the plague?
> Methinks I feel this youth's perfections
> With an invisible and subtle stealth
> To creep in at mine eyes.
>
> (I.v.279–82)

Love at first sight, love coming through the eye—they are clichés,
and earlier in the scene such clichés were mocked; but here their
power is finally acknowledged. But if Viola has broken down
Olivia's inhibitions, there are obvious ironies in her achievement.
She arouses in Olivia a passion for herself, as Cesario, that she
cannot gratify. She will now have to see unrequited love from a
new, unexpected point of view: the willow cabin is at her own
gate. The scene ends with a flurry of frustration—Olivia's painful
faux pas of offering Viola money, Viola's indignant exit and Olivia's
hurried expedient of sending the ring. Some barriers have fallen,
some contact has been made, but in the end the women are more
deeply embroiled than ever in the problems of a love that can
reach out but not touch its object.[6]

Viola's reaction when she realizes what has happened is "Disguise, I see thou art a wickedness/Wherein the pregnant enemy
does much" (II.ii.25–6). Disguise has allowed her the freedom to
serve both her master and herself, in the way she handles her
mission to Olivia; it has allowed her a freedom to comment about
love, both mocking it and acknowledging its power without hav-

ing to admit openly her own special interest. But disguise is also a barrier: it prevents Olivia from seeing how misdirected her love is, and it prevents Orsino from knowing how far his affection for Cesario may really go. Viola herself continually strains against the disguise, dropping broad hints: "I am not that I play" (I.v.173); "I am not what I am" (III.i.138). Orsino unwittingly looks behind the disguise to the reality:

> For they shall yet belie thy happy years
> That say thou art a man: Diana's lip
> Is not more smooth and rubious; thy small pipe
> Is as the maiden's organ, shrill and sound,
> And all is semblative a woman's part.
>
> (I.v.29–33)

Normally, when another character describes one of these disguised heroines, the emphasis is on the pert boyishness one imagines as a quality of the boy actor himself. This emphasis on the femininity of Cesario is unusual; it is as though Orsino is trying to wish the disguise away. In her indirect declaration of love, Viola also struggles against the barriers imposed by the disguise, depicting this time a woman in the semblance of a man:

> *Orsino:* What kind of woman is't?
> *Viola:* Of your complexion.
> *Orsino:* She is not worth thee, then. What years, i'faith?
> *Viola:* About your years, my lord.
>
> (II.iv.25–7)

The scene in which she makes this declaration is an interesting parallel to her first scene with Olivia. As Olivia's reserve is broken down, so (at first) is Orsino's self-indulgence. He begins by presenting himself as a pattern of love:

> Come hither, boy. If ever thou shalt love,
> In the sweet pangs of it remember me;
> For such as I am all true lovers are,
> Unstaid and skittish in all motions else
> Save in the constant image of the creature
> That is belov'd.
>
> (II.iv.14–19)

But his interest in Cesario's love draws him out of himself, and shows him capable of a wry detachment from his own posturing:

For, boy, however we do praise ourselves,
Our fancies are more giddy and unfirm,
More longing, wavering, sooner lost and won,
Than women's are.

(II.iv.31–4)

The detachment, however, does not last. Feste's song, "Come away, come away, death," establishes a mood of languid grief all too congenial for Orsino, and under its spell he returns to his old posture. When Viola asks him to imagine a woman who loves him as much as he loves Olivia, he declares,

There is no woman's sides
Can bide the beating of so strong a passion
As love doth give my heart; no woman's heart
So big to hold so much; they lack retention.
Alas, their love may be call'd appetite—
No motion of the liver, but the palate—
That suffer surfeit, cloyment, and revolt;
But mine is all as hungry as the sea,
And can digest as much.

(II.iv.92–100)

At this point—as in the earlier scene with Olivia—attendants have been dismissed and they are alone. And once again, Viola creates a set piece on unrequited love, describing her sister, who

lov'd a man,
As it might be perhaps, were I a woman,
I should your lordship.

(II.iv.106–8)

and who, in suffering this love "sat like Patience on a monument,/ Smiling at grief" (II.iv.113–14). The image, as before, is drawn from her own experience, yet generalized. This time, she is urging Orsino to recognize that she can feel the same passions as he does; indeed she strives to go him one better:

We men may say more, swear more, but indeed
Our shows are more than will; for still we prove
Much in our vows, but little in our love.

(II.iv.115–17)

They are virtually in competition, seeing which can outdo the other in declarations of constancy. She is also asking him, by

implication, to remember his own words about woman's constancy and man's fickleness. He is clearly fascinated and sympathetic; and in the ensuing dialogue we sense that they are drawing
very close to each other:

> *Orsino:* But died thy sister of her love, my boy?
> *Viola:* I am all the daughters of my father's house,
>   And all the brothers too—and yet I know not.
>   Sir, shall I to this lady?
> *Orsino:* Ay, that's the theme.
>   To her in haste. Give her this jewel; say
>   My love can give no place, bide no denay.
>   (II.iv.118–23)

Viola's riddling reply comes breathtakingly close to breaking the
disguise altogether; but still the barrier holds. With an audible
effort, they change the subject, and the feelings she has roused in
him are redirected towards Olivia. To some degree, it is the
disguise that has kept them apart; but there is also something in
the images of love they have created that stands in the way of
fulfilment. Orsino depicts his love as an active, selfish, insatiable
appetite; Viola portrays hers as passive, selfless, but at bottom
sterile and self-enclosed, like his own. The two are complementary and therefore drawn to each other; but neither suggests any
capacity for sharing or for mutual sympathy. The irony is that
Orsino and Viola, in exchanging experiences as they do, demonstrate a sympathy they cannot express: the images they have
found for love belittle and even betray it, concentrating on its
privateness, but the interplay of minds that surrounds these
images suggests a deeper capacity for love than either of them can
make articulate. The scene ends, like the scene with Olivia, on a
note of frustration.

Both scenes are lively and moving in their depiction of the
efforts people make to reach each other across the barriers of
situation and personality. As in *The Merchant of Venice*, characters
react to a fantastic situation with behaviour that is convincingly,
frustratingly human. As in *Much Ado*, more is expressed in the
subtext than appears on the surface of the dialogue. And one of
the basic problems of Shakespearian comedy is here explored
eloquently: we see the conventions of speech, the literary images,
that characters use in an attempt to make contact with each

other; and we see that these conventions both help and betray them, just as Viola's disguise frees and imprisons her at the same time. There is nothing didactic in this: it is not an abstract exploration of the nature of language. Rather, it is a theatrical demonstration of language in action, of the complex dilemmas involved in the characters' efforts, spurred on by love, to break out of the privateness of the individual mind.

The comic figures operate in quite a different way, and their scenes are dramatically simpler. There is no subtext, for there are no hidden depths of feeling: the self-indulgence, the pretensions, and the mutual hostility are out in the open. And while the lovers struggle with misunderstandings they have not created and cannot solve themselves, the misunderstandings of the comic plot, centred on Malvolio, are deliberately manufactured by Maria and her cohorts. Here, the barriers that separate people are actually fortified. The hostility between Malvolio and the rest of the household has a sharpness unusual among Shakespeare's comic figures. When Malvolio threatens Sir Toby with dismissal from his comfortable position in the household, or when Sir Toby retorts "Art any more than a steward?" (II.iii.108), we see that each man knows, as if by instinct, the other's most sensitive spot. The air is filled with grudges and threats:

> *Sir Toby:* Wouldst thou not be glad to have the niggardly rascally sheep-biter come by some notable shame?
> *Fabian:* I would exult, man; you know he brought me out o' favour with my lady about a bear-baiting here.
> *Sir Toby:* To anger him we'll have the bear again; and we will fool him black and blue.
>
> (II.v.4–9)

This passage introduces Malvolio's letter scene; and Sir Toby's last speech suggests that now Malvolio himself will be the bear. Bear-baiting is not a bad image for the sport Malvolio's enemies have with him—a single ungainly figure surrounded by nimble adversaries.

Malvolio's letter scene shows how radically different are the dramatic methods Shakespeare employs in the two plots. Instead of the subtle mingling of sympathy and concealment in the scenes with the lovers, we are shown two quite separate trains of thought, operating independently. Malvolio figuratively enclosed in his private fantasy, and the listeners literally enclosed in their boxtree, engage in competition rather than dialogue:

> *Malvolio:* To be Count Malvolio!
> *Sir Toby:* Ah, rogue!
> *Sir Andrew:* Pistol him, pistol him.
> *Sir Toby:* Peace, peace!
> *Malvolio:* There is example for't: the Lady of the Strachy married the yeoman of the wardrobe.
> *Sir Andrew:* Fie on him, Jezebel!
> *Fabian:* O, peace! Now he's deeply in; look how imagination blows him.
> *Malvolio:* Having been three months married to her, sitting in my state—
> *Sir Toby:* O, for a stone-bow to hit him in the eye!
>
> (II.V.32–43)

This is the Jonsonian device of putting a character on display, while others make sardonic remarks about him[7] (a device Shakespeare uses again in Parolles's drum scene in *All's Well That Ends Well*). The effect is not so much to provide a comic dislocation of Malvolio—that is hardly necessary, for he is sufficiently ridiculous on his own—as to let each party strike sparks off the other. While all the obvious laughter of the scene is against Malvolio, the fact that he is utterly unaware of the jests hurled at him gives him, theatrically, a comic integrity: his private world is so utterly self-sufficient that nothing can pierce it. The number and volubility of the interruptions emphasize the point. His listeners talk almost as much as he does, and the fact that he hears nothing, though it is of course a convenient theatrical convention, is also a way of dramatizing his complete isolation from reality.[8] He even (like Parolles) scores a few points of his own, creating in his private world a passive and deferential Sir Toby, against whom the real Sir Toby can only fume indignantly, and mentioning "a foolish knight" whom Sir Andrew immediately recognizes as himself. Most of the laughs are against Malvolio, but not all of them.

The scene also includes yet another set piece describing unrequited love—though this time it is not a literary convention expressing truth, but a pure and simple sham:

> Jove knows I love,
>   But who?
> Lips, do not move;
>   No man must know. . . .
> I may command where I adore,
>   But silence, like a Lucrece knife,
> With bloodless stroke my heart doth gore;
>   M.O.A.I. doth sway my life.
>
>   (II.v.89–99)

This reads like a parody of the attitude struck by Viola in her
"Patience on a monument" speech in the previous scene. Here the
glib rhymes and mechanical rhythm make us see the attitude as
pure cliché. And Malvolio's reaction is quite different from those
of Olivia and Orsino. Instead of moving him to sympathy with
the imagined Olivia, or even to recognizing in her plight an image
of his own, the letter releases in him only another flood of
egotistical self-satisfaction:

> I will be proud, I will read politic authors, I will baffle Sir
> Toby, I will wash off gross acquaintance, I will be point-
> devise the very man. I do not now fool myself to let imagina-
> tion jade me; for every reason excites to this, that my lady
> loves me. She did commend my yellow stockings of late, she
> did praise my leg being cross-garter'd; and in this she mani-
> fests herself to my love, and with a kind of injunction drives
> me to these habits of her liking. I thank my stars I am happy.
>
>   (II.v. 143–51)

I, I, I. Viola created generalized images of unrequited love, that
both concealed and revealed her true situation, and struck re-
sponsive chords in her listeners. The image Maria creates is a
comic fraud, and draws out of Malvolio a feeling expressed by
none of the serious lovers in the play—a smug satisfaction at
being the object of love. We might notice, however, that the
delight of his listeners in the gulling of their victim is equally
smug. The scene is splendidly funny in performance, and we do
not ask awkward questions about the characters' behaviour. But
like so many great comic scenes it is based on a view of humanity—in this case, of competing egotists—that is anything but
sanguine. The lovers' awkward but earnest attempts at contact
are thus thrown into relief. The difference between the two plots

is finally not just a matter of dramatic idiom or technique, but a basic difference of vision.

We see this difference emphasized in a single long scene, III. iv, in which comic and romantic figures become embroiled with each other in a manner unusual for the play—Viola challenged by Sir Andrew and Malvolio attempting to court Olivia. Malvolio presents a comic variation on the unrequited loves of the main plot. When he addresses Olivia there is a complete breakdown of understanding, as words not only fail to communicate but cease to have any significance at all:

> *Malvolio:* 'Be not afraid of greatness.' 'Twas well writ.
> *Olivia:* What mean'st thou by that, Malvolio?
> *Malvolio:* 'Some are born great'—
> *Olivia:* Ha?
> *Malvolio:* 'Some achieve greatness,'—
> *Olivia:* What say'st thou?
> *Malvolio:* 'And some have greatness thrust upon them.'
> *Olivia:* Heaven restore thee!
> *Malvolio:* 'Remember who commended thy yellow stockings'—
> *Olivia:* 'Thy yellow stockings?'
> *Malvolio:* 'And wish'd to see thee cross-garter'd?'
> *Olivia:* 'Cross-garter'd?'
> *Malvolio:* 'Go to, thou art made, if thou desir'st to be so;'—
> *Olivia:* Am I made?
> *Malvolio:* 'If not, let me see thee a servant still.'
> *Olivia:* Why, this is very midsummer madness.
>
> (III. iv. 37–53).

He flings what he thinks are her own words back at her, and she, so far from recognizing them, does not even understand them. To compound the joke, he does not notice her bewilderment; her interjections have no more effect than those of the eavesdroppers in the earlier scene. For all the contact they make with each other they might be speaking pure gibberish. The egotism of Malvolio's "love" is nowhere better demonstrated, and beside him the figures of the love plot, for all their self-absorption, appear quite sensitive to each other.

Sir Andrew as the valiant duellist cuts an equally ridiculous figure, in some ways parallel to Malvolio's posture as a lover. But unlike Malvolio he cannot even imagine himself as truly valorous. When Malvolio breaks up the revels, Sir Andrew's dormouse valour can rise no higher than "to challenge him the field, and then to break promise with him and make a fool of him" (II.iii.120–1). However, in a world of comic deception, the appearance of valour is what matters. Sir Toby advises him:

> so soon as ever thou see'st him, draw; and as thou draw'st, swear horrible; for it comes to pass oft that a terrible oath, with a swaggering accent sharply twang'd off, gives manhood more approbation than ever proof itself would have earn'd him.
>
> (III.iv.168–72)

Not trusting Sir Andrew to achieve even this much, Sir Toby takes charge of the affair himself, and creates false images of both Sir Andrew and Cesario as valiant fighters. While productions usually emphasize the visual comedy of the scene, inherent in such lines as "Fabian can scarce hold him yonder" (III.iv.269), much of the comedy is in fact verbal. In Malvolio's courtship words become meaningless; here, they become liars, as Sir Toby creates two deadly fighters out of words alone. Viola, out of her depth in this world (as Malvolio is in the world of love) is just as much fooled as Sir Andrew. Her own deceptions—describing an imaginary sister, for example—have grains of truth in them, and she is not equipped to deal with a pure comic deception like this one.

But the final, crucial difference between the two plots lies in the manner of their respective endings. The deceptions of the love plot are partly the result of chance, and chance can take a hand in resolving them. But the deceptions of the comic plot are manmade, the result of fixed, antagonistic, personalities. And there is no easy or satisfying solution for this plot. After our initial amusement, we become aware of the inherent cruelty of the jokes against Malvolio. We have seen in earlier plays, notably *The Merchant of Venice* and *Much Ado*, that wit is not always in season, and in *Twelfth Night* the same realization grows towards the end. We are not bothered by the letter scene, whose pace and *brio* prevent any awkward emotional involvement; but when Malvolio is shut in a dark room, begging for light, we see the victim's sufferings a little too clearly, and our laughter acquires an edge of distaste. In the practical jokes against Katherina the Shrew and Christopher Sly there was in the jokers a civilized detachment, a lack of animosity towards the victim, that prevented the jokes from going too far. There is no such detachment here. The jokers' reaction when their victim is down is to hit him again:

> *Maria:* Nay, pursue him now, lest the device take air and taint.
> *Fabian:* Why, we shall make him mad indeed.
> *Maria:* The house will be the quieter.
>
> (III.iv.125–8)

No end is postulated except their own exhaustion with the jest: "We may carry it thus, for our pleasure and his penance, till our very pastime, tired out of breath, prompt us to have mercy on him" (III.iv.131–3). But in the end they never show mercy. The joke simply turns sour, and Sir Toby wishes to rid his hands of it, but has no idea how: "I would we were well rid of this knavery. If he may be conveniently deliver'd, I would he were; for I am now so far in offence with my niece that I cannot pursue with any safety this sport to the upshot" (IV.ii.65–8). Sir Toby feels no compassion for the victim; merely a weariness with the joke, and a growing fear for his own position.

Malvolio in his dark room is the play's most vivid image of the trapped, isolated self. The scene is almost an emblematic one, with Malvolio "within," reduced to a crying voice, Sir Toby and Maria remaining aloof even from their own jest (as they have always been aloof from its victim) and Feste reducing objective reality to a mad jumble by impersonating two different characters and assuring Malvolio that the windows of his house are "transparent as barricadoes" (IV.ii.36). Malvolio insists that his chamber is dark "as hell" (Iv.ii.35), and in fact it is something like a comic image of hell. The scene brings to a head references to hell and devils scattered throughout the play: Malvolio's apparent madness is of course associated with demonic possession; and Sir Toby has declared that he will follow Maria "To the gates of Tartary, thou most excellent devil of wit" (II.v.184–5). Even the confusions of the love plot have been attributed to devilish interference, as in Viola's "Disguise, I see thou art a wickedness/

Wherein the pregnant enemy does much" (II.ii.25-6) and Olivia's startling cry, "A fiend like thee might bear my soul to hell" (III.iv.207). The dark-room scene itself ends with Feste's bizarre song of the Vice and the Devil. Egotism and loveless solitude are a kind of damnation, and the imprisoned Malvolio is our clearest image of this.

This scene of darkness and confusion is followed immediately by Sebastian's

> This is the air; that is the glorious sun;
> This pearl she gave me, I do feel't and see't;
> And though 'tis wonder that enwraps me thus,
> Yet 'tis not madness.
>
> (IV.iii.1-4)

The two characters are mirror-opposites.[9] Malvolio, assured of Olivia's love, is the victim of a conventional comic deception in which his senses betray him; Sebastian, actually presented with Olivia's love, wonders if it is a fantastic illusion. Malvolio insists, vainly, that he is not mad. Sebastian thinks so too, but with greater hesitation, wondering whether to trust his senses or not:

> I am ready to distrust mine eyes
> And wrangle with my reason, that persuades me
> To any other trust but that I am mad,
> Or else the lady's mad; yet if 'twere so,
> She could not sway her house, command her followers,
> Take and give back affairs and their dispatch
> With such a smooth, discreet, and stable bearing,
> As I perceive she does.
>
> (IV.iii.13-20)

Like Christopher Sly, like the lovers of *A Midsummer Night's Dream*, he is poised between dream and reality, unsure which is which. And, like Antipholus of Syracuse, he is prepared to surrender to a dream, and accept the happiness it holds for him: "Let fancy still my sense in Lethe steep;/If it be thus to dream, still let me sleep!" (IV.i.61-2).

Viola had said of Olivia, "Poor lady, she were better love a dream" (II.ii.24)—but now Olivia's dream is coming true. And Sebastian will find that his dream, too, is reality. The comic plot is conventionally full of false images—Maria's letter, Feste's dis-

guise, Sir Toby's description of Sir Andrew as a dangerous swords-
man. And when Malvolio adopts the external shows of love, in
yellow stockings, cross-gartered and relentlessly smiling, the result is simply absurd. In this plot, images and appearances have no
validity except as signs of comic confusion. But the romantic plot
operates by a different set of rules. In her first scene Viola is
prepared to trust the Sea Captain on appearance alone:

> There is a fair behaviour in thee, Captain;
> And though that nature with a beauteous wall
> Doth oft close in pollution, yet of thee
> I will believe thou hast a mind that sits
> With this thy fair and outward character.
>
> (I.ii.47–51)

Throughout the romantic plot, a trust in appearances, though it
may lead to temporary confusion, is justified in the long run. To
Orsino, Cesario looks like a woman; he is a woman. To Olivia, he
looks like a man; he is a man. Antonio loves Sebastian for his
appearance, and cries out against false seeming when he thinks he
has been betrayed:

> And to his image, which methought did promise
> Most venerable worth, did I devotion. . . .
> Virtue is beauty; but the beauteous evil
> Are empty trunks, o'erflourished by the devil.
>
> (III.iv.346–7; 353–4)

This charge is misdirected: Antonio has been deceived, but only in
a limited, technical way; his original trust in Sebastian's appearance was sound enough. Only for the clowns is it dangerous to go
by looks, as Sir Andrew finds when he strikes the wrong Cesario.

This trust in images is made possible by the special handling of
the figure of Cesario, in which the extension of personality implied in disguise is taken further, and exploited in a more daring
way, than in any previous comedy of Shakespeare's. When Viola
and Sebastian meet at the end of the play, the reactions of the
others suggest something more than the simple discovery that
there are two characters who look alike. Orsino exclaims "One
face, one voice, one habit, and two persons! / A natural perspective, that is and is not" (V.i.208–9). Antonio asks "How have you

made division of yourself?" (V.i.214), and even Sebastian holds
back for a moment the natural explanation of the seeming miracle:

> Do I stand there? I never had a brother;
> Nor can there be that deity in my nature
> Of here and everywhere.
>
> (V.i.218–20)

The reunion of the twins is a moment of still, poised formality:
action freezes in the contemplation of a miracle, and natural
explanations emerge only slowly. Theatrically this moment
counts for more than the pairing of the lovers, and so it should.
The joining of the twins is the crucial action; after it has been
accomplished the lovers can slip easily into couples, for the problem is already solved. But the plot significance of this moment is a
clue to something deeper. The single being in a double body is an
image of love to set against the opposing image of the solitary
ego—Malvolio in his dark room. It recalls the fable of Aristo-
phanes in Plato's *Symposium*: a single being, divided into two bodies, seeks reunion, and this is the source of love. The singleness of
personality is broken down.[10] Orsino continues to address Viola
as "boy" and "Cesario" (V.i.259, 371), and the jokes have a certain
resonance: unlike Rosalind, Viola keeps her male attire to the end.
Sebastian's pun about his own virginity also suggests a blurring
of distinctions, even a blurring of sexes:

> You would have been contracted to a maid;
> Nor are you therein, by my life, deceiv'd;
> You are betroth'd both to a maid and man.
>
> (V.i.253–5)

He has, in an earlier scene, admitted something feminine in his
own nature: "My bosom is full of kindness, and I am yet so near
the manners of my mother that, upon the least occasion more,
mine eyes will tell tales of me" (II.i.35–7). Viola's almost telepathic
sympathy, in taking her own escape as a guarantee of Sebastian's
safety, suggests another way of breaking down the exclusiveness
of personality (I.ii.19–21). In other comedies a single personality is
extended by disguise, but the extension is temporary and finally
withdrawn; this is the only case in which the new figure created

by disguise has also an objective reality, a life of its own. Viola's
creation of Cesario is confirmed, as no ordinary comic pretence
could be, by the existence of Sebastian. It is as though mind has
actually created matter, and the distinction between spirit and
body, like other distinctions, is blurred:

> *Viola:* If spirits can assume both form and suit,
>   You come to fright us.
> *Sebastian:* A spirit I am, indeed,
>   But am in that dimension grossly clad
>   Which from the womb I did participate.
>
> (V.i.227-30)

The human spirit may be bound to a particular body, or a particular mind; but that is not necessarily its permanent or natural
condition. This idea is parodied in the comic plot, in Feste's exchange with Malvolio on "the opinion of Pythagoras concerning
wild fowl" (IV.ii.48-58); but here it is one of the serious implications that surround the idea of love.

The resolution of the love plot does not depend on the will, or
the knowledge, of individuals. It is an impersonal, organic process:
confusion gathers to a head, and breaks.[11] Sebastian has no
Prospero-like authority: he solves the lovers' problems not by
what he knows, but by what he is. He provides a true version of
the false, comic images of the subplot—a real lover for Olivia, a
real fighter who can put the two knights in their place.[12] And he
is to some degree an outsider, bringing with him (like Bassanio)
the fresh air of a different world: in his second scene, we hear for
the first time of a Plautine seaport town, with lodgings, markets
and monuments. But his role as one half of Cesario is what
matters most, and his most important action is simply to appear
when Viola is on stage. Viola may seem to have more will, and
more initiative. But when we compare her with Rosalind we see
how much she is the creature rather than the creator of the plot.
We never hear the reason for her sea voyage,[13] nor is her disguise
ever justified in a literal way. Other heroines offer rationaliza-
tions for their disguises, usually based on the dangers of travel.
But in this case the decision is simply presented to us, justified in
the most cryptically general terms:

> Conceal me what I am, and be my aid
> For such disguise as haply shall become
> The form of my intent.
>
> (I.ii.53-5)

In the predicaments created by her disguise Viola submits to destiny, rather than trying to solve the problem herself: "O Time, thou must untangle this, not I;/It is too hard a knot for me t'untie!" (II.ii.38-9). Olivia also submits to destiny in acknowledging her love for Cesario: "Fate, show thy force: ourselves we do not owe;/What is decreed must be; and be this so!" (I.v.294-5). The lovers in fact are in a situation beyond the control of any individual; only a benevolent fate, by bringing the twins together, can solve their problems. As in the image of love presented by Cesario, the importance of the individual is broken down—a process that disturbs initially but ultimately brings joy. As in Shakespeare's last plays, the sea is invoked throughout, and carries suggestions of a power beyond human will—frightening, destructive, yet finally benevolent—the devouring sea of Orsino's love fantasies, and the life-giving sea of Viola's "Tempests are kind, and salt waves fresh in love" (III.iv.368).[14] The sea has the same function here as the impersonal cycles of nature in earlier comedies: it suggests the characters' dependence on forces beyond their control.

The pairing of the lovers in the final scene is likewise beyond considerations of individual temperament. It is, like the meeting of the twins, a generalized image of love. Within the image, the pairing of Orsino and Viola carries some psychological conviction: their interest in each other is already established, and even when Olivia appears, Orsino's greeting, "Here comes the Countess; now heaven walks on earth" (V.i.91), is rendered perfunctory by the speed with which he goes back to what really interests him—a conversation about Cesario. His joking with Feste, and the references to the sea fight, suggest that Orsino's personality may be more balanced and complete, and his capacities wider, than mere indulgence in love melancholy. There is enough material here to make us see his match with Viola as satisfying, if we are inclined to ask for satisfaction in psychological terms. Even so, Orsino's actual transfer of affection is too swift and simple to bear much

literal-minded inspection. And Olivia's marriage to Sebastian,
seen literally, would be a clear case for immediate annulment. We
are not, however, encouraged to take it this way. Olivia never
speaks to Sebastian after she has learned the truth, and her only
reference to her marriage is addressed to Orsino, stressing its
formal aspect:

> My lord, so please you, these things further thought on,
> To think me as well a sister as a wife,
> One day shall crown th'alliance on't, so please you,
> Here at my house, and at my proper cost.
>
> (V.i.303-6)

Her pairing with Sebastian is part of a formal design, and we are
encouraged to think of it in those terms alone. Expecting more
than this, some critics have asked, as S. C. Sen Gupta does, "Can
we call this a happy ending? Or rather shall we look upon such a
conclusion to a comedy as a fitting prelude to the dark comedies
and great tragedies?"[15] Clifford Leech describes the ending as "an
exposure of the triviality of human desire";[16] and Philip Edwards
concludes that the union of the lovers is treated sardonically,
Shakespeare having become tired of such endings.[17] Other critics
see the mating of the lovers as a purging of folly and a return to
normality.[18] That too seems to be imposing on the ending significance of a kind that it is not designed to bear. There are no
apologies or statements of forgiveness as the lovers join hands;
indeed their minds are hardly examined at all.[19] The ending takes
little account of the reasons for particular attachments; it is, on
the contrary, a generalized image of love.

     As such, its significance is limited. We can easily think of
Rosalind and Orlando married and producing children, for they
think of themselves that way; but the union of lovers in *Twelfth
Night* is more a freezing of the moment of romantic contemplation, before the practical business of marriage: Viola is to be
"Orsino's mistress, and his fancy's queen" (V.i.374). Feste has a
few marriage jokes in his repertoire (I.v.18; III.i.30-3), but the
lovers themselves never consider the realities of wedlock as Rosalind does. The happiness they have achieved is more stylized and
conventional. It is also both miraculous and exclusive: it cannot
touch the ordinary world. While Touchstone and Audrey can join

the procession of couples in *As You Like It*, the comic figures of *Twelfth Night* pass through the final scene untouched by its harmony. Sebastian, the agent of release for the lovers, has given the knights nothing but a sound beating. Sir Toby's false friendship for Sir Andrew has collapsed: for the first time, the lean knight is insulted to his face. Malvolio, like Viola, has seen himself in the hands of a benevolent fate: "Well, Jove, not I, is the doer of this, and he is to be thanked" (III.iv.77-8). But his faith is rudely shattered. For the lovers, time is held in abeyance by a static moment of fulfilment; for the clowns, time goes relentlessly on. To Feste's "thus the whirligig of time brings in his revenges," Malvolio replies "I'll be reveng'd on the whole pack of you" (V.i.364). The whirligig shows no sign of ever stopping.

In *As You Like It* time was primarily the medium of fulfilment; it was also admitted to be the medium of decay, but that view was firmly placed as secondary. In *Twelfth Night* the two views are more closely balanced. Time brings the lovers to each other, untangling the knot as Viola said it would; but we are constantly reminded that time does other work as well. The two verses of "O mistress mine" strike a balance: in the first, "Journeys end in lover meeting"; in the second, "Youth's a stuff will not endure" (II.iii.42-51). Orsino and Viola contemplate the transience of beauty: "For women are as roses, whose fair flow'r/Being once display'd doth fall that very hour"(II.iv.37-8). Other pleasures decay, too: Feste is warned, "your fooling grows old, and people dislike it" (I.v.104). Sir Toby's revels end with the cold chill of morning: "Let's to bed, knight. Thou hadst need send for more money" (II.iii.171-2). At the end, this sense that time finally destroys our illusions and brings us to decay is centred on the broken figures of the clowns. Time as the medium of fulfilment belongs to the lovers. And the special moment of the play's title shares this double significance: Twelfth Night celebrates the Epiphany, the showing forth of a miraculous birth; but it is also the last night of a revel, before the clod of winter closes in.

The last scene is neither a still point of harmony nor a simple dying fall: it is the busiest, most complex scene in the play, as the private, magic happiness of the lovers vies for attention with the larger, uncontrollable world of time inhabited by the clowns. The two plots affect each other slightly: Sir Toby's brisk mating with

Maria is underplayed, but it may show them achieving their own kind of harmony; and when we hear that the Sea Captain who has Viola's "woman's weeds" is "in durance, at Malvolio's suit" (V.i.268), there may be a suggestion that the full happiness of the lovers is conditional on a reconciliation with Malvolio. Orsino commands, "Pursue him, and entreat him to a peace;/He hath not told us of the captain yet" (V.i.366–7). But for the most part Shakespeare prefers to maintain the tension by swift alternations between the happiness of the lovers and the battered condition of the clowns. Sebastian's entrance is preceded by the entrance of the bleeding knights; the vows of the lovers are interrupted by Malvolio. And while the lovers seem to have escaped from ordinary reality, it is still in the background: even the reunion of the twins is touched by a reference to their father's death (V.i.236–40). And the ending as a whole is placed within the larger sweep of time: since Olivia and Sebastian were contracted, says the Priest, "my watch hath told me, toward my grave,/I have travell'd but two hours" (V.i.156–7). The twins' father "died that day when Viola from her birth/Had numb'red thirteen years" (V.i.236–7). The miracle of Cesario is thus played off against the uncontrollable world of time. This kind of tension is basic to Shakespearian comedy: it is at bottom a tension between stylized and realistic art. The lovers, having engaged our feelings as human beings, are now fixed in a harmony we can believe in only by trusting the power of fantasy; the clowns, stylized in their own way at first, have lost some of the immunity of comedy and now present an image of defeat that is uncomfortably real.

The tension is resolved, unexpectedly, in Feste's last song. It seems at first to belong to the vision of the comic plot. Feste sings of our decay through time, from the folly of childhood to the knavery of manhood to a drunken collapse in old age. The lovers have disappeared, and there is a solitary figure on stage. His experience, as often in the comedies, is linked to ours through the medium of nature—this time the wind and the rain. Yet before we sink too easily into melancholy, the song concludes: "But that's all one, our play is done,/And we'll strive to please you every day" (V.i.393–4). In *As You Like It* the play was put aside as an illusion, but its vision of humanity walking to the Ark in pairs was confirmed by the audience itself. In *Twelfth Night* the triumph of love is put at a distance, as a strange and special miracle that cannot touch everyone. But the vision of decay that opposes it is also, in the last analysis, one more illusion, part of a play. The one thing that is permanent is the work of art itself: tomorrow it will be there to entertain us again, even if we are all a day older. As in Shakespeare's sonnets, art is a means, perhaps the only means, of cheating time, of holding human experience in permanent form. Orsino says of "Come away death,"

> Mark it, Cesario; it is old and plain;
> The spinsters and the knitters in the sun,
> And the free maids that weave their thread with bones,
> Do use to chant it. . . .
>
> (II.iv.42–5)

It has survived through time; it can entertain the simplest folk of the working-day world and the most sophisticated courtiers. We have seen in the play as a whole the power of conventional images to touch their hearers. The same may be true of the stylized image of the lovers in the final scene: the fact that it is obviously a matter of literary artifice does not make it invalid; on the contrary, its bold stylization strikes through to the heart of experience. When Feste is left alone on stage the vision of an uncontrollable world of time and decay may seem for a moment to overwhelm the happiness of the lovers. But just as, in *As You Like It*, satire fights a sudden rearguard action at the end, so in *Twelfth Night* there is, against all odds, a final rescue for artifice.

NOTES

1. "The tragic theatre," *Essays and Introductions* (London, 1961), p. 214.
2. See, for example, Paul Mueschke and Jeannette Fleischer, "Jonsonian elements in the comic underplot of *Twelfth Night,*" *Publications of the Modern Language Association of America*, XLVIII (1933), pp. 722–40; and Herbert Howarth, *The Tiger's Heart* (London, 1970), pp. 102–19.
3. In David William's production at Stratford, Ontario in 1966, Sir Toby cracked a whip as Sir Andrew danced; their relations were those of trainer and performing animal.
4. On the treatment of language throughout the play, see Terence Eagleton, "Language and reality in *Twelfth Night,*" *Critical Quarterly*, IX

(Autumn 1967), pp. 217–28. Eagleton stresses the power of language to create an illusory world, divorced from reality.

5. *Shakespeare: A Survey* (Harmondsworth, 1964), p. 41.

6. This scene is analysed from a similar point of view by Charles Tyler Prouty, "*Twelfth Night,*" *Stratford Papers 1965–67,* ed. B. A. W. Jackson (McMaster University Press, 1969), pp. 118–22. However, he takes a different view of Viola's "Make me a willow cabin at your gate. . . .," which he sees as more purely artificial than I do; he views the whole scene as game-like from beginning to end.

7. Cf. *Every Man in his Humour,* III.iv and *Every Man out of his Humour,* II.ii.

8. The point is often emphasized in production by the comic inadequacy of the conspirators' attempts to hide. In Tyrone Guthrie's production at Stratford, Ontario in 1957, Sir Toby, Sir Andrew and Fabian hid behind the pillars which are part of the permanent stage, and which are considerably thinner than the average actor. As Malvolio moved about the stage, the other actors revolved slowly around the pillars, keeping (in theory) out of his angle of vision. At one point, Sir Andrew actually read the letter over Malvolio's shoulder, spelling out the words with him.

9. The connection between the two characters was emphasized in John Barton's production for the Royal Shakespeare Company in 1969: as Sebastian assured himself he was not mad, there were lingering cries from Malvolio in the cellarage.

10. See Walter N. King, Introduction to *Twentieth Century Interpretations of Twelfth Night* (Englewood Cliffs, 1968), pp. 10–12.

11. As the confusion intensifies, the tone of the love plot darkens temporarily, with Antonio's painful mistake about Viola and the brief flurry of melodrama at the start of the final scene—Orsino willing to kill Viola, Viola willing to die, Olivia demanding a husband who denies her, and Orsino believing (like Antonio) that he has been betrayed. The effect of all this is to sharpen our sense of relief when the confusion is suddenly dispelled.

12. C. L. Barber describes the sense of sheer relief when Sebastian strikes Sir Andrew: "The particular implausibility that there should be an identical man to take Viola's place with Olivia is submerged in the general, beneficent realization that there is such a thing as a man." See *Shakespeare's Festive Comedy* (Cleveland, 1967), p. 246.

13. See John W. Draper, *The Twelfth Night of Shakespeare's Audience* (Stanford, 1950), p. 133.

14. In John Barton's production the sound of the sea was heard at crucial moments; most effectively, at the reunion of the twins. Besides direct references to the sea, the play's dialogue is full of nautical

jokes: "Will you hoist sail, sir? Here lies your way" (I.v.190): "Then westward-ho!" (III.i.132); "you are now sail'd into the north of my lady's opinion; where you will hang like an icicle on a Dutchman's beard" (III.ii.24–6).

15. *Shakespearian Comedy* (London, 1950), p. 173.
16. *Twelfth Night and Shakespearian Comedy* (Toronto, 1968), p. 7.
17. *Shakespeare and the Confines of Art* (London, 1968), pp. 68–9.
18. See, for example, Larry S. Champion, *The Evolution of Shakespeare's Comedy* (Cambridge, Mass., 1970), p. 88; and Harold Jenkins, "Shakespeare's *Twelfth Night*," *The Rice Institute Pamphlet*, XLV (January 1959), p. 21.
19. See John Russell Brown, *Shakespeare and his Comedies* (2nd edition, revised: London, 1968), p. 33.

Karen Greif

Plays and Playing in "Twelfth Night"

I

"The purpose of playing," says Hamlet, is "to hold as 'twere the mirror up to nature: to show virtue her feature, scorn her own image, and the very age and body of the time his form and pressure."[1] Hamlet himself employs "playing," in various guises, as a means of penetrating false appearances to uncover hidden truths, but he also discovers how slippery illusions can be when their effects become entangled in the human world. Like *Hamlet*, but in a comic vein, *Twelfth Night* poses questions about "the purpose of playing" and about whether illusion is perhaps too deeply embedded in human experience to be ever completely separated from reality.

Virtually every character in *Twelfth Night* is either an agent or a victim of illusion, and often a player will assume both these roles: as Viola is an impostor but also a prisoner of her own disguise, or as Sir Toby loses control of the deception he has contrived when he mistakes Sebastian for his twin. Illyria is a world populated by pretenders, which has led one critic to describe the action as "a dance of maskers . . . for the assumption of the play is that no one is without a mask in the serio-comic business of the pursuit of happiness."[2] In the course of the story, many of these masks are stripped away or willingly set aside; but illusion itself plays a pivotal yet somewhat ambiguous role in this process. While Viola's masquerade serves to redeem Orsino and Olivia from their romantic fantasies and ends in happiness with the final love-

Reprinted from *Shakespeare Survey*, vol. 34 (1981), by permission of Cambridge University Press. Copyright © 1981 by Cambridge University Press.

matches, the more negative aspects of deception are exposed in the trick played against Malvolio, which leads only to humiliation and deeper isolation.

Role-playing, deceptions, disguises, and comic manipulations provide the fabric of the entire action. So pervasive is the intermingling of illusion and reality in the play that it becomes impossible at times for the characters to distinguish between the two. This is not simply a case of illusion becoming a simulated version of reality. "I am not that I play," Viola warns her fellow player (1.5.184); but, as the subtitle suggests, in *Twelfth Night* one discovers that "what you will" may transform the ordinary shape of reality.

The fluidity of the relationship between "being" and "playing" is indirectly illuminated at the beginning of act 3, in the play's single face-to-face encounter between Viola and Feste, who share the distinction of being the only pretenders in Illyria who do not wear their motley in their brains. They match wits in a contest of wordplay, which moves the Fool to sermonize: "To see this age! A sentence is but a chev'ril glove to a good wit. How quickly the wrong side may be turn'd outward!" (3.1.11–13). According to Feste, words have become like kidskin gloves, pliable outside coverings readily yielding to manipulation by a good wit. Viola's response echoes this sense; those who know how to play with words "may quickly make them wanton" (l.15). Men may expect words to operate as constant symbols of meaning, faithfully reflecting the concrete outlines of reality; but, in fact, words prove to be flighty, untrustworthy mediators between human beings and experience:

> *Clown.* But indeed, words are very rascals since bonds dis-
> grac'd them.
> *Viola.* Thy reason, man?
> *Clown.* Troth, sir, I can yield you none without words, and
> words are grown so false, I am loath to prove reason with
> them.
>
> (ll.20–5)

Rather than serving as a medium for straightforward communication, words have become bent to the purposes of dissembling. Feste declares himself a "corrupter of words" (l.36), and throughout the play he demonstrates how chameleon-like words can become in the mouth of an expert dissembler like himself. Yet Feste is also recognized by his audience and many of his fellow players as a kind of truth-teller; under the guise of fooling and ingenious word-play, he reminds those around him of truths they have blocked out of their illusion-bound existences. The Fool's dialogue with Viola suggests that "since bonds disgrac'd them," words have fallen under suspicion within the world of *Twelfth Night*, at least among those who admit their own dissembling. But for those who possess wit and imagination, the protean nature of words also affords an exhilarating form of release. Dexterity with language becomes a means of circumventing a world that is always shifting its outlines by exploiting that fluidity to the speaker's own advantage.

The same ambiguity that is characteristic of words pervades almost every aspect of human experience in *Twelfth Night*. Illyria is a world of deceptive surfaces, where appearances constantly fluctuate between what is real and what is illusory. Out of the sea, there comes into this unstable society a catalyst in the form of the disguised Viola, who becomes the agent required to free Orsino and Olivia from the bondage of their self-delusions. Equilibrium is finally attained, however, only after the presence of Viola and her separated twin has generated as much error and disturbance as Illyria could possibly contain.

Moreover, this resolution is achieved not by a straightforward injection of realism into this bemused dreamworld, but by further subterfuge. "Conceal me what I am," Viola entreats the Sea Captain after the shipwreck (1.2.53), setting in motion the twin themes of identity and disguise that motivate so much of the action in *Twelfth Night*. Identity, it is important to bear in mind, includes both the identity that represents the essence of one's being, the "what I am" that separates one individual from another, and also the identity that makes identical twins alike; and the comedy is concerned with the loss and the recovery of identity in both these senses.

Viola's plan to dissemble her true identity proves to be ironically in keeping with the milieu she has entered. But the fact that Viola, left stranded and unprotected by the wreck, assumes her guise as Cesario in response to a real predicament sets her apart from most of the pretenders already dwelling in Illyria. Surfeiting on fancy, they endlessly fabricate grounds for deceiving others or themselves. Orsino and Olivia are foolish, in part, because it is apparent that the roles of unrequited lover and grief-stricken lady they have chosen for themselves spring more from romantic conceits than from deep feeling or necessity. The games-playing mania of Sir Toby Belch and his cohorts carries to comic extremes the Illyrian penchant for playing make-believe. Just as words, in Sir Toby's hands, are rendered plastic by his Falstaffian talent for making their meaning suit his own convenience, so he manufactures circumstances to fit his will.

The kind of egotism that stamps Sir Toby's perpetual manipulation of words and appearances, or Orsino and Olivia's wilful insistence on their own way, is far removed from Viola's humility as a role-player. Although she shares Feste's zest for wordplay and improvisation, Viola never deludes herself into believing she had absolute control over either her own part or the actions of her fellow players. Musing over the complications of the love triangle into which her masculine disguise has thrust her, Viola wryly concedes "O time, thou must untangle this, not I,/It is too hard a knot for me t'untie" (2.2.40-1). Viola's outlook is unaffectedly realistic without the need to reject imaginative possibilities. Her own miraculous escape encourages her to hope her brother has also survived the wreck, but throughout most of the play she must continue to act without any certainty he is still alive. She accepts the facts of her dilemma without self-pity and begins at once to improvise a new, more flexible role for herself in a difficult situation; but she also learns that the freedom playing permits her is only a circumscribed liberty. For as long as the role of Cesario conceals her real identity, Viola is free to move at will through Illyria, but not to reveal her true nature or her love of Orsino.

The first meeting between Cesario and Olivia creates one of the most demanding tests of Viola's ability to improvise. She meets the challenge with ingenuity, but Viola also insists, with deliberate theatricality, on the disparity between her true self and the role that she dissembles:

> *Viola.* I can say little more than I have studied, and that
> question's out of my part. Good gentle one, give me

> modest assurance if you be the lady of the house, that I
> may proceed in my speech.
> *Olivia.* Are you a comedian?
> *Viola.* No, my profound heart; and yet (by the very fangs of
> malice I swear) I am not that I play.
>
> (1.5.178–84)

In her exchanges with Olivia, Viola is able to treat the part she plays with comic detachment; but the somewhat rueful tone underlying her awareness of the ironies of her relation to Olivia turns to genuine heartache when this separation between her true identity and her assumed one comes into conflict with her growing love for Orsino.

Unable to reveal her love openly, Viola conjures for Orsino the imaginary history of a sister who

> lov'd a man
> As it might be perhaps, were I a woman,
> I should your lordship.
>
> (2.4.107–9)

As long as Orsino clings to his fancied passion for Olivia and she herself holds on to her disguise, Viola can vent her true feelings only by more dissembling, so she masks her secret love for the Duke with the sad tale of this lovelorn sister. Yet her fiction also serves to present her master with a portrait of genuine love against which to measure his own obsession for Olivia. "Was this not love indeed?" she challenges him:

> We men may say more, swear more, but indeed
> Our shows are more than will; for still we prove
> Much in our vows, but little in our love.
>
> (ll.116–18)

Her story is a touching one, and for once Orsino's blustering is stilled. He is moved to wonder "But died thy sister of her love, my boy?"; but she offers only the cryptic answer "I am all the daughters of my father's house,/And all the brothers too—and yet I know not" (ll.119–21). Viola's veiled avowal of her love is perhaps the most delicate blend of imagination and truth in the play, and this fabrication will finally yield its reward when Cesario is free to disclose "That I am Viola" (5.1.253).

Role-playing, whether it be a deliberate choice like Viola's disguise or the foolish self-delusions that Orsino, Olivia, and Malvolio all practise upon themselves, leads to a general confusion of identity within Illyria. In the second encounter between Olivia and Cesario, this tension between being and playing is given special resonance:

> *Olivia.* I prithee tell me what thou think'st of me.
> *Viola.* That you do think you are not what you are.
> *Olivia.* If I think so, I think the same of you.
> *Viola.* Then think you right: I am not what I am.
> *Olivia.* I would you were as I would have you be.
> *Viola.* Would it be better, madam, than I am? I wish it might,
>   for now I am your fool.

> (3.1.138–44)

Like a tonic chord in a musical passage, Viola's riddles always come back to the idea of "what you are" and "what I am," the enduring truth of one's real identity. But this note of resolution is never a stable one. Viola warns Olivia that she has deluded herself into acting out fantasies with no basis in reality, first in her vow of celibacy to preserve her grief and then in her pursuit of the unattainable Cesario. In turn, she herself admits that "I am not what I am." Olivia, meanwhile, is obsessed with "what thou think'st of me" and what "I would have you be." She is less interested in the truth about Cesario or her own nature than in making what is conform to what she would like it to be. On the one hand, the facts of nature ensure that she will be frustrated in her wooing, and yet her beloved will indeed be transformed into what she would have him be when the counterfeit Cesario is replaced by the real Sebastian.

The compression of so many levels of meaning within this passage suggests how complicated and paradoxical the relationship is in *Twelfth Night* between what actually is and what playing with reality can create. Viola's exchange with Olivia follows directly upon her encounter with Feste, and the second dialogue translates into terms of identity and role-playing the same attitudes towards words appearing in the first. The Fool claims that "since bonds disgrac'd them," words have no static nature—that no unchanging identification between the-thing-itself and the word symbolizing it is ever possible—and the condition of being, the identity belonging to "what I am," is in a comparable state of flux throughout most of the action.

The separation between being and playing, like the disjunction between words and concrete reality, may lead to a sense of disorientation closely akin to madness. This is the condition that the release of imagination creates in Malvolio. When he exchanges the reality of what he is for the make-believe part he dreams of becoming, he begins to act like a madman. Viola's charade as Cesario produces a welter of mistaken identities that so disorient her fellow players no one is quite certain of his or her sanity. Yet another variation of the madness which springs from unleashing the effects of imagination upon reality is seen in the escapades of Sir Toby Belch. His reign of misrule is fuelled by his refusal to allow reality to interfere with his desires, and this unruliness drives his associates to wonder repeatedly if he is mad.

Yet, just as Feste finds means of communicating truth by playing with words, so does the unstable relationship between being and playing allow at least a few of the players in Illyria to discover a more flexible sense of identity that can accommodate both enduring truths and changing appearances. The same loosening of the bonds governing identity that can lead to bewildering confusion may also open up a fresh sense of freedom in shaping one's own nature. What you will may indeed transform what you are.

The point at which all these attitudes converge is in the recognition scene of the final act. At the moment when Viola and Sebastian finally come face to face upon the stage, the climactic note of this motif is sounded in Orsino's exclamation of wonder:

> One face, one voice, one habit, and two persons,
> A natural perspective, that is and is not!
>
> (5.1.216–17)

For the onlookers, who are still ignorant both of Viola's true identity and of the existence of her twin, the mirror image created by the twins' confrontation seems explicable only as an optical illusion of nature. Yet the illusion proves to be real; this "natural perspective" is the stable reality underlying the mirage of shifting appearances caused by mistaken identity.

This dramatic revelation of the identity that has been obscured by illusory appearances, but is now made visible in the mirror image of the twins, is deliberately prolonged as Viola and Sebastian exchange their tokens of recognition. Anne Barton has drawn attention to the fact that the recognition scene provides

> a happy ending of an extraordinarily schematized and 'play-like' kind. Viola has already had virtual proof, in Act III, that her brother has survived the wreck. They have been separated for only three months. Yet the two of them put each other through a formal, intensely conventional question and answer test that comes straight out of Greek New Comedy.[3]

The recognition of identity is at first an experience involving only the reunited twins; but, as the facts of their kinship are brought forth, the circle of awareness expands to include Orsino and Olivia. They appreciate for the first time their shared folly in desiring the unobtainable and both discover true love in unexpected forms by sharing in the recognition of the twins' identities. As Orsino vows,

> If this be so, as yet the glass seems true,
> I shall have share in this most happy wrack.
>
> (5.1.265–6)

The reflections of identity that have been present throughout the play are now openly acknowledged and sealed by the bonds of marriage and kinship. The similarities between Viola and Olivia, for example—the lost brother, the unrequited love, the veiled identity—which are echoed in the names that are virtually anagrams, are now confirmed by the ties of sisterhood when each wins the husband she desires.

Paradoxically, what allows this dramatic moment of epiphany[4] to occur at all is the same loss and mistaking of identities that caused the original confusion. It is the separation of the twins and Viola's subsequent decision to "Conceal me what I am" which gives emotional intensity to the moment when identity is recognized and regained. This final scene, moreover, makes it clear that the regaining of lost personal identity—the individuality that distinguishes Viola from Sebastian—is closely tied to the recognition of the likeness that makes the twins identical. The recognition scene, with its ritual-like ceremony of identification, suggests that men and women must recognize how much they are identical, how much alike in virtues and follies and in experiences and desires, before they can affirm the personal identities that make them unique.[5] These twin senses of identity converge in the final act, dramatically embodied in the reunited twins who share "One face, one voice, one habit, and two persons."

But at what point do the reflections stop? Beyond the onlookers upon the stage who behold this ceremony of recognition is the larger audience of the illusion that is *Twelfth Night*. The play itself is "a natural perspective, that is and is not": a mirror held up to nature intended to reflect the contours of reality and simultaneously a work of imagination that incarnates the world of being in a world of playing. What the audience encounters in the mirror of the play is its own reflected identity in the characters who play out their experiences upon the stage. In sharing the experience of *Twelfth Night*, we come to recognize the ties of identity that link our own world of being to the imagined world of the play; and, on a more personal level, we identify our private follies and desires in our fictional counterparts upon the stage. In acknowledging this kinship of resemblance, we too gain a fresh awareness of the nature of "what I am," the true self concealed beneath the surface level of appearances. Moreover, having witnessed how deeply life is ingrained with illusion within Illyria, we may awake from the dreamworld of the play to wonder if "what we are" in the world outside the playhouse is perhaps less static and immutable than we once believed. At this point, imagination and truth may begin to merge in our own world: "Prove true, imagination, O, prove true" (3.4.375).

If art possesses this creative power, however, there remains the problem of dealing with the more troubling issues raised by the gulling of Malvolio. The plot contrived to convince the steward of Olivia's passion for him is enacted with deliberately theatrical overtones, and the conspirators employ deception to feed and then expose Malvolio's folly in much the same way that a playwright manipulates illusion and reality upon the stage. Yet Malvolio's enforced immersion in the world of make-believe in no way reforms him. Nor does it enable him to gain a more positive understanding of either his own identity or the ties that bind him to his fellow men. Malvolio remains isolated and egotistical to the end. What is more, the mockers who have seen their own follies reflected in Malvolio's comic performance are no more altered by the experience than he is.

The plot against Malvolio is originally planned along the traditional lines of Jonsonian "humour" comedy: the victim's folly is to be exposed and purged by comic ridicule to rid him of his humour. Maria explains the scheme in such terms to her fellow satirists:

> . . . it is his grounds of faith that all that look on him love him; and on that vice in him will my revenge find notable cause to work. . . . I know my physic will work with him.
>
> (2.3.151–3; 172–3)

But there is also a strong dose of personal spite in their mockery. The pranksters are really more eager to be entertained by Malvolio's delusions of grandeur than they are to reform him. Maria guarantees her audience that "If I do not gull him into an ayword, and make him a common recreation, do not think I have wit enough to lie straight in my bed" (ll.134–7). It is certainly in this spirit that the revellers take the jest. "If I lose a scruple of this sport," Fabian pledges as the game begins, "let me be boil'd to death with melancholy" (2.5.2–3).

Maria plants the conspirators in the garden box-tree like spectators at a play, bidding them: "Observe him, for the love of mockery; for I know this letter will make a contemplative idiot of him" (ll.18–20). Malvolio, who "has been younder i' the sun practising behavior to his own shadow this half hour" (ll.16–18), is a natural play-actor; and he immediately takes the bait of this improvised comedy. The megalomania suppressed beneath his Puritan façade is comically set free by the discovery of Maria's forged letter, and he is soon persuaded to parade his folly publicly by donning the famous yellow stockings.

Maria's letter cleverly exploits Malvolio's conceit, but he himself manufactures his obsession. With only the flimsiest of clues to lead him on, Malvolio systematically construes every detail of the letter to fuel his newly liberated dreams of greatness, never pausing to consider how ludicrous the message really is:

> Why, this is evident to any formal capacity, there is no obstruction in this. And the end—what should that alpha-

betical position portend? If I could make that resemble something in me! ... M.O.A.I. This simulation is not as the
former; and yet, to crush this a little, it would bow to me, for
every one of these letters are in my name.

(ll.116–20; 139–41)

The deception deftly juggles appearances to prompt Malvolio to
his own undoing, but there is always the danger inherent in such
games of make-believe that the dupe will no longer be able to cope
with reality once his self-fabricated fantasies are stripped away
from him. "Why, thou hast put him in such a dream," Sir Toby
laughingly tells Maria, "that when the image of it leaves him he
must run mad" (ll.193–4). But no such qualms disturb these
puppet-masters. When Fabian echoes this warning, Maria replies
"The house will be the quieter" (3.4.134).

Although it is the letter that persuades Malvolio to play out
his fantasies in public, his audience has already been treated to a
display of his fondness for make-believe. While the conspirators
impatiently wait for him to stumble on the letter, Malvolio muses
on his dream of becoming the rich and powerful "Count Malvolio." As he paints the imaginary scene of Sir Toby's future humiliation and expulsion, the eavesdroppers find themselves unexpectedly drawn into the performance they are watching. Sir Toby, in
particular, becomes so enraged at this "overweening rogue" (l.29)
that Fabian must repeatedly warn him to control his outbursts:
"Nay, patience, or we break the sinews of our plot!" (ll.75–6).
Malvolio's audience prove to be as uncertain as their gull about
the boundaries separating fiction from fact, as will be made comically evident in the miscalculations and confusions that result
from the duel contrived between Sir Andrew and Cesario. Taken
unawares by Malvolio's tableau of future triumph, the three spies
inadvertently become participants in the comedy they are observing.

Malvolio's private playlet of revenge and his discovery of the
letter are staged in a deliberately theatrical manner, played before
the unruly audience of Sir Toby, Sir Andrew, and Fabian. His
play-acting exposes Malvolio's folly to comic perfection; but it
also, in its own topsy-turvy fashion, holds the mirror up to nature
for both the spectators in the box-tree and the audience beyond
the stage. It is a glass more like a funhouse mirror than the

symmetry of a "natural perspective," but in Malvolio's absurd performance the pranksters are presented with a comically distorted image of their own follies and delusions. Malvolio's folly is made more ludicrous by the charade that openly exposes the overweening ambition and conceit normally held within respectable bounds by the sanctimonious steward, but the difference between the performer and his audience is simply one of degree.

If Malvolio is treated by these practical jokers as a puppet on a string, a "trout that must be caught with tickling" (2.5.22), Sir Andrew is no less Sir Toby's own "dear manikin" (3.2.53). His auditors deride Malvolio's pretensions to his mistress's love; but Sir Andrew's wooing of Olivia is equally preposterous, and his hopes are based entirely on Sir Toby's counterfeit assurances. Sir Toby may ridicule Malvolio's determined efforts to "crush" the letter's message to accommodate his own desires, but the assertion of imagination over concrete reality is no less a characteristic trait of Sir Toby himself, who has earlier insisted that "Not to be a-bed after midnight is to be up betimes" (2.3.1–2). The only difference in their dealings with words is that Malvolio uses logic as a crowbar to twist and hammer meanings into a more gratifying form, while Sir Toby chooses to suspend logic altogether. The steward's obsessive instinct for order is simply the inverted image of Sir Toby's own mania for disorder. Even their plot to put an end to Malvolio's authority is dramatized for the spectators in a parody version supplied by Malvolio's own dream of revenge.

The spectators are in their own ways as much drowned in excesses of folly and imagination as their gull. But as they mock the woodcock nearing the gin, the onlookers fail to realize that the "play" itself is an imaginary snare for the woodcocks in its audience. Sir Andrew's reaction to Malvolio's fictive dialogue with a humbled Sir Toby exemplifies the fatuity of his fellow auditors:

> *Malvolio.* "Besides, you waste the treasure of your time with
>   a foolish knight"—
> *Andrew.* That's me, I warrant you.
> *Malvolio.* "One Sir Andrew"—
> *Andrew.* I knew 'twas I, for many do call me fool.
>   (2.5.77–81)

Sir Andrew makes the correct identification but remains oblivious to the intended reprimand. In the same fashion, all the members of Malvolio's audience observe their reflected images in the mirror of the comedy without recognition, thus comically fulfilling Jonathan Swift's famous dictum that "Satyr is a sort of Glass, wherein Beholders do generally discover every body's Face but their own."[6]

By the time Malvolio encounters Olivia again after reading her supposed declaration of love, his perceptions have become completely mastered by his delusions. To those around him who are unaware of the deception, Malvolio appears quite mad. "Why, this is very mid-summer madness," (3.4.56) cries Olivia in response to the incoherent ramblings of this smiling, cross-gartered apparition. From his own perspective, however, he is unquestionably sane, and it is the rest of the world that is behaving strangely. Unlike Viola or Feste, Malvolio has no talent for improvisation. His rejection of a rigidly defined identity, although it gives him a temporary release from social bonds, affords Malvolio no room for flexibility.

Faced with the fluidity of the world of playing in which he suddenly finds himself, Malvolio insists on trying to marshal shifting appearances back into regimented formation:

> Why, every thing adheres together, that no dram of a
> scruple, no scruple of a scruple, no obstacle, no incredulous
> or unsafe circumstance—What can be said?
>
> (3.4.78–81)

But Malvolio's efforts to control the flux are like trying to sculpt water into solid shapes; the material itself refuses static form. His obstinate insistence that the words and actions of those around him should conform to his will makes him appear mad to his fellow players, while they seem equally insane to him.

The quandary over who is mad and who is sane becomes even more entangled in the dialogue between the incarcerated steward and the Fool, disguised as Sir Topas. Malvolio is entirely just in his charge that "never was man thus wrong'd. . . . they have laid me here in hideous darkness" (4.2.28–30). From his perspective, the darkness is tangible and his madness the fantasy of those around him. Yet it is also true, as "Sir Topas" insists, that the darkness is symbolic of the shroud of ignorance and vanity through which Malvolio views the world:

> *Malvolio.* I am not mad, Sir Topas, I say to you this house is
> dark.
> *Clown.* Madman, thou errest. I say there is no darkness but
> ignorance, in which thou art more puzzled than the Egyp-
> tians in their fog.
> *Malvolio.* I say this house is as dark as ignorance, though
> ignorance were as dark as hell; and I say there was never
> man thus abus'd. I am no more mad than you are.
> (4.2.40-8)

His "confessor's" riddles seem designed to force Malvolio to a new understanding of his identity as a fallible and often foolish human being. But "Sir Topas" is himself a fake—a self-avowed corrupter of words whose disguised purpose is not to heal Malvolio's imagined lunacy, but to drive him deeper into madness. Feste juggles words with ease because he understands that they are "very rascals since bonds disgrac'd them," but Malvolio stubbornly insists on making rascal words behave with as much decorum as he believes they should. Throughout this scene, Malvolio returns to his claim "I am not mad" with the same tonic emphasis as Viola reverts to "what I am" in her dialogue with Olivia (act 3, scene 1). But being incapable of Viola's playful attitude, Malvolio rejects any imaginative interpretation of his dilemma.

His rigidity toward both language and experience leaves him incapable of comprehending any truth beyond the concrete limits of reality. "I tell thee I am as well in my wits as any man in Illyria" (4.2.106-7), Malvolio insists with absolute justice; but how far from madness are the other inhabitants of Illyria? In a very ironic sense, Malvolio gets what he deserves when he is imprisoned in his cell. Having persisted in imposing his arbitrary order upon capricious words and appearances, he is himself confined in a guardhouse for his own caprices.

Whatever his deserts, there is nonetheless considerable justice to Malvolio's charge that he has been much abused by the deceivers who have made him "the most notorious geck and gull/That e'er invention play'd on" (5.1.343-4). Ironically, Malvolio's absurdly inflated ego and his isolation are only hardened by his satiric treatment. Even in making his defence, Malvolio stubbornly maintains yet another delusion, that Olivia is personally responsible for his torment. Humiliated beyond endurance, Malvolio stalks off the stage with a final ringing assertion of his vanity and alienation: "I'll be reveng'd on the whole pack of you" (l.378). Malvolio stands as an isolated figure in a festive world from beginning to end because never once does he honestly perceive his own nature, the true identity of "what I am," or the corresponding ties of identity that bind him to his fellow players.

The pranksters, in spite of their fondness for "fellowship," do not fare much better. They have already demonstrated a failure to detect their own follies in Malvolio's pretensions, and it is therefore appropriate that the beguilers as well as their gull should be missing from the witnesses at the recognition scene and the subsequent revelations. Sir Toby, in particular, suffers for his failures of identification. After having challenged Sebastian to a fight in the mistaken belief he was the timorous Cesario, Sir Toby rages onto the stage with a bloody head, angrily spurning the comfort of his friend Sir Andrew: "Will you help?—an asshead and a coxcomb and a knave, a thin-fac'd knave, a gull!" (5.1.206-7).

Whereas the mistaken identities and role-playing in the romantic plot centring on Viola ultimately lead, in the recognition scene, to a renewal of identity and the human bonds of kinship and marriage, Malvolio's immersion in a world of make-believe yields no such beneficial rewards. The ironic counterpart to the recognition scene with its unravelling of identities is Malvolio's dungeon scene. There, Malvolio is literally enclosed in darkness in a cell cutting him off from all direct human contact, and he is bedevilled by tricksters who would like to drive him into deeper confusion. Nor does his audience there or in the garden scene gain any greater insight into their own characters. This failure of imagination, set against Viola's own miraculous success, reflects ironically on the supposedly therapeutic value of "playing" and the dubious morality of the would-be satirists as much as it does on Malvolio's own recalcitrance. Malvolio's final words and his incensed departure add a discordant note to the gracefully orchestrated harmonies of the final act.

Malvolio's response to his comic purgatory stirs unresolved

questions about the value of playing with reality. Whereas Viola's part in the comedy reveals how the release that playing allows can lead to a renewed sense of identity and human bonds, Malvolio's role exposes the other side of the coin, the realm in which release of imagination leads only to greater isolation and imperception. Fabian's jest about Malvolio's absurd play-acting, "If this were play'd upon a stage now, I could condemn it as an improbable fiction" (3.4.127–8), like the theatrical overtones of Viola's improvisations and the playlike quality of the recognition scene, deliberately opens up the vistas of the play by reminding us that we are witnesses of a play, "a natural perspective, that is and is not." But amusing as Malvolio's surrender to playing is, it raises the most disturbing questions in the play. Can men, in fact, ever perfectly distinguish what is real from what is imagined or intentionally spurious? Can they ever come to know the truth about themselves, the identity appearances have concealed from them?

Twelfth Night itself offers no pat solutions. In a comic world devoted to playing and yet mirroring the actual world of being, in which identities are both mistaken and revealed, in which deception can both conceal truths and expose them, and in which bonds have disgraced the words on which men are dependent for communication, no permanent resolution of these ambiguities is ever possible. Shakespeare himself shrugs off the task of providing any final illumination with delightful finesse. As the play draws to a close with Feste's epilogue song and the world of playing begins to dissolve back into the world of being, the Fool concludes:

> A great while ago the world begun,
> With hey ho, the wind and the rain,
> But that's all one, our play is done,
> And we'll strive to please you every day.

NOTES

1. 3.2.20–4. Quotations from Shakespeare are from *The Riverside Shakespeare*, ed. G. Blakemore Evans *et al.* (Boston, 1974).
2. Joseph H. Summers, "The Masks of *Twelfth Night*," *The University Review*, 22 (1955), 26.
3. " 'As You Like It' and 'Twelfth Night': Shakespeare's Sense of an

Ending," in *Shakespearian Comedy*, ed. Malcolm Bradbury and David Palmer, Stratford-upon-Avon Studies, 14 (1972), p. 175.

4. It is relevant to recall that the festival of Twelfth Night, in addition to its popular associations with the holiday release of Misrule festivities, was also a religious celebration of the Feast of Epiphany.

5. Discussing the use of identical twins in *The Comedy of Errors*, Northrop Frye argues: ". . . I feel that one reason for the use of two sets of twins in this play is that identical twins are not really identical (the same person) but merely similar, and when they meet they are delivered, in comic fashion, from the fear of the loss of identity, the primitive horror of the döppelganger which is an element in nearly all forms of insanity, something of which they feel as long as they are being mistaken for each other." (*A Natural Perspective* [New York, 1965], p. 78)

6. *A Tale of a Tub, With Other Early Works, 1696–1707*, ed. Herbert Davis (Oxford, 1957), p. 140.

Jörg Hasler

The Dramaturgy of the Ending of *Twelfth Night*

The final resolution of *Twelfth Night* evolves from a process which engages the whole of the play's last scene. Furthermore, there is no lack of consistent theatrical notation in this scene. Employed with remarkable singleness of purpose, it is instrumental in shaping the build-up towards the strong impact of Viola's revelation. Apart from the unusually extensive control of the action, a study of this ending also invites us to glance back at some features of earlier comedies. The view of *Twelfth Night* as the consummation of Shakespearian comedy is widely accepted.[1] At the same time, few commentators neglect to mention the extent to which Shakespeare here draws on his preceding experiments. Barrett Wendell even went so far as to "recognize the *Twelfth Night*—with all its perennial delights—a masterpiece not of invention, but of recapitulation."[2] This remark has been much quoted, though it perhaps unduly neglects the transmutations that go with Shakespeare's self-borrowings. Harold Jenkins sums up this particular aspect of *Twelfth Night* when he suggests that

> . . . in however short a time Shakespeare ultimately wrote this play, he had in a sense been composing it during the previous decade.[3]

The final scene begins very quickly. Orsino has decided to go and see Olivia himself. At her house he meets Feste who, irked a little by Orsino's condescension,[4] does a stint of his most artful begging. The mood is relaxed, as so often in Illyria; we get an

Reprinted by permission of Cooper Monographs (Switzerland), from *Shakespeare's Theatrical Notation: the Comedies* (1974), by Jörg Hasler.

impression of unlimited leisure and time to jest away. Having exhausted Orsino's bounty, Feste leaves to inform Olivia of her visitor, when suddenly the scene darkens and Viola's trials begin. Antonio is brought in by officers. Viola is first to notice them:

> Here comes the man, sir, that did rescue me
>
> V.1.44

she says to Orsino. This is more than the usual formula for putting the spotlight on an actor making his entry. We infer that Viola has obviously told Orsino about the duel Toby inflicted on her. Her reference to that adventure, however, is vague enough to be misunderstood: she thinks of the duel and how this strange seaman got her out of it, but Antonio most likely relates her words to the shipwreck where he rescued Sebastian. To him, her remark sounds like an acknowledgement of their acquaintance, and this can only deepen his grief at her renewed denials later on. As he explains to Orsino why, in spite of the grave risk involved, he exposed himself to "the danger of its adverse town," he points an accusing finger at Viola:

> . . . A witchcraft drew me hither:
> *That most ingrateful boy there by your side*[5]
> From the rude sea's enrag'd and foamy mouth
> Did I redeem; . . .   70

Antonio very forcefully directs the focus of attention on the young "culprit." What is more, he "places" Viola at Orsino's side, stressing that at this juncture she is very much the Duke's loyal servant. She is where she most desires to be. This is important in view of the imminent, explosive encounter with Olivia.

Viola's predicament, with Olivia doting on her while she secretly pines for Orsino, is quite enough to have to bear without the puzzling complaints of Antonio. The heavy deictic emphasis is kept up throughout his indictment of the "youth," and must contribute not a little to Viola's embarrassment.

> . . . for his sake,
> Did I expose myself, *pure for his love,*
> Into the danger of this adverse town; . . .   76

There is no time to investigate the matter further, however.

Orsino forgets the moving accents of the seemingly betrayed man when Olivia approaches:

> Here comes the Countess; now heaven walks on earth 91

he fatuously exclaims. His hyperbole is too blatantly out of tune with reality: it soon becomes ridiculous in the light of the reception he gets from the Countess, and the childish wrath with which he tries to force her affections. Dismissing Antonio for the time being, he stuns him with his assertion that

> Three months this youth hath tended upon me. 93

Olivia and her attendants are not allowed to obliterate the person around whom everything turns in this scene. Almost immediately "this youth" is back in focus, in preparation for what follows, viz. Olivia's most astonishing breach of etiquette inspired by her love for Cesario.

> *Oli.* What would my lord, but that he may not have,
> Wherein Olivia may seem serviceable?
> Cesario, you do not keep promise with me.
> *Vio.* Madam?
> *Duke.* Gracious Olivia—
> *Oli.* What do you say, Cesario? Good my lord—⁶ 95

Olivia sees her "husband" at Orsino's side, still posing, she thinks, as a servant. This sight is enough to make her forget her manners. She begins by addressing Orsino—then she interrupts herself to speak to the page at his side. The baffled Orsino tries to regain her attention, but she is only interested in Cesario. The tension now mounts rapidly, to Viola's embarrassment. She steadfastly sticks to her rôle as Orsino's man:

> My lord would speak; my duty hushes me. 101

This—almost a rebuke—is all that Olivia gets out of her, and it does not improve the Countess' temper at all. She adopts a quite unprecedented tone to rid herself of Orsino:

> If it be aught to the old tune, my lord,
> It is as fat and fulsome to mine ear
> As howling after music. 102

Rejected more bluntly than ever, Orsino indulges in positively childish tantrums which, even at this later hour, make one wonder whether he will ever grow up. He elects to try his hand at a new posture, that of "a savage jealousy That sometime savours nobly." Since Olivia reserves her love for Cesario, he will do away with Cesario:

> But *this your minion*, whom I know you love,
> And whom, by heaven I swear, I tender dearly,
> Him will I tear out of that cruel eye
> Where he sits crowned in his master's spite.
> *Come, boy, with me;* my thoughts are ripe in mischief:
> I'll sacrifice the lamb that I do love
> To spite a raven's heart within a dove.   119

Viola, still by his side, is ready—"most jocund, apt, and willingly,"—to be sacrificed like a lamb. Olivia now tastes the same bitter cup as Antonio. "Where goes Cesario?" she asks as Viola obediently follows Orsino. Viola's answer is a passionate declaration of love for the irate Duke, curious enough on the lips of a "youth." The Countess is brought so low by this that she begins to sound like the adolescent lovers of *A Midsummer Night's Dream* in their most plaintive despair:

> Ay me, detested! How am I beguil'd!   113

In her ignorance of Sebastian's existence, let alone of what has occurred between him and Olivia, Viola is bound to appear shamefully, heartlessly, false:

> Who does beguile you? Who does do you wrong?   134

Orsino and "Cesario" have almost disappeared when Olivia finally says the électrifying word that stops them in their tracks:

> Whither, my lord? Cesario, husband, stay.   137

There now develops a tug-of-war between the outraged Duke of Illyria and the injured, deeply disappointed Olivia. They both turn on Viola, Orsino with the vehemence of a nobleman betrayed by his servant ("Her husband, sirrah?"), Olivia lamenting the "baseness" of Cesario's "fear." This naturally brings about a visible shift: Viola is no longer at the side of her amazed, incredulous master, but rather half-way between him and Olivia. Duke and Countess both stare at her in disbelief. All eyes, in fact, are on her, the mortified, confused bone of contention. Bernard Beckerman has observed that in the last scene of *Twelfth Night*

> Orsino and Olivia . . . jointly direct the uncovering of the mystery by calling upon others to act rather than by acting themselves. The focus thus lies between them.[7]

Between them, until Sebastian appears, stands Viola. Caught in the middle as she is, her situation steadily worsens. In her love of Cesario, Olivia appeals to him to show some manly courage. Ironically, she now actually echoes Maria's letter to Malvolio urging the steward not to be afraid of greatness:

> Fear not, Cesario, take thy fortunes up; 142

Viola may well begin to doubt her own sanity when the Priest enters. He comes at Olivia's request to unfold in her words

> . . .—what thou dost know
> Hath newly pass'd between this youth and me. 148

After a glance at "this youth" the Priest promptly asserts that "A contract of eternal bond of love" has indeed been confirmed, attested, strengthened and sealed only two hours ago. The grave Priest's report, essentially not a narrative but a listing of the symbolic gestures of the formal betrothal, is curiously abstract, drained of all life and devoid of any individualizing details:

> A contract of eternal bond of love,
> Confirm'd by mutual joinder of your hands,
> Attested by the holy close of lips,
> Strength'ned by interchangement of your rings;
> And all the ceremony of this compact
> Seal'd in my function, by my testimony;
> Since when, my watch hath told me, toward my grave,
> I have travell'd but two hours. 150

The whole emphasis is on the awesome solemnity and binding power of the ceremony he performed. Against such testimony Viola is helpless. Meanwhile Orsino has recovered the power of speech, and she has to listen to his wild abuse of her:

> *O thou dissembling cub!* What wilt thou be,
> When time hath sow'd a grizzle on thy case?   158

What is worse, he is now quite prepared to give up Cesario, as
well as to renounce Olivia:

> Farewell, and take her; but direct thy feet
> Where thou and I henceforth may never meet.   162

The finality of the closing couplet strongly suggests that Orsino
is again on the point of leaving. Viola can only protest, knowing
that it is of no avail against the word of the Priest. She follows
Orsino in despair:

> *Vio.* My lord, I do protest—
> *Oli.*   O, do not swear!
>   Hold little faith, though thou has too much fear.   164

As "Cesario" walks away from her once again, even the doting
Olivia loses patience with him: she interrupts him immediately.
The incident causes the three figures to be spaced out more
widely across the stage. In view of the sequel it is essential that
Viola, in pursuit of Orsino, should move away from Olivia. For
one thing, Sir Andrew does not see "Cesario" until he is pointed
out to him. What is more, Sebastian does not notice his sister for
quite some time. This can only be managed without awkwardness
if Viola stands at a sufficient distance from Olivia, quite apart
from the symmetrical arrangement of the twins, which also requires some space between them.

    This time Orsino is prevented from actually leaving by the
comic-pathetic appearance of Sir Andrew with his head "broken,"
clamouring for a surgeon. Like all the preceding arrivals, he has a
grievance against Cesario. His case, though, is an amusing variation on this recurrent motif. He is not aware of Cesario's presence—probably he enters with his mauled head bent down. He
also assumes that everyone knows whom he is talking about:

> *Oli.* What's the matter?
> *Sir And.* Has broke my head across, and has given
>   Sir Toby a bloody coxcomb too.   168

Olivia therefore has to ask "Who has done this, Sir Andrew?" and
on hearing that it was "The Count's gentleman, one Cesario," it is

Orsino's turn to be amazed. After all, he has long ago declared that "Diana's lip Is not more smooth and rubious" than that of his lovely page, whose whole person "is semblative a woman's part." It is therefore with understandable scepticism that he makes sure:

> My gentleman, Cesario? 175

Sir Andrew's reaction indicates that Orsino incredulously points to "Cesario" as he asks the question. The effect on Aguecheek is quite spectacular:

> Od's lifelings, here he is! You broke my head for nothing; . . . 176

The foolish knight recoils from the mere sight of Viola—what could be more incriminating? But there is more to come. The pace accelerates as new accusers turn up at ever shorter intervals. Aguecheek is followed by Sir Toby. In contrast to Sir Andrew, he is above—or past—complaining. In answer to Orsino's questions, he will only say:

> That's all one; has hurt me and there's th' end on't . . . 188

He can walk only slowly, with difficulty. He has overheard Sir Andrew berating Cesario:

> If a bloody coxcomb be a hurt, you have hurt me 182

before he is near enough to be noticed by his friend: "Here comes Sir Toby halting . . ." For once there is no accusing finger for Viola. Toby seems too overwhelmed with the fact that the stripling was equal to hurting him—there is certainly no more than a tired nod in the direction of Viola.

This is the last we see of these knights, for Olivia promptly sends them off to bed. The striving for symmetry begins to make itself felt. The two votaries of cakes and ale have played their part; there is no room for them in the final tableau.[8] Moreover, at this stage any confrontation between Toby (or Maria) and Malvolio must be avoided.

While the audience is aware that Sebastian is somewhere about Olivia's house, and bound to turn up sooner or later, Viola has gone from bad to worse. She is caught in a maze from which it must seem to her impossible to extricate herself. On an increasingly crowded stage she finds herself surrounded by accusers. Surveying the portion of the scene we have so far discussed, we see that it definitely belongs to Viola. Until Sebastian's entrance baffles all, Shakespeare consistently keeps the focus of attention on her, in spite of the fact that she has little to say. The situation and the technique employed are reminiscent of Hero's arraignment in church. As in the case of Hero, of course, everybody talks about Viola. She is the target of a general wrath. We have seen how at every stage, the gestic impulses of passionate address, and especially the gestic force of that basic tool, the demonstrative, help to keep Viola at the calm centre of the tornado. The others make all the noise, but while they come, have their say, and then make room for the next plaintiff, Viola remains, always involved, always concerned.

A comedy, in the words of Harold Jenkins, "is a play in which the situation holds some threat of disaster but issues in the achievement of happiness."[9] This may remind us more immediately of the merchant Antonio or of Aegeon. In *Twelfth Night* the concrete threats against Viola do not materialize before the finale. Viola's experience here is not unlike that of Isabella. In *Measure for Measure* it is the accuser who goes through an ordeal until at last she is taken seriously, listened to, and then vindicated by Mariana's and ultimately the Duke's own testimony.

It is instructive to examine the way in which Viola's ordeal is given its dramatic form. We have observed how every new arrival brings his own, incomprehensible accusations. J. L. Styan has briefly surveyed this technique of "successive entrances" from *Henry VI* to *King Lear*.[10] The ending of *Twelfth Night* he views primarily in terms of control. At the end of *As You Like It* and *Twelfth Night*, he says, Shakespeare orders

> a crowded stage for a scene of artificial symmetry, the visual pattern acquiring some of the qualities of tableaux. Yet Shakespeare had also to overcome the disadvantage of the confusing impact of a full stage . . .
> One method of controlling the action was to fill the stage by a mechanical procession of entrances. The spectator's attention is taken by each new figure and each new voice.[11]

The final scene of *Twelfth Night* blends this technical advantage of successive entrances with the purpose the device serves in the histories and tragedies, when a series of messengers with progressively worsening news creates a feeling of calamity and imminent doom, or tests the endurance of the hero.[12] We can now see that the passage under review represents an elaborate adaptation of that pattern to the needs of comedy. The mere messengers have been replaced by important figures with whom we are well acquainted, and who all confront the treacherous youth of their imagination in their own characteristic way: the honest, devoted "pirate" Antonio meets Cesario with forthright indignation at his ingratitude; the noble, enamoured Olivia with more restrained, yet deep disappointment; Aguecheek with undisguised terror, Toby still bemused with the shock of being beaten by the young stripling of a gentleman. Furthermore, there is of course a final entrance, Sebastian's, which sets things right again.

An incidental, comic adaptation of the same pattern in its basic form occurs in *The Merry Wives of Windsor*. Dr. Caius and Evans revenge themselves on the Host of the Garter: one after the other, in a sequence blatantly pre-arranged, Bardolph, Evans and Caius appear like messengers at the door, just long enough to shout their increasingly alarming news about the "Germans" who have stolen the Host's horses.[13] There is another succession of entrances, again comically calamitous, at the end of the play. Here, Page and his wife are both thwarted by a counter-plot of their daughter Anne. Slender, Master Page's favourite choice for Anne, first returns with a tale of woe: his white fairy turned out to be "a great lubberly boy." No sooner has Mistress Page explained the misfortune by revealing her own stratagem in favour of Caius, than the doctor bursts on the scene in one of his rages: the fairy in green was a boy too. Now the successful Fenton brings in his Anne to ask pardon of his good father and mother. To our delight, the parental plotters are outplotted, but we are also pleased to see that resentment is remarkably short-lived.

Earlier, in the finale of *The Taming of the Shrew*, Shakespeare had used a witty inversion of the successive entrances pattern. There the wager between the three husbands causes them, one by one, to send for their wives. Now it is precisely the non-appearance of the first two wives that spells disaster. Lucentio "bids" his mistress to come to him, but Biondello returns alone. Hortensio, though he cautiously "entreats" the widow to come, fares no better: Biondello has only a defiant message for him. Thus the effect is all the more breathtaking when Kate, "commanded" to come, appears in the doorway:

> *Bap.* Now, by my holidame, here comes Katherina!
>
> *TS* V.ii.99

In these cases, as in *Twelfth Night*, the series of entrances strikes us as a formal pattern of more or less transparent artificiality. The sequence works towards a final, important effect. This is not the same as, for instance, the entirely "natural" yet carefully spaced-out returns of Portia and Bassanio, each preceded by a harbinger, from Venice to Belmont.

As Toby and Aguecheek limp away, attended by Feste and Fabian, Sebastian hurries in. There is no time for anyone to mirror his approach, as had been done in the case of Antonio, Olivia and Toby. Yet his is surely the most effective entrance of them all. Eager to justify himself to Olivia, he makes straight for her, ignoring everyone else. This partly explains why he does not notice Viola at first. His entrance, of course, is the one that will undo all the confusion caused by the preceding ones. It sheds light on everything at a stroke. Nevertheless, before meeting his sister, he is made to settle very quickly the various questions, one by one. Almost every line he speaks solves a problem. As the audience knows everything already, no time is wasted in dwelling on this, and Sebastian cannot ignore Viola too long without artificiality.

> I am sorry, madam, I have hurt your kinsman.
>
> V.i.201

His apology solves the mystery of Toby's "hurt." The contrite offender mirrors Olivia's consternation at the sight of this second Cesario:

> You throw a strange regard upon me, and by that
> I do perceive it hath offended you.   204

His next words confirm the Priest's account of a secret betrothal:

> Pardon me, sweet one, even for the vows
> We made each other but so late ago.   206

Olivia must begin to grasp that *this* is her husband. Next, he recognizes a familiar face, and his most affectionate greeting disposes of the riddle which has so oppressed Antonio:

> Antonio, O my dear Antonio!
> How have the hours rack'd and tortur'd me
> Since I have lost thee!   210

Full of joyful emotion himself, Sebastian still spreads nothing but amazement around him. As with Olivia, Sebastian notices the extreme astonishment of Antonio, and again he misunderstands it:

> *Ant.* Sebastian are you?
> *Seb.* Fear'st thou that, Antonio?   213

For Olivia, Orsino, Antonio and Viola everything falls into place in the whirlwind of Sebastian's entrance. His preoccupation with Olivia and then with Antonio must be quite intense and passionate to keep him from noticing Viola. At the same time it is quite likely that the spectators—who do not need to be enlightened—will not give Sebastian's words their full attention. They are inevitably absorbed by the visual impact of the twins, simultaneously present for the first time. Orsino and Antonio draw our attention to this very emphatically:

> One face, one voice, one habit, and two persons!
> A natural perspective, that is and is not.   208
> How have you made division of yourself?
> An apple cleft in two is not more twin
> Than *these two creatures*. Which is Sebastian?   214

Both stress the stage-picture created by the resemblance of brother and disguised sister, Sebastian very animated, Viola transfixed. These baffled reactions are not meant as "asides." At the very moment when Orsino speaks, Sebastian discovers his friend Antonio; it looks as if he is too rapt to heed the strange talk about a "natural perspective." In contrast to this he does listen to Antonio's stunned comment, and prompted by the deictic "*these* two creatures" he finally becomes aware of Viola.

When their eyes meet at last, the result is an immediate slowing down of the pace, even a momentary halt, very effective after the tempo sustained since Sebastian's exciting entrance.

> *Seb.* Do I stand there? I never had a brother;
> Nor can there be that deity in my nature
> Of here and everywhere. I had a sister
> Whom the blind waves and surges have devour'd.   218

There follows the exquisitely beautiful duologue in which the twins gradually identify each other. Their meeting having been put off until now, the positive recognition, viz. the revelation of Viola, is thus further delayed. They are not allowed to race into each other's arms. Nevill Coghill has an excellent passage describing why a delayed recognition can be so particularly moving. He rightly stresses the visual element in this:

> It is in the delay that we taste the recognition most feelingly: for with our eyes we see that a longed-for thing is about to happen, even before it has begun: we see the certainty of a joy to come, delayed in order to prolong the thrill of having it in prospect. This is an experience in art that I think can most feelingly be given through the medium of theatre . . .[14]

As to the peculiar delicacy and restraint of the twins' duologue, Alice Shalvi has observed how

> the use of the third person in their mention of Viola is a beautifully subtle method of indicating the way in which neither wants to be overwhelmed by emotion, even while it excellently conveys the emotion that is pent up, and implied by, their words.[15]

As regards gesture and grouping, Viola's speech concluding the recognition-passage is particularly interesting:

> If nothing lets to make us happy both
> But this my masculine usurp'd attire,
> Do not embrace me till each circumstance
> Of place, time, fortune, do cohere and jump
> That I am Viola; which to confirm,
> I'll bring you to a captain in this town,
> Where lie my maiden weeds; by whose gentle help
> I was preserv'd to serve this noble Count.

All the occurrence of my fortune since
Hath been between this lady and this lord.   241

The desire to withhold the inner surge of joy until the last
shadow of a doubt has been removed is most clearly in evidence
when Viola requests her brother not to embrace her. This however seems to pose a real problem in performance. Whereas
scholars may easily take Viola's words at their face-value, there
are few producers who can deny their Sebastian the emotional
relief of a brotherly embrace. Alice Shalvi, pursuing her theme of
restraint, finds it significant that

> Shakespeare even makes Viola delay her brother's happy
> embrace until she shall have abandoned her doublet for a
> gown, and the same is true of her betrothal to Orsino.[16]

This is very persuasive, and soundly based on the text. Yet
when it comes to producing the scene, Viola's cautious reserve
seems to overtax our strength and even to border on the unnatural. The principle of postponing the happy celebrations is here
driven to its limits. Producers must feel that before Sebastian can
turn to Olivia to stress the lighter side of what has occurred,

So comes it, lady, you have been mistook,   251

"each circumstance . . ." has surely cohered and jumped. In accor-
dance with this, the beginning of Viola's critical sentence tends to
get slurred over, while the end, "That I am Viola," is detached
from the rest as much as possible and given the special emphasis
of a solemn affirmation.

In Viola's concluding line Shakespeare again hints at the intended stage-picture. During much of the scene, when she was
the bone of contention, and again now, when the twins meet at
the centre of the stage, Viola has been placed between "this lady
and this lord." The dangers inherent in her false position between
Orsino and Olivia had only been latent before this final scene.
Now it has all come to a head. Viola's place on stage therefore
symbolizes the "occurrence" of her fortune since she came to
Illyria, her ambiguous rôle as a go-between

. . . between *this lady* and *this lord*.   250

Her last words contain a strong gestic impulse to stress her
position in the danger zone between the two proud, noble personages, at the very point when this scenic image is about to be
replaced by a new constellation. After the arrival of Sebastian and
the ensuing revelation of Viola, the happy, permanent equilibrium of two couples is substituted for the uneasy, precarious
symmetry of the triangle.

Sebastian, as we have seen, is a resolving figure *par excellence*,
since his mere entrance at the right moment disposes of all the
confusions at a stroke. To achieve this startling effect, Shakespeare exploits a theme he has introduced into the play only at a
very late stage. Harold Jenkins has pointed out that in *Twelfth Night*
the dramatist "is, in fact, combining the plots of *The Two Gentlemen
of Verona* and *The Comedy of Errors*":

> He does not, however, combine them in equal degree. The
> heartsick heroine who in page's disguise takes messages of
> love to another woman provided little more than an episode
> in the complicated relations of the two gentlemen of Verona;
> but in *Twelfth Night* this episode has grown into the central
> situation from which the play draws its life. On the other
> hand, the confusion of twins which entertained us for five
> acts in *The Comedy of Errors* appears now as little more than an
> adroit device to bring a happy ending.[17]

This hardly overstates the case. The theme of mistaken identity
only begins to make its contribution when Sebastian and Antonio
have at last found their way to the capital of Illyria. From the first,
of course, there is the similarity in the shipwreck stories of *The
Comedy of Errors* and *Twelfth Night*, but not before III.iv. does Antonio mistake Viola for Sebastian. In IV.i. Feste for his part believes
Sebastian to be Viola. Sebastian's exasperation on that occasion
recalls the atmosphere of Ephesus:

> Are all the people mad?
>
> TNIV.i.26

he exclaims, in a mood of frustration not unlike that of the
Syracusan Antipholus when he concludes that

> There's none but witches do inhabit here.
>
> CEIII.ii.154

In line with Jenkins' observation, however, most echoes of *The Comedy of Errors* occur in the last scene. Antonio's sad experience reminds us most strongly of Shakespeare's first comedy. Like Aegeon, he believes himself shamefully betrayed by one he loves.[18] Just as Duke Solinus of Ephesus confounds Aegeon:

> I tell thee, Syracusian, twenty years
> Have I been patron to Antipholus,
> During which time he ne'er saw Syracusa,
>
> CEV.i.325

so Duke Orsino of Illyria reduces Antonio to silence with an unanswerable rebuttal:

> . . .—fellow, thy words are madness.
> Three months this youth hath tended upon me—. . .
>
> TNV.i.92

At the point when everyone stands amazed by the likeness of the twins, there is even a literal echo. Duke Solinus, beholding the Dromios and Antipholuses together, had wondered:

> One of these men is genius to the other;
> And so of these. Which is the natural man,
> And which the spirit? . . .
>
> CEV.i.331

Pointing at Sebastian in disbelief ("So went he suited") Viola says to Sebastian her brother:

> Such a Sebastian was my brother too;
> So went he suited to his watery tomb;
> If spirits can assume both form and suit,
> You come to fright us.
>
> TNV.i.225

Yet even such a verbal parallel in a similar situation does not necessarily imply the simple repetition of an old idea. In *Twelfth Night*, "spirit" takes on an additional meaning: it is beyond a Dromio or Antipholus to answer, like Sebastian:

> A spirit I am indeed,
> But am in that dimension grossly clad
> Which from the womb I did participate.   228

Solinus thinks in terms of *genius* as the attendant spirit of a man, Viola at first fears she has to deal with her brother's "ghost" returned from the grave, like a Hamlet senior or a Banquo, and Sebastian uses the same word to refer to his immortal soul. Olivia now faces her real husband, and it is all visibly too much for her. Orsino reassures her with new-found consideration and sympathy:

> Be not amaz'd; right noble is his blood.   256

Then it is time for him to grapple with the changed situation himself, to address himself to the newly revealed Viola. Whereas Sebastian, having served his turn, is heard of no more, the fate of his sister remains the central concern of the audience. Orsino now gives the first, veiled, and as yet conditional intimation of his intentions towards the girl:

> If this be so, as yet the glass seems true,
> I shall have share in this most happy wreck.[19]   257

Though he could easily be more specific, his meaning is obviously in the spectators' mind when he now faces Cesario/Viola. Addressing her still as a "boy," he reminds her of her former pledges which, now he knows she is a woman, take on a new significance:

> Boy, thou hast said to me a thousand times
> Thou never shouldst love woman like to me.   259

This gives Viola her second opportunity to express the full depth of her love for him. His response to her fervent and solemn declaration is ambiguous, to say the least: his gestic reaction may give her hope, but his words are strangely guarded and reserved.

> Give me thy hand;
> And let me see thee in thy woman's weeds.   264

Now as before, the writing focuses on Viola. Explicit gestic notation, such as Orsino's imperative ("Give me thy hand") invariably refers to her. In contrast to this, we do not know what is going on between Olivia and her husband. In their case, everything is already settled, whereas Orsino quite understandably needs some time to adjust himself: he cannot transfer his affections from

Olivia to Viola too fast, or he risks appearing in too comic a light. It is almost as if he reserved his position until he knows whether Viola's true "outside" can charm him as her male disguise had charmed Olivia. The awkwardness of his situation must explain the discrepancy between his instinctive gesture and his non-committal words.

Nevertheless, things seem to be drawing to a close. Yet there is still that other matter, the strange frenzy of Olivia's steward, who even now languishes in the "dark house." Orsino's reference to her "woman's weeds" reminds Viola of the captain with whom she left her things in I.ii. That self-same sea-captain, she reveals, "Is now in durance, at Malvolio's suit . . ." This—Viola's last speech, by the way—in turn reminds Olivia of her steward. The *New Cambridge Shakespeare* notes that "we have heard nothing before of this lawsuit" and explains: "it is Shakespeare's device for bringing Malvolio back upon the scene."[20] Yet Shakespeare goes out of his way to show that he does not need the mysterious lawsuit to bring Malvolio back. Before Olivia can even send for the "madman," Feste comes in, unbidden by anyone, with Malvolio's letter of complaint. *Enter Clowne with a letter, and Fabian,* as the Folio direction puts it. Evidently there must be some other point to this curious coincidence which led to a case, "Malvolio vs. Captain." Our recollection of the trusty Captain and of Viola's high opinion of him[21] engages our sympathies on his side. The wrong done to Malvolio, on the other hand, will shortly be so much emphasized that we might mistakenly conclude he was more sinned against than sinning. So Clifford Leech may well be right with his reading:

> It is evident that the ambitious steward has exercised authority with a long arm: our realization of that moderates our pity for him.[22]

A sizeable section of the scene is now set aside for the conclusion to the Malvolio-intrigue; the upshot, however, will be that it cannot be truly concluded at all. Olivia and the gull himself must at least learn what really happened. Fabian, who was not among the instigators, is the ideal man to tell them.[23] Viola has had no part in all this, yet Shakespeare does not allow her to be totally eclipsed for such a long time. Having heard Malvolio's letter, Olivia sends for him. While we are waiting, she uses the lull to attend to her own business:

> My lord, so please you, these things further thought on,
> To think me as well a sister as a wife,
> One day shall crown th'alliance on't, so please you,
> Here at my house, and at my proper cost.   303

Some reflection has taught her that there is really nothing left to prevent her and Orsino being friends. She moves towards reconciliation. At the same time, she already deals with an important point which is normally part of the closing-speech: she will arrange for the festivities to come. She foresees a double marriage: a curious feature of her speech is the request to Orsino

> To think me as well a sister as a wife.   304

She hopes she will be no less acceptable to him as a sister-in-law than she would have been as his wife. Yet Orsino, as we have seen, has not really committed himself to Viola as yet. Could it be that Olivia, sympathizing with Viola in her predicament, indulges in a bit of gentle prompting on behalf of the girl she once fell in love with?[24] If so, it certainly works: Orsino briefly thanks her and then again turns to Viola:

> Your master quits you; and, for your service done him,
> So much against the mettle of your sex,
> So far beneath your soft and tender breeding,
> And since you call'd me master for so long,
> Here is my hand; you shall from this time be
> Your master's mistress.   308

Now he no longer speaks to "Cesario." He recognizes and indeed stresses her womanhood and her noble birth, acknowledging all she has done for him. This is not without irony when we remember the vanity with which he used to pontificate about the inferiority of a woman's love to that of a man. He repeats his former gesture, and even here the change from "Give me thy hand" (264) to "Here is my hand" is surely significant. It looks more like a pledge this time—and he comes out with a well-nigh unequivocal proposal. In the case of Viola, we know very well that

the Duke's proposal is welcome, but no more than Isabella in
Measure for Measure is she permitted to respond. We never hear
another word from her after her mention of Malvolio's suit
against the Captain. Perhaps the promise in Orsino's words makes
her speechless, but there is also the fact that "the madman" now
comes in, escorted by the ever-useful Fabian. The investigation of
Malvolio's misadventure is resumed.

This short interlude (from Fabian's *exit* to his return with the
steward) inserted into the segment devoted to Malvolio helps to
achieve two important effects. It has a bearing on Orsino's switch
from Olivia to Viola, which requires to be handled with delicacy
and tact. The interlude is a device which allows the change to be
effected in three evenly spaced-out steps, so that it appears like a
gradual process which is not truly completed even at the end of
the play, while assuring us of Viola's future happiness. The other
consequence of this insertion concerns Malvolio and his influence
on the mood of the ending: many things usually left until the end
are already settled before Malvolio enters, so that very little will
be left for Orsino's closing-speech. As a result, the totally unreconciled, defiant exit-line

> I'll be reveng'd on the whole pack of you   364

hits the audience as late as possible, only ten lines before everyone else withdraws too, leaving us alone with Feste and his
epilogue-song. This harsh and jarring note, placed where it has
maximum effect, justifies the view that "the most interesting
thing in *Twelfth Night* is its ultimate drawing back from a secure
sense of harmony."[25] Malvolio's last words reverberate in Olivia's
sympathetic reaction:

> He hath been most notoriously abus'd   365

which is doubly effective because it echoes Malvolio's first, solemn (if mistaken) accusation when he came in:

> Madam, you have done me wrong,
> Notorious wrong.   315

The sorry business is even allowed to spill over into Orsino's
closing-speech:

> Pursue him, and entreat him to a peace;
> He hath not told us of the captain yet.   366

It is remarkable how consistently Shakespeare discourages too simple, black-and-white judgements of the issue. In referring to the Captain, Orsino provides an immediate corrective to Olivia's sympathy for her steward. We may already have winced at the word "pack," and now, lest we feel too much pity, we are further reminded of the nasty streak in Malvolio. With the steward in the "dark house," Maria's jest has no doubt gone a little too far, but on the other hand Malvolio himself is apparently quite prepared to put decent men in prison. It will not be easy to placate him, but Orsino will at least try.

Even if we avoid the gross mistake of turning Malvolio into a tragic figure, his appearance in V.i. is bound to have a sobering effect on the play's ending. With his furious departure, however, his person at least is removed from sight before the actual conclusion. Shakespeare continues to tidy up the stage for the final speech when Orsino says:

> Pursue him, and entreat him to a peace.   366

Though there is no stage-direction in the Folio, and modern editors refrain from supplying one, it would look absurd if no one stirred at Orsino's command. No doubt the invaluable Fabian, perhaps with one or more of Orsino's men, leaves in pursuit of the "madly-us'd" Malvolio. When therefore Orsino closes the play, the two couples have to share the stage only with Antonio and Feste, who are at a respectful distance with attendants, officers, and possibly the Priest.

After all the thoughtful preparation by Olivia, there are no loose threads left for Orsino to tie up:

> He hath not told us of the captain yet.
> When that is known, and golden time convents,
> A solemn combination shall be made
> Of our dear souls. Meantime, sweet sister,
> We will not part from hence, Cesario, come;
> For so you shall be while you are a man;

> But when in other habits you are seen,
> Orsino's mistress, and his fancy's queen.   367
> [*Exeunt all but the Clown.*

Even at the very end Orsino's tone remains singularly
subdued. However beautiful his phrase about "golden time," he
still rather ungraciously insists on checking the truth of Viola's
story. We, the audience, shall of course never know the circumstances which delivered the Captain into the power of Malvolio.
When Orsino knows, and when Viola sheds her disguise, the
marriage will take place. In looking forward to the consummation
of Viola's desires, Orsino speaks almost with the gravity of the
Priest: "A solemn combination Of . . . souls" will be made. He
avoids all mention of "triumphs," "mirth," "revels" or "jollity." We
are not invited, as in earlier comedies, to think in terms of merry-
making festivity.

Then he addresses Olivia, and one short sentence now suf-
fices to set all things aright between them. In calling her "sweet
sister," taking up her own word of l.313, he accepts her offer of
friendship together with the invitation to stay at her house.
"Cesario, come" prepares the imminent departure: most likely he
takes her by the hand a third time. He will lead her out. Orsino
and Viola leave as a couple, like Olivia and Sebastian. Nevertheless, his restraint keeps the upper hand to the end:

> . . . Cesario, come;
> For so you shall be while you are a man.   371

The last time he spoke to her, he had been mindful of her "soft
and tender breeding," now he playfully reverts to treating her
according to her male disguise. Only the final couplet reassures
us that Viola will reap her reward. Orsino reiterates his proposal
in much the same terms as he had used before:

> But when in other habits you are seen,
> Orsino's mistress, and his fancy's queen.   373

In keeping with the theatrical notation throughout the scene,
the place of honour belongs to Viola. Orsino's final gesture is
addressed to her, and so are the last words of the play.

NOTES

1. There has been little change in this since H. B. Charlton, in his *Shakespearian Comedy* (London, 1938) discussed the play, together with *Much Ado About Nothing* and *As Your Like It*, in a chapter entitled "The Consummation."
2. *William Shakespeare* (London, 1894), p. 209.
3. "Shakespeare's *Twelfth Night*," in *Shakespeare's Comedies*, ed. Kenneth Muir (Englewood Cliffs, 1965), p. 72.
4. *Duke.* Belong you to the Lady Olivia, friends?
   Clo. Ay, sir, we are some of her trappings.   V.i.7
5. Italics mine throughout this chapter.
6. Whereas the *New Variorum* edition (1901) says this "probably accompanied by a gesture to the Duke to keep silent and let Cesario speak" (l.110, n., p. 286), it has become "a polite request to Orsino to let Viola speak first" in M. M. Mahood's *New Penguin* edition of 1968 (l.104, n., p. 180). The distinction may be a nice one, but Olivia's next speech rather indicates that she is beyond making polite requests.
7. *Shakespeare at the Globe 1599-1609* (New York, 1962), p. 210.
8. In *The Two Gentlemen of Verona*, Speed and Launce never make it to the forest of the outlaws. In *A Midsummner Night's Dream* the mechanicals are withdrawn first, to make room for Theseus' closing-speech and the incantations of the fairies. In The *Merchant of Venice* Launcelot Gobbo only just fleets across the stage, announcing the return of Bassanio. Even this brief intrusion into Belmont has been much resented. In *Much Ado About Nothing*, Dogberry is remunerated and firmly dismissed before the last scene begins. The elimination of Sir Andrew and Sir Toby has thus numerous precedents. While clowns are withdrawn, however, the fool will return. Feste has a word to say to Malvolio, and he is even entrusted with the epilogue-song. Similarly, *As You Like It* has room for Touchstone and his Audrey.
9. Jenkins, p. 73. One cannot help suspecting that Orsino's extravagant threat to kill Cesario owes something to the desire to frighten us with a sufficiently lurid disaster. Northrop Frye's statement that "comedy contains a potential tragedy within itself" also comes to mind here: "Even in New Comedy, the dramatist usually tries to bring his action as close to a tragic overthrow of the hero as he can get it and reverses his movement as suddenly as possible." "The Argument of Comedy," in *Essays in Shakespearian Criticism*, ed J. L. Calderwood and H. E. Toliver (Englewood Cliffs, 1970), p. 53.
10. *Shakespeare's Stagecraft* (Cambridge U.P., 1967), p. 109ff.

11. Styan, p. 109.

12. Styan, p. 111, shows the ultimate refinement of this method in *Lear*, II.iv., where "the succession of entrances is used to . . . jar upon the nerves of the hero, each entrance a signal for the redoubling of his fury."

13. *The Merry Wives of Windsor*, IV.v. 58ff.

14. *Shakespeare's Professional Skills* (Cambridge U.P., 1964), p. 25.

15. *The World and Art of Shakespeare* (Jerusalem, 1967), p. 167.

16. Shalvi, p. 167.

17. Jenkins, p. 73.

18. *Aege.*   . . . but perhaps, my son,
Thou sham'st to acknowledge me in misery.   CEV.i.320
Ant.   . . . his false cunning,
Not meaning to partake with me in danger,
Taught him to face me out of his acquaintance,
And grew a twenty years removed thing
While one would wink; . . .   TNV.i.80

19. The central position of *Twelfth Night* in Shakespeare's work and the peculiar wealth of this play are both illustrated by the fact that while it harks back to his first comedy, it also looks forward to his last plays. Viola's
> Tempests are kind, and salt waves fresh in love!
>
>   III.iv.368

and Orsino's reference to "this most happy wreck" evoke an idea which is central to *Pericles* and important in *The Tempest*. Likewise, the delayed recognition between Viola and Sebastian looks like a sketch for the much more protracted, almost painfully moving reunion of Pericles and Marina in *Pericles*, V.i.

20. *Twelfth Night* (1930), ll.274–275, n., p. 167.

21. See I.ii.47:

> There is a fair behaviour in thee, Captain;
> And though that nature with a beauteous wall
> Doth oft close in pollution, yet of thee
> I will believe thou hast a mind that suits
> With this thy fair and outward character.

22. *"Twelfth Night" and Shakespearian Comedy* (Toronto U.P., 1965), p. 45.

23. Malvolio's appearance in V.i. is so important to Shakespeare that he breaks one of his rules. The audience is informed of what it already knows. However, we are rewarded with a piece of authentic, and welcome, news: Toby has married Maria after all.

24. H. H. Furness, in the *New Variorum* edition (1901), l.333, n., p. 308,

sees her motive as somewhat more selfish. According to him, Olivia
"wishes to silence the Duke's importunities for ever, by marrying
him to Viola." Since Olivia is as good as married to Sebastian,
however, it would appear that Orsino is already silenced.

25. Leech, p. 38. In earlier comedies, villains and others who threaten to
jeopardize the sense of harmony are either removed long before the
end (Shylock), or converted and then allowed to participate in the
happy ending (Oliver), or we hear that they will be duly punished
(Don John). Some remove themselves because they cannot abide
what others call happiness (Jaques). Malvolio is in a quite different
category. His case produces a much more subtle effect, as Clifford
Leech points out in his account of the peculiar uneasiness we sometimes feel in Illyria:

> To put Malvolio on a tragic level is to disregard the general effect of
> his appearance on the stage: rather, he is one of those comic figures
> at whom it is too easy to laugh, so easy that, before we know it, we
> have done harm and are ashamed. (*"Twelfth Night" and Shakespearian
> Comedy*, p. 44).

Even if we add to this the agonizing experience of Antonio, for
example, it remains an exaggeration to maintain that "the predomi-
nant mood" in *Twelfth Night* is "one of suffering." (Shalvi, p. 168).
When Malvolio is on stage in V.i., we may be disturbed even while
the theatre echoes with our laughter. A comparable incident, though
much less disturbing, is Dr. Caius' furious departure at the end of
The Merry Wives of Windsor. He too voluntarily withdraws from the
festive community, and storms out with the cry: ". . . be gar, I'll raise
all Windsor." (V.v.198). His exit has however no appreciable effect
on the good humour of the ending. It is eclipsed by the generous
rehabilitation of Falstaff, the "villain" who threatened the social
order of Windsor. Once he is punished and even turned into a victim
by the vicious "fairies," he is invited to Mistress Page's "country
fire."

Anne Barton

Shakespeare's Sense of an Ending in *Twelfth Night*

All of *Twelfth Night*, up to the final scene, takes place in a heightened world. There is no contrasting environment, no Athens or Duke Frederick's court, to set against Illyria. Messaline, the place from which Viola and Sebastian have come, is even more shadowy than Syracuse in *The Comedy of Errors*, or those wars from which Don Pedro, Claudio and Benedick find release in Messina. Messaline has no character whatever, and certainly no claim to be regarded as that normal world to which characters have so often returned at the end of a Shakespearian comedy. Illyria itself, on the other hand, has a very distinct character and declares it from the opening moments of the play. The sea-captain, appealed to by Viola for information about the country in which she has so unexpectedly arrived, might just as well have said to her what the Cheshire Cat says to Alice: "They're all mad here." Even before the unsettling appearance of twin Cesarios, both the ruler of Illyria and his reluctant mistress have ma-noeuvred themselves into unbalanced states of mind. They are surrounded, moreover, by characters even madder than they: Sir Toby Belch, Sir Andrew Aguecheek, or Feste, the man whose profession is folly. Malvolio in his dark room may seem to present the play's most extreme image of insanity, yet Olivia can confess that "I am as mad as he,/If sad and merry madness equal be"

Reprinted by permission of Edward Arnold Publishers, Ltd., Stratford upon Avon studies series, from *Shakespearian Comedy* by Anne Barton. Originally titled, "*As You Like It* and *Twelfth Night*: Shakespeare's Sense of an Ending."

(III.iv.14–15). Sebastian, bewildered by Olivia's passionate claims upon him, will earnestly debate the question of his own sanity. Antonio, already bewitched as he sees it by Sebastian, is accused of madness by Orsino's officer when he tries to explain his situation.

The eruption onto the stage of identical twins is calculated to make people distrust the evidence of their own senses. *The Comedy of Errors*, which plays the same game of mistaken identity in a doubled form, had also made use of images of madness. Yet the lunacy of *Twelfth Night* is both more widespread and more various. It is part of the whole atmosphere of the Feast of Fools suggested by the play's title, not simply a product of the failure to understand that there are two Cesarios and not just one. For Elizabethans this title would have stirred immemorial and continuing associations with a period of time in which normal rules were suspended, in which the world turned ritually upside down, allowing the plain man to become king and pleasure to transform itself into a species of obligation. Certainly the spirit of holiday reigns in Illyria, particularly in the household of the mourning Olivia. The countess herself may disapprove from a distance of the nightly chaos presided over by Sir Toby: only Malvolio tries in earnest to repress it. As soon as he does so, he places himself in danger. He becomes the churl at the banquet, the sobersides at the carnival. The revellers, forgetting their own private dissensions, recognize him at once for the common enemy and hunt him from their midst. As feasters, men living in a celebratory world that, temporarily at least, is larger than life, they instinctively protect themselves against the niggard who refuses to yield himself to the extraordinary.

As members of the *Twelfth Night* audience, we too are sharers in the extraordinary, a fact which perhaps explains why Malvolio has found tender-hearted apologists in the study but very few sympathizers in the playhouse. His humiliation at the hands of Feste, Maria, Fabian and Sir Toby removes a threat to our own equilibrium, to the holiday mood induced by the comedy in its early stages. We make common cause with Sir Toby and the Fool against Malvolio because we do not want him to spoil fun which in a sense is ours as well as that of characters actually on the stage. By means of laughter, we too cast Malvolio out. As soon as the steward has pieced together the meaning of the mock letter to his own satisfaction, as soon as he has swallowed the bait, he ceases to be a threat. Yellow-stockinged and cross-gartered, trying to produce some rusty approximation to a smile, Malvolio has become part of precisely that heightened world of play-acting, revelry and lack of control which he so despised. Festivity has made him its unwilling prey. Thereafter, it will do with him what it likes, until the moment of awakening.

This moment of awakening is in some ways the most distinctive feature of *Twelfth Night*. Sir Toby is the first to scent the morning air. At the end of Act IV, he is wishing that "we were well rid of this knavery," that some means of releasing Malvolio "conveniently" might be devised before the mood of holiday inconsequence breaks (IV.ii.65–8). Act V displays a marked harshening of tone. It begins by massing together images of death in a fashion that harks back to Shakespeare's preferred comic practice in the plays written before *As You Like It*. In this respect, as in its renewed emphasis on plot, *Twelfth Night* breaks away from the classicism of its predecessor. Orsino, confronting Antonio in his fetters, remembers that when last he saw this face "'it was besmeared/As black as Vulcan in the smoke of war" (V.i.46–7). To the grim realities of combat and mutilation now recalled there is added the agony of Antonio's account of his friend's treachery. The appearance of Olivia only makes matters worse. Orsino, half-crazed with jealousy of Cesario, threatens publicly to "kill what I love" (V.i.113):

> Him will I tear out of that cruel eye
> Where he sits crowned in his master's spite.
> Come, boy, with me; my thoughts are ripe in mischief:
> I'll sacrifice the lamb that I do love
> To spite a raven's heart within a dove.
>
> (V.i.121–5)

The situation is further complicated by the priest's confirmation of Olivia's marriage, a marriage so recent that since its solemnization "my watch hath told me, towards my grave,/I have travell'd but two hours" (V.i.156–7). Between sincere and passionate affirmation on the one side and, on the other, equally sincere and passionate denial, the deadlock is complete. Only Sebastian can

untangle this knot. The next character to enter is not, however,
Sebastian but the wretched Sir Andrew Aguecheek. He comes,
surprisingly, as the victim of real violence:

> For the love of God, a surgeon! Send one presently to Sir
> Toby. . . . Has broke my head across, and has given Sir Toby
> a bloody coxcomb too. For the love of God, your help! I had
> rather than forty pound I were at home.
>
> (V.i.166–71)

Sebastian has levelled precisely those inequalities upon which
Sir Toby battened. Predator and prey have been used alike despite
the considerable difference in their swordsmanship and general
efficiency. And indeed something more than a pair of coxcombs
has been broken.

Surgeons, after all, belong to a sober reality of sickness and
disease outside the limits of festivity. This, at least, ought to be
their territory. Feste's reply to Sir Toby's question, "didst see Dick
Surgeon, sot?," is less than consoling: "O, he's drunk, Sir Toby,
an hour agone; his eyes were set at eight i' th' morning" (V.i.189–
91). Sir Toby himself has hitherto turned day into night and night
into day. He has argued in Falstaffian terms that "to be up after
midnight and to go to bed then is early; so that to go to bed after
midnight is to go to bed betimes" (II.ii.7–9). For the reveller, the
only meaningful chronicity is the one Prince Hal attributed to
Falstaff, one in which hours are "cups of sack, and minutes
capons, and clocks the tongues of bawds and dials the signs of
leaping houses" (1 *Henry IV*, I.ii.5–11). Bleeding and in pain, forced
to recognize another and harsher kind of time, Sir Toby demands
the services of the surgeon, only to discover that this functionary,
like himself in happier state, has sat up all night revelling and is
now blissfully asleep in just those daylight hours when he is
wanted. It is bad enough to be jolted unceremoniously into reality, but even more bitter to find that the surgeon you urgently
require is still, in an unregenerate fashion, disporting himself at
the carnival. Condemned to suffer pain without relief, Sir Toby
gives vent to the uncharacteristic utterance, "I hate a drunken
rogue" (V.i.193).

In the next moment, he turns savagely on Sir Andrew's well-meant offer of assistance and companionship in misery. "Will you help—an asshead and a coxcomb and a knave, a thin-fac'd knave, a gull?" (V.i.196–9). Only a moment before, Sir Andrew had wished "for forty pound" that he was safely at home again. It was the genuine accent of the reveller for whom the party has suddenly become poisonous, who wishes now that he had never set out from the familiar, homely world to the masked ball; the man for whom day breaks after a night of abandon and fruitless pursuit of profit in a garish and essentially shaming way. On top of all this comes the sudden treachery, the revelation in his true colours of a supposed friend. Sir Andrew does not reply to Sir Toby's abuse. He simply vanishes, never to reappear in the comedy. Sir Toby leaves the stage too, not to be seen again. Subsequently it will be revealed that he has married Maria, as a recompense for her plot against the steward. For him, as for Sir Andrew creeping back to his depleted lands, holiday has been paid for in ways that have real-life consequences

At precisely this point, as the two broken revellers are being helped away in a state of debility and antagonism, Shakespeare exchanges prose for verse and radically alters the mood of the scene. He allows Sebastian, that comedy resolution personified, at last to confront his twin sister, to assure Olivia of his faith, to renew his friendship with Antonio and to enlighten Orsino. There will be a happy ending. It is, however, a happy ending of an extraordinarily schematized and "playlike" kind. Viola has already had virtual proof, in Act III, that her brother has survived the wreck. They have been separated for only three months. Yet the two of them put each other through a formal, intensely conventional question and answer test that comes straight out of Greek New Comedy:

> *Viola:* My father had a mole upon his brow.
> *Sebastian:* And so had mine.
> *Viola:* And died that day when Viola from her birth
>   Had numb'red thirteen years.
> *Sebastian:* O, that record is lively in my soul!
>   He finished indeed his mortal act
>   That day that made my sister thirteen years.
>   (V.i.234–40)

This recognition scene is intensely moving. Its emotional force and purity derive, however, from consonances that are recognizably fictional. In the theatre, the fact that an audience will always be more struck by the *dissimilarity* in appearance of the actors playing Viola and Sebastian than by that marvellous identity hailed so ecstatically by the other characters, also serves to drive a wedge between tact and literary invention.[1] We are dealing here, Shakespeare seems to announce, with a heightened, an essentially implausible world.

For Olivia and Sebastian, Viola and Orsino, this heightened world perpetuates itself. For them, there will be no return from holiday, no need to leave Illyria. Yet the little society which they form at the end of the play is far more fragmentary and insubstantial than the one that had been consolidated in Arden. The final pairings-off are perfunctory. Olivia accepts Sebastian for himself. Orsino, rather more surprisingly, accepts a Viola he has never seen as a woman. Rosalind had returned in her own guise as a girl at the end of *As You Like It*, uniting Ganymede with the lady Orlando loved first at Duke Frederick's court. Considering the abruptness of Orsino's resolve to substitute Viola for Olivia in his affections, an unknown Viola only guessed at beneath her "masculine usurp'd attire" (V.i.242), Shakespeare might well have done something similar here. Instead, he treats this joining of hands summarily, and turns away at once to the very different issue of Malvolio.

In the final act of *Twelfth Night*, a world of revelry, of comic festivity, fights a kind of desperate rearguard action against the cold light of day. It survives only in part, and then by insisting upon an exclusiveness that is poles apart from the various and crowded dance at the end of *As You Like It*. Viola and Orsino, Olivia and Sebastian may no longer be deluded, yet it is still Illyria in which they live: an improbable world of hair's-breadth rescues at sea, romantic disguises, idealistic friendships and sudden, irrational loves. This is not quite the country behind the North Wind, but it approaches those latitudes. The two romantic couples stand on the far side of a line dividing fiction from something we recognize as our own reality, and the society they epitomize is too small to initiate a dance.[2] Of the other main characters, no fewer than four are conspicuous by their absence. Maria, Sir Toby and

Sir Andrew are not present to witness the revelations and accords of the closing moments. Malvolio intrudes upon them
briefly, but entirely uncomprehendingly. Like Sir Toby and Sir
Andrew, he comes as a figure of violence and leaves unreconciled,
meditating a futile revenge. For him too, the dream is over and
the moment of awakening bitter. Jaques had walked with dignity
out of the new society; Malvolio in effect is flung.

There is only one character who can restore some sense of
unity to *Twelfth Night* at its ending, mediating between the world
of the romantic lovers and our own world, which is (or is about to
be) that of the chastened Sir Andrew, the sobered Belch and the
unbending Malvolio. In a sense, he has been doing just this all
along in preparation for some such ultimate necessity. Throughout *Twelfth Night*, Feste has served as commentator and Chorus,
mocking the extravagance of Orsino, the wasteful idealism of
Olivia's grief, Viola's poor showing as a man. He has joined in the
revels of Sir Toby and Sir Andrew while remaining essentially
apart from them, aware of their limitations. Most important of
all, he has kept us continually aware of the realities of death and
time: that "pleasure will be paid one time or another" (II.iv.70),
that "beauty's a flower" (I.v.37) and youth "a stuff will not endure" (II.iii.51). Two contradictory kinds of time have run parallel
through the comedy, diverging only at its end. One is the time of
holiday and of fiction, measureless and essentially beneficent, to
which Viola trusts when she remains passive and permits the
happy ending to work itself out with no positive assistance from
her (II.ii.38-9). The other time is remorseless and strictly counted.
Although even Viola and Orsino catch glimpses of it, its chief
spokesman has been Feste.

At the very end of *Twelfth Night* these two attitudes towards
time distinguish two groups of characters, dividing a world of
fiction from one of fact. The audience leaving the theatre faces its
own jolt into reality, into the stern time of a world beyond
holiday, but at least it is given Feste and not Malvolio as its guide.
Left alone on the stage, Feste sings his song about the ages of
man, a song which draws its material from the same source as
Jaques' pessimistic catalogue. This time, there will be no attempt
at qualification or correction. Yet the song itself is curiously
consoling. It leads us gently and in a way that is aesthetically

satisfying from the golden world to the age of iron which is our own. A triumph of art, it builds a bridge over the rift which has opened in the comedy at its conclusion.

Feste is tolerant as Jaques, on the whole, was not. He does not attempt to judge, or even to reason. He simply states fact. The child is allowed his fancies: a foolish thing is but a toy. When he grows up he pays for them, or else discovers that the self-deceptions in which he is tempted to take refuge are easily penetrated by the world. Marriage ultimately becomes tedious, and so do the infidelities to which it drives a man. The reality of wind and rain wins out, the monotony of the everyday. The passing of time is painful, may even seem unendurable, but there is nothing for it but resignation, the wise acceptance of the Fool. All holidays come to an end; all revels wind down at last. Only by the special dispensation of art can some people, Viola and Orsino, Olivia and Sebastian, be left in Illyria. For the rest of us, the play is done; fiction yields to fact, and we return to normality along with Sir Toby and Maria, Sir Andrew and Malvolio.

NOTES

1. Jonson claimed, according to Drummond (*Works*, ed. C. H. Herford and P. Simpson (Oxford, 1925), vol. I, p. 144), that he had never undertaken any adaptation of the *Amphitruo* of Plautus because it was impossible to find actors who were identical twins. Shakespeare, writing a different kind of comedy, one concerned to explore the relationship between illusion and reality, accepted and indeed built upon the obstacle which Jonson found insuperable, here and in *The Comedy of Errors*.
2. It consists, in fact, only of themselves and the minor figure Fabian. There is no place for this Antonio, as there was for his namesake in the love/friendship resolution of *The Merchant of Venice*. In John Barton's 1969 Stratford production of *Twelfth Night*, Antonio made his exit alone at the end, in a direction different from that taken by the lovers.

Bibliography

Barber, C. L., *Shakespeare's Festive Comedy* (Princeton, 1959).

Barton, Anne, From "*As You Like It* and *Twelfth Night*: Shakespeare's Sense of an Ending," in *Shakespearian Comedy* (Stratford-upon-Avon Studies 14, 1972).

Beerbohm, Max, *More Theatres* (1969).

Bradley, A. C., "Feste the Jester," from *A Book of Homage to Shakespeare*, ed. Israel Gollancz (1916).

Brown, John Russell, "Directions for *Twelfth Night*," from *Shakespeare's Plays in Performance* (1966).

Evans, Bertrand, *Shakespeare's Comedies* (Oxford, 1960).

Granville-Barker, Harley, "*Twelfth Night* at the Vieux Colombier," from *The Observer*, 1 January, 1922.

Greif, Karen, "Plays and Playing in *Twelfth Night*," from *Shakespeare Survey* 34 (Cambridge, 1981).

Hasler, Jörg, *Shakespeare's Theatrical Notation: The Comedies* (Berne, 1974).

Hotson, Leslie, *The First Night of "Twelfth Night"* (1957).

Jenkins, Harold, "Shakespeare's *Twelfth Night*," Rice Institute Pamphlets 45, pp. 19–42.

Lamb, Charles, "On Some of the Old Actors," from *Essays of Elia* (1823).

Leggatt, A. S., *Shakespeare's Comedy of Love* (1974).

Levin, Harry, "The Underplot of *Twelfth Night*," from *Shakespeare and the Revolution of the Times* (Oxford, 1976).

Morley, Henry, *The Journal of a London Playgoer 1851–1866* (1891).

Priestley, J. B., *The English Comic Characters* (1925).

Salingar, L. G., "The Design of *Twelfth Night*," from *Shakespeare Quarterly* 9 (1958).

Sprague, Arthur Colby, *Shakespeare and the Actors* (Cambridge, Mass., 1944).

Walker, Roy, From "The Whirligig of Time," *Shakespeare Survey* 12 (Cambridge, 1959).

Woolf, Virginia, "*Twelfth Night* at the Old Vic," from *Collected Essays*, 1 (1966).